THE
PROPHETIC ACHIEVEMENT

THE
PROPHETIC ACHIEVEMENT

BY

C. F. WHITLEY
M.A., B.D., PH.D.

LECTURER IN SEMITICS AND OLD TESTAMENT,
UNIVERSITY COLLEGE OF NORTH WALES, BANGOR

LEIDEN
E. J. BRILL
1963

PRINTED IN THE NETHERLANDS

CONTENTS

Page

Preface   VII

Abbreviations   IX

    I The Nature of Canonical Prophecy   1

   II The Originality of the Prophets   24

  III Basic Prophetic Principles   45

  IV The Prophetic Attitude to the Cult   63

   V The Mediators of Monotheism   93

  VI The Divine Justice   129

 VII Repentance and Grace   152

VIII Fulfilment in Service   176

Appendix: Pre-exilic Prophecy and Eschatology . . .   199

Index.   221

PREFACE

'There was great distress in Israel such as had not been since the time that prophets ceased to appear among them' (I Mac. 9 : 7). Such is the testimony of a writer of the second century B.C. to the significance of the prophets in the life of ancient Israel.

Prophecy is, of course, a familiar subject, and in one aspect or another has long engaged the attention of scholars. A generation or so ago the prophets were studied primarily from an interest in their ethical teaching. Recent work, on the other hand, has been mainly concerned with such questions as the relationship of the prophets to the cult, the transmission of the prophetic literature, and the psychology of prophetic inspiration. Accordingly the time seems now ripe to consider the prophetic message as a whole. An attempt is therefore made in the following pages to assess the contribution of the great prophets to Hebrew religious thought. On any grounds this contribution must be judged considerable, but perhaps the greatest achievement of the prophets lies in the originality of their teaching and in its particular relevance to the historical and political developments of their time.

As far as possible these figures have been allowed to present their own message, and all quotations are in the text of the Revised Standard Version.

Bangor, June 1962.   C. F. WHITLEY.

ABBREVIATIONS

A.J.S.L.	American Journal of Semitic Languages and Literature.
A.N.E.T.	Ancient Near Eastern Texts Relating to the Old Testament (edited by J. B. Pritchard, 2nd edn., Princeton 1955).
B.D.B.	A Hebrew and English Lexicon of the Old Testament, by Brown, Driver and Briggs (corrected impression 1952), Oxford.
B.J.R.L.	Bulletin of the John Rylands Library.
B.W.A.N.T.	Beiträge zur Wissenschaft vom Alten und Neuen Testament.
E.B.	Encyclopaedia Biblica.
E.T.	Expository Times.
H.D.B.	Hastings' Dictionary of the Bible.
H.T.R.	Harvard Theological Review.
H.U.C.A.	Hebrew Union College Annual.
I.C.C.	International Critical Commentary.
J.B.L.	Journal of Biblical Literature.
J.N.E.S.	Journal of Near Eastern Studies.
J.S.S.	Journal of Semitic Studies.
J.T.S.	Journal of Theological Studies.
LXX	The Septuagint.
R.B.	Revue Biblique.
R.S.V.	Revised Standard Version.
T.R.	Theologische Rundschau.
V.T.	Vetus Testamentum.
Z.A.W.	Zeitschrift für die alttestamentliche Wissenschaft.
Z.S.T.	Zeitschrift für systematische Theologie.

CHAPTER ONE

THE NATURE OF CANONICAL PROPHECY

The great canonical prophets are at once the most engaging and creative figures in the Old Testament. They claim our attention not only because of the ethical and spiritual nature of their teaching, but because the period of their activity coincided with the most critical years of Israel's history. From the eighth to the sixth centuries B.C., when the Hebrews were demoralised by the threat of invasion and conquest, the prophets appeared as both the spiritual and political counsellors of the hour. From the Assyrian invasion of Judah in the days of Isaiah to the Babylonian conquest of the land in the time of Jeremiah, it was the prophetic voice alone that conveyed the word of God to Israel. When the Jews in Babylon were languishing under the humiliation of the exile it was the ministry of Ezekiel that enabled them to accept their environment and to orientate their lives anew. When these same exiles were confronted with the splendour and pageantry of Babylonian worship it was, again, the teaching of Deutero-Isaiah that confirmed them in their belief in Yahweh and convinced them of the inanity of idols. His interpretation of the coming of Cyrus as the instrument of their liberation and as the realisation of a long ordained purpose of God assured them, moreover, of the divine sovereignty over all historical events.

Of course, prophecy was known in Israel long before the appearance of its great classical representatives. Indeed it may be claimed that prophecy of a kind was common to the Semitic world as a whole. In the sagas and legends of the ancient Egyptians we find oracles which are prophetic in character, while in the myths and literary fragments of the Babylonians we meet with utterances which bear some resemblance to prophecy. [1] Texts deriving from eighteenth-century Mari, on the Middle Euphrates, similarly represent the god Dagan as having a messenger who performed prophetic functions. [2] Again, when visiting the Phoenician coast in the eleventh century B.C. an Egyptian temple official, Wen-Amon by name, claims to have seen a youth possessed of prophetic frenzy. [3] The pages of I Samuel (6 : 2), moreover, relate that the Philistines had diviners as well as priests, while according to the Book of Numbers (chs. 22-24) Balaam, the Aramean, was capable of delivering oracles of Yahweh. Such considerations lead some scholars to the conclusion that Israelite prophecy was but a deve-lopment from the prophetic phenomena which was generally characteristic of the peoples of the ancient Near East. [4] Other scholars like Hölscher have argued that inasmuch as Israelite prophecy was ecstatic it must have been indebted to the prophecy of the region of Syria and Asia-Minor where alone in the ancient world such prophecy was found. [5] On this view prophecy was not practised by the Israelites

---

[1] For Egyptian oracles and prophecies, see J. A. Wilson, *A.N.E.T.*, pp. 441-449, and for Babylonian oracles and prophecies R. H. Pfeiffer *ibid.*, pp. 449-452. See also Hugo Gressmann 'Foreign Influences in Hebrew Prophecy', *J.T.S.*, 27, 1926, pp. 241-254.

[2] Martin Noth, *B.J.R.L.*, 32, 1949-50, pp. 197 f.

[3] *A.N.E.T.*, p. 26b.

[4] E.g., A. Haldar, *Associations of Cult Prophets among the Ancient Semites*, 1945, pp. 110 f., A. Neher, *L'Essence du Prophétisme*, 1955, pp. 17 f.; cf. also W. F. Albright, 'The Near East and Israel', *J. B. L.*, 59, 1940, pp. 99 ff., for Israel's place in the ancient Near East.

[5] G. Hölscher, *Die Profeten*, 1914, pp. 132 ff.; A. Jepsen, *Nabi*, 1934, pp. 143 ff. For the ecstatic character of Greek religion see E. R. Dodds, 'Maenadism in the Bacchae', *H.T.R.* July 1940, pp. 155 f.

during the early years of their history, and its adoption on their entrance to the land of Canaan is but an example of the religious and cultural influences which the Canaanites exerted on them. However this may be, we know from ancient texts that the Canaanite god Baal certainly had his prophets, [1] and we even read in the Old Testament of their activities in Israelite circles (I Kgs. 16 : 31-33; 18 : 19). We likewise hear of the frenzied behaviour to which they resorted in order to induce the mantic state. Not only was it their practice to dance round the altars uttering loud cries, but they 'cut themselves after their custom with swords and lances until the blood gushed out' (I Kgs. 18 : 26-29). It was, thus, probably under such Canaanite influence that the prophets of Yahweh used 'harp, tambourine, flute and lyre' (1 Sam. 10 : 5) to stimulate prophetic utterance. Elisha too seemed dependent on stimulus of this nature, for it is recorded that he called for the services of a minstrel before 'the power of the Lord came upon him' (2 Kgs. 3 : 15). The excitement and enthusiasm evoked by these means was no doubt infectious and capable of influencing others. On meeting a band of ecstatic prophets Saul was seized by an irresistible desire to prophesy (I Sam. 10 : 10), while on another occasion his messengers were similarly affected 'when they saw the company of the prophets prophesying' (I Sam. 19 : 20). This wild, mantic experience was particularly susceptible to excitation by collective effort, and that is probably why such prophets traversed the countryside in companies (I Sam. 19 : 5; I Kgs. 22 : 16). Figures like Elijah (I Kgs. 17) and Micaiah ben Imlah (I Kgs. 22 : 7) appear to have been engaged in more individualistic activities, but even Elisha had close associations

---

[1] J. A. Wilson, *A.N.E.T.*, p. 250a, n. 13.

with 'the sons of the prophets' whose leader he seems to have been (2 Kgs. 2 : 15; 4 : 38).

The Yahwistic enthusiast of this period was known as נביא (*nabi*; pl. *nebiim*). And as the canonical prophets were also called by this name some interest has naturally been manifested in the meaning of the term. Influenced perhaps by the voluble utterances characteristic of the prophetic guilds, older scholars such as Gesenius and Kuenen associated the word with the root נבע (*nabaʿ*) which has the meaning of 'gushing' or 'bubbling forth'. [1] But it has been more commonly connected with an Arabic root signifying 'utterance' or an Assyrian root suggesting 'calling' or 'proclaiming'. [2] Observing that the word is passive in form Stade regarded it as expressing the persistence of a condition, [3] while Alfred Guillaume conceived of it as denoting 'the passive recipient of something which is manifested in' the prophet's 'condition as well as in his speech'. [4] W. F. Albright likewise favours a passive interpretation of *nabi*, and connecting it with the Akkadian *nabu* (to call) says, 'The correct meaning of the word is . . . "one who is called (by God), one who has a vocation (from God)" . . .'. [5] Haldar too derives the word from the same Akkadian root, and thinking that 'the etymology is clear' takes it to mean 'speaker'. [6] On the basis of Exodus 7 : 1 where Aaron is designated *nabi* and fulfils the function of a spokesman, T. J. Meek similarly concluded that the

---

[1] F. H. W. Gesenius, *Hebrew and Chaldee Lexicon*, Eng. trans. by S. P. Tragelles, 1846, p. 525b; A. Kuenen, *Prophets and Prophecy in Israel*, Eng. trans. by A. Milroy, 1877, p. 42.

[2] So *B.D.B.*, p. 611. See also Hölscher, *op.cit.*, p. 139, n. 3.

[3] B. Stade, *Lehrbuch der hebräischen Grammatik*, 1879, p. 152.

[4] *Prophecy and Divination*, 1938, pp. 112 f.

[5] *From the Stone Age to Christianity*, 1940, p. 231.

[6] *Op. cit.*, p. 109.

word means 'speaker' in the sense of a spokesman of God. [1]
Again, following the more novel proposal of W. R. Arnold,
R. H. Pfeiffer regarded the term as 'probably a passive
(niphal) participle of the verb *bô'* (enter), meaning *"entered"*
by the divine spirit'. [2] Robertson Smith was, however,
more cautious in his approach and thought that the etymological meaning of the term must remain in dispute since there
is nothing in what remains of Hebrew literature to enable
us to determine it. The two verbal forms which we find, the
Niphal and Hithpael, are denominatives of the noun *nabi*
which itself has no known root in Hebrew. The fact that
the *nebiim* were common amongst Baal worshippers led
Smith, however, to think that the word is hardly older than
the Israelite settlement in Canaan. He consequently inclined
to the view that it was of Canaanite origin and concluded,
'In this case the etymology becomes comparatively unim-
portant, and in any case the origin of the name lies too
remote from the historical development of Hebrew prophecy
to be of value in illustration of the conception of a prophet
among the Israelites'. [3] Lods, likewise, doubted if the word
nabi is of Hebrew origin and seemed rather to associate it
with the ecstatic practices of the Phoenician prophets. [4]

In view, then, of the uncertainty attaching to both the
origin and history of *nabi* it is doubtful if the etymological
approach in itself can be regarded as determinative in investigating the connotation of the term. [5] Nor will an examination

---

[1] *Hebrew Origins*, 2nd edn., 1950, p. 148.
[2] *Religion in the Old Testament*, 1961, p. 83.
[3] *The Prophets of Israel*, 2nd edn., 1895, p. 390.
[4] A. Lods, *Israel*, Eng. trans. by S. H. Hooke, 1932, p. 445.
[5] We may note here that the word *nabi* appears for the first time
in non-biblical texts in the Lachish Letters of the early sixth century
B.C.; see D. Winton Thomas, *Documents From Old Testament Times*
(also edited by him), 1958, p. 215.

of the verbal forms of the word reflect much light on its meaning. It is true that the *Niphal* is chiefly used during the period of canonical prophecy, but as it is used indiscriminately with the *Hithpael* for earlier and later periods it is doubtful if we can draw any definite inference from the forms which the verb assumes. [1] A more confident attitude is, however, noticeable in T. H. Robinson's treatment of the question. Regarding the reflexive forms of the verb as adequate evidence for an ecstatic view of prophecy, he declared, 'The fact is that Nabi meant an ecstatic, and it is difficult to see how the term could have been applied to a people who had nothing of the ecstatic about them'. [2]

But the question as to whether or not the canonical prophets were themselves subject to ecstatic experiences is one of the most controversial in the whole field of prophecy. Although 'ecstasy' had long been predicated of the prophets [3] it was the appearance of Hölscher's *Die Profeten* in 1914 which brought the question into prominence. For Hölscher not only regarded 'ecstasy' as an essential feature of the earlier *nebiim* but, also, as characteristic of the great classical prophets. [4] This view received sympathetic consideration from more than one subsequent scholar. Writing in 1922 John Skinner said: 'The recent tendency of criticism has been on the whole to hold that the visions recorded by the prophets were actually experienced by them in a condition of comparative ecstasy', and he, himself, regarded such a view

---

[1] Cf. Jepsen, *op.cit.*, p. 8; Wheeler Robinson, *op.cit.*, pp. 174 f.

[2] *The Expositor*, Series 8, 21, 1921, pp. 224-225.

[3] Cf., e.g., August Knobel, *Der Prophetismus der Herbräer*, 1837, who had a chapter entitled 'Die Ekstasie und Vision', pp. 155-178. See also H. H. Rowley, 'The Nature of Prophecy in the Light of Recent Study', *H.T.R.*, 38, 1, 1945, pp. 1 ff.

[4] The assumption underlies the whole book, but see especially pp. 6 ff.

as being 'consistent with the directness and objectivity of the prophet's narration'. [1] A decade later T. H. Robinson could say, 'Scarcely a doubt exists that in one form or another, Hölscher's theory will for the future hold the field'. [2] Elsewhere he wrote: 'the only authority which' the prophet 'could fully accept was that which came to him through the ecstatic state', while on a later page we read, 'The ecstasy, both to the prophet and to his hearers, was a guarantee of Yahweh's presence and message'. [3] Similarly, speaking of the attempt to relegate to the background the elements common to the great prophets and the earlier *nebiim* Lods said: 'This is a mistake. The form—and the term includes not only the outward manifestation of prophecy, but also the psychic phenomena which characterised it—remained essentially the same for the new prophets as for their predecessors'. [4] It is, again, the opinion of W. C. Klein that 'A candid reading of what the prophets themselves have written shows how rash it would be to deny that they had anything at all to do with ecstasy, and indeed so extreme a stand is out of the question unless one restricts the term to spectacular paroxysms'. [5] Like Hölscher, Harold Knight maintains that ecstatic prophecy was Canaanite in origin and therefore 'The prophet cannot wholly escape the influence with which he is confronted in Palestine, but he imparts to these unusual psychic states a new significance'. [6] Nevertheless, with definite reference to

---

[1] *Prophecy and Religion*, p. 11.
[2] 'Neuere Propheten-Forschung', *T.R.*, N.F., 3, 1931, p. 89.
[3] *Prophecy and the Prophets in Ancient Israel*, 2nd edn., 1953, pp. 45 and 46.
[4] *The Prophets and the Rise of Judaism*, Eng. trans. by S. H. Hooke, 1937, p. 52.
[5] *The Psychological Pattern of Old Testament Prophecy*, 1956, p. 83.
[6] *The Hebrew Prophetic Consciousness*, 1947, p. 53.

the writing prophets he says, 'The very manner of their speech stamps them as "ecstatics" ' (p. 79). In conformity with his view that prophecy was a characteristic of the Semitic peoples, Haldar claims that the canonical prophets too experienced the common phenomenon of ecstasy. Having asserted that 'the Hebrews ... used incense, alcohol and other drugs in the service of cult ecstasy' he comments: 'This is a type of ecstasy which we found among the Sumero-Accadians and in the Canaanite region and which is also characteristic of the early *nebiim*. And thence there is an unbroken continuity down to the later pre-exilic prophets. This point must be heavily underlined in confutation of all those who contend that we are faced by an entirely different type of ecstasy in the "scriptural prophets" '. [1]

But while such scholars are representative of the ecstatic interpretation of prophecy others have expressed a more moderating if not opposite view. Thus, J. M. Powis Smith maintained that 'Hebrew prophecy at its best almost wholly repudiated ecstasy, trance, and fanaticism and abandoned all efforts to superinduce such experiences'. [2] Again, while admitting 'that the word ecstatic may be applied to the Hebrew prophets', Guillaume remarked, 'It is a mistake to lay such emphasis on the physical phenomena of ecstasy-dancing, leaping, stabbing the body, swallowing hot coals and so on—as to imply that the physical phenomenon are primary and the spiritual experience secondary'. [3] Wheeler Robinson similarly wrote: 'The so-called "ecstatic" features, though not entirely absent, are certainly removed from the centre to the circumference of the prophetic experience'. [4]

---

[1] *Op. cit.*, p. 119.
[2] *The Prophet and his Problems*, 1914, p. 47.
[3] *Prophecy and Divination*, p. 291.
[4] *Inspiration and Revelation in the Old Testament*, 1946, p. 174.

So, in his Commentary on Amos, R. S. Cripps expressed the
view that 'evidence is entirely lacking that the primitive or
lower kind of *ecstasy*, which was the characteristic feature
of earlier "prophecy" was part of Amos's equipment', [1]
while with reference to the canonical prophets as a whole
he said, 'Nor does there seem to be sufficient evidence to
conclude that their messages were *delivered* in ecstasy' (p. 19).
According to Abraham Heschel it was the prophetic sympathy (*Sympathie*) with the divine Pathos (*göttliches Pathos*)
which was the source of their inspiration. [2] But this
'sympathy' is of a special religious nature and is the very
opposite of that which might be attained by ecstasy (p. 168).
R. B. Y. Scott is similarly prepared to regard the prophetic
consciousness of the word of God in terms of the ecstasy
experienced by the mystic. It was, however, an ecstasy which
'expressed itself in a new kind of ecstatic speech, clearly
intelligible, direct and radical, and charged with strong
emotional force'. [3] But I. G. Matthews could discern nothing
mystical or ecstatic in the utterances of the great prophets.
On the contrary 'They claimed no superior gifts, had no
esoteric, preparatory training, were the recipients of no
special information through trance or ecstasy'. [4] So in his
investigation of the revelatory experiences of Amos, Isaiah
and Jeremiah, I. P. Seierstad came to the conclusion that
ecstasy cannot be regarded as the medium of this experience. [5]

In recent years the most determined attempt to establish
the unique place of the canonical prophets has come from
the pen of Alfred Jepsen. In his book *Nabi* he has contended

---

[1] *The Books of Amos*, 1955 edn., p. 18.
[2] *Die Prophetie*, 1936, pp. 166-167.
[3] *The Relevance of the Prophets*, 1944, p. 88.
[4] *The Religious Pilgrimage of Israel*, 1947, p. 131.
[5] *Die Offenbarungserlebnisse der Propheten Amos, Jesaja und Jeremia*,
Oslo, 1946, p. 183.

that they were of a very different type from the *nebiim*, or professional prophets, of their day. The characteristics of the *nebiim* were not even Israelite in origin, but are to be traced to the inhabitants of pre-Israelite Canaan. [1] Jepsen argues that it was Samuel who first adopted this means of prophecy in Israel, for, having lost the ancient ephod oracle, he had no choice but to resort to the means of prophecy then current amongst the Canaanites (pp. 99 ff.). But the *nebiim* cannot be regarded as the predecessors of the classical prophets; for, these outstanding figures neither displayed the physical characteristics of the *nebiim* nor indeed called themselves by that name (pp. 132 ff.). The *nebiim* were accomplished in the use of professional techniques which they used as occasion demanded, while by contrast the canonical prophets only delivered their oracles when moved by God himself. The initiative rested entirely with God and when he chose to act the genuine prophet could not but prophesy (p. 215).

There is doubtless much that is true in the distinction made here between the *nebiim* and the canonical prophets. But in denying the name *nabi* to the great prophets Jepsen has had to resort to considerable textual alteration, or rather deletion. Thus in Amos 2 : 11 we read that God raised up prophets (*nebiim*) for Israel, but Jepsen regards the passage as an interpolation of the *nebiim* themselves. He in fact argues that the *nebiim* subjected the text of the Old Testament to an extensive revision. Hence the many instances in which Jeremiah is called a *nabi* as well as those in which Jeremiah himself is represented as referring to the 'prophets' as the servants of God (*e.g.*, Jer. 7 : 25; 25 : 4; 29 : 19) are all attributed to the redactional pen of the *nebiim* (p. 139 f.). In

---

[1] *Nabi*, pp. 144 ff.

accordance with his belief that visions are especially characteristic of the *nebiim* Jepsen emphasizes that they are not mentioned in the oracles of Hosea, but he makes no comment on the visions referred to in the Book of Amos although he stresses that Amos himself was very different from the *nebiim* of his day (pp. 132 f.). Jepsen, however, accepts the authenticity of the term *nabi* as applied to Jeremiah in the account of his call (1 : 5), while he also accepts as original, instances in which *nabi* is predicated by Yahweh himself of Ezekiel (Ezek. 2 : 5; 33 : 33); but in these cases he regards the term as meaning nothing more than 'Spokesmen of God' and as not used in the technical sense of a member of a professional class (p. 141 f.). But even if the term *nabi* had by now acquired this meaning it indicates that however far removed the classical prophets were from the professional *nebiim* they did not at any rate object to the name by which they were called. [1] Moreover, Jepsen seems to underestimate the element of compulsion in the utterances of the *nebiim*; and consequently the distinction which he makes between them and the canonical prophets in this respect can scarcely be supported by the biblical evidence. In times prior to the classical prophets we read of utterances of a 'prophetic' nature made under some sort of compulsion. We are told that 'the spirit of God came upon the messengers of Saul and they ... prophesied' (I Sam. 19 : 20), while a later passage relating to Saul himself states that 'the spirit of God came upon him also, and as he went he prophesied ... (I Sam. 19 : 23). Moreover, a distinguished prophet in the time of Ahab, Micaiah ben Imlah by name, was constrained to confess that he could speak only what Yahweh commanded him (I Kgs. 22 : 14).

---

[1] Cf. here the criticisms of Wheeler Robinson, *op.cit.*, pp. 176-177.

But while we may question certain aspects of Jepsen's position we will scarcely find the opposing view of Hölscher any more acceptable. For, as we have noted, this scholar maintains that even the great prophets were subjected to the most violent ecstatic experiences. [1] Not only is ecstasy attended by acute psychical experiences, but the muscles, heart, and the circulation of the blood undergo drastic biological changes (p. 5). Ezekiel is regarded as an example of the ecstatic who is powerless to control the wild, convulsive movements of his feet and hands, while Jeremiah's cries and moanings are typical of ecstatic utterances (p. 7). Normal consciousness is suppressed by an obsession imposed from without and the behaviour of the subject is thenceforth involuntary and fanatical (p. 16). The resulting psychical state is consequently one of dissolution, as the mind, far from being composed, is emotionally seized by an impulsive and irrational force (p. 20). But, says Hölscher, 'This condition of madness is essentially characteristic of the ecstatic prophet and in professional prophecy the intentionally desired goal of ecstatic exercises' (*ibid.*). However descriptive this may be of the professional ecstatic it can have but little relevance to the canonical prophets. It is true that later in his work (p. 187) Hölscher speaks of ecstasy as a diminishing factor in the rational utterances of the great prophets, but it is difficult to regard his conception of prophetic ecstasy as being applicable even in a limited way to the religious experiences of these figures. [2]

The question of the manner of the inspiration of the classical prophet, however, remains. Was his inspiration

---

[1] *Op. cit.*, pp. 4 ff.

[2] Harold Knight notes here that while 'ecstasy involves a unification and enhancement of consciousness producing vivid realisation Hölscher defines ecstasy as a state of mind involving disintegration and loss of balance', *op. cit.*, p. 93.

mediated through some form of ecstasy or was he a mere
passive recipient of the divine word? In so far as the biblical
material enables us to suggest an answer to this question it
appears that in receiving his message the prophet underwent
some form of psychic experience. Visions would seem to be
the media by which both Amos (1 : 1) and Isaiah (1 : 1)
received their call and inspiration. [1] And in the book of
Hosea we hear Yahweh saying:

> 'I spoke to the prophets;
> it was I who multiplied visions,
> and through the prophets gave parables' (12 : 10).

But however 'the word of the Lord . . . came to Hosea'
himself (1 : 1) it was said in his day that 'the prophet is a
fool, the man of the spirit is mad' (9 : 7). Certainly Jeremiah's
own description of his sensations would seem to suggest
that he was in some way subject to abnormal psycho-physical
experience:

> 'My anguish, my anguish, I writhe in pain!
> Oh, the walls of my heart!
> My heart is beating wildly;
> I cannot keep silent' (4 : 19).

And again,

> 'Whenever I speak, I cry out,
> I shout, "Violence and Destruction"! . . .' (20 : 8).

On yet another occasion he confessed that the burden of his
message had an intoxicating effect on him:

> 'I am like a drunken man,
> like a man overcome by wine,
> because of the Lord
> and because of his holy words' (23 : 9).

---

[1] H. Th. Obbink, however, remarks, 'With the genuine prophets in
Israel the visionary element is confined to their vision of their calling',
'The Forms of Prophetism', *H.U.C.A.*, 14, 1939, p. 26.

Similarly 'the hand of the Lord' which came upon Ezekiel (1 : 3; 2 : 22) was attended by unusual phenomena. He sees visions of God against a background of abnormal atmospheric conditions and strange creatures having at once the characteristics of man, bird and beast. (1 : 1-28). Under the influence of his encounter with God he eats a roll which tastes as honey (3 : 1-2), while on a later occasion he becomes dumb and remains so till God intervenes (3 : 26-27). His hair is, again, pulled out and becomes a means of endowing him with extraordinary powers (8 : 3); for, as if in levitation, he is transported from Babylon to distant Jerusalem and displays a most detailed knowledge of the temple and its precincts (chs. 8-11). [1]

Much of the experience and behaviour of the canonical prophets is, moreover, reminiscent of the *nebiim* of earlier times. The 'hand of Yahweh' which exerted such influence over Isaiah (8 : 11) and Ezekiel (1 : 3; 3 : 14) was also laid upon Elijah (1 Kgs. 18 : 46). We are told that when prophesying before Samuel, Saul 'stripped off his clothes . . . and lay naked all that day and . . . night' (I Sam. 19 : 24), but it is related of Isaiah too that he walked 'naked and barefoot' (Is. 20 : 2). [2] One of the *nebiim* of the court of Ahab made horns of iron as an indication of the manner of the defeat of the Syrian army (I Kgs 22 : 11), but we also find that Jeremiah, under divine instructions, made thongs and yoke-bars as symbols of the power which Nebuchad-rezzar would wield over the western states (Jer. 27 : 2-3). It is noteworthy, again, that the symbolic names which

---

[1] Cf. here G. Widengren, *Literary and Psychological Aspects of the Hebrew Prophets*, 1948, pp. 102-107.

[2] Cf. also Micah 1 : 8 where concerning the idolatry of Samaria Yahweh is represented as saying: 'For this I will lament and wail, I will go stripped and naked.'

Isaiah (8 : 1-4) and Hosea (1 : 2-9) call their children find
a parallel in an Akkadian text in which the boatman of the
nether world is designated by a term signifying 'Remove
hastily'. [1] The symbolism to which Ezekiel more than once
resorted (*e.g.*, 3 : 16; 4 : 1 f.; 5: 1-4) has, likewise, many
affinities with the religious beliefs and practices of the
ancient Orient. [2]

But although characteristics of this nature seem to have
persisted in the behaviour of the canonical prophets, these
figures cannot be explained in terms of mere development
from earlier prophecy. As R. B. Y. Scott observed, 'Something new emerged in such men—a manifestation of spiritual
power which brought them to an altogether different plane
of religious experience and insight, and which gives them
unique significance'. [3] Again, while such abnormal experiences may have contributed to the mediation of the divine
word they are not in themselves the measure of inspiration.
For inspiration is independent of all such phenomena and
ultimately derives from God himself. Wheeler Robinson
claims that 'The theology of revelation has for its counter-
part, or rather for its necessary constituent, the psychology
of inspiration'. [4] But while we may make certain assertions
as to the nature of Hebrew psychology it is doubtful if we
are able to reconstruct satisfactorily a psychology of prophetic
inspiration. And however the phenomena associated with
'ecstasy' may be amenable to psychological analysis it is
questionable if the term is at all descriptive of the religious
experience of the Hebrews. For it is based on a Greek notion

---

[1] E. A. Speiser, *A.N.E.T.*, p. 109 b.
[2] See here G. Fohrer, *Die symbolischen Handlungen der Propheten*, 1953,
pp. 34-46.
[3] *The Relevance of the Prophets*, p. 40.
[4] *Op. cit.*, p. 173.

of personality whereby the soul is conceived of as detaching itself from the body to become re-united in mystical fashion with the divine source of its being. [1] The Hebrews on the other hand regarded the *nephesh*, or soul, as having no existence apart from the body and consequently incapable of disembodiment in the manner in which the Greeks conceived of the incarnate soul. The *nephesh* was the breath-soul endowing the body with life but was nonetheless an integral part of it. The soul, in the words of Pedersen, 'is a force acting through all its parts. The whole of the soul is in the reins, in the heart, in the flesh, just as, on the other hand, the flesh stamps the whole of the character of the soul'. [2] It was not through an exclusively psychical operation of the mind but through the psycho-physical activity of seeing and hearing that prophets like Amos (1 : 1) and Isaiah (1 : 1) became conscious of their call and commission. So when Ezekiel tells us that the 'spirit' (*ruach*) lifted him by a lock of his hair and brought him 'in visions of God to Jerusalem' (8 : 3) he implies that his experience was no mere transportation of the *nephesh* but that his whole personality was involved. The invasive spirit of God was accordingly conceived as affecting the entire structure of the body; and so realistically was this believed that not only the *nephesh*, but other organs of this complex psycho-somatic structure are

---

[1] Cf. the remarks of Wheeler Robinson, *op.cit.*, p. 180; Harold Knight, *op. cit.*, p. 63, and R. S. Cripps, *op. cit.*, p. 89, n. 1.

[2] J. Pedersen, *Israel: its Life and Culture*, I-II, 1926, p. 178. Cf. also W. C. Klein: 'In common with other pre-metaphysical peoples, the Hebrews are at once materialists and spiritualists in the sense that they think, not of spirit in contrast with matter, nor of spirit as delicate matter, nor of matter as gross spirit, but of one fundamental stuff, which is less readily palpable and perceptible in some of its manifestations than others: as there is no immaterial spirit, so there is no matter that is not at least capable of animation', *op. cit.*, pp. 16-17.

represented as expressing a desire for a close relationship with God. The Psalmist could thus say:

> 'O God thou art my God, I seek thee,
> My soul thirsts for thee;
> my flesh faints for thee' (63 : 1).

Again in Psalm 84 we read:

> 'My soul longs, yea faints
> for the courts of the Lord;
> my heart and my flesh sing for joy
> to the living God' (vs. 2).

Describing the sinful state of a rebellious people Isaiah says:

> 'The whole head is sick,
> and the whole heart faint.
> From the sole of the foot even to the head,
> there is no soundness in it' (1 : 5-6).

So Jeremiah's reaction against the corruptness of the priests and false prophets is one of the entire personality:

> 'My heart is broken within me,
> all my bones shake' (23 : 9).

This attribution of psychical properties to the physical organs, with the consequent notion that the several members and faculties of the body are alike subject to the invasive influence of God, is, therefore, indicative of the complex nature of the Hebrew religious consciousness. It appears clear, however, that religious experience is attained through God's initiative in invading the human personality. Hence any view of prophetic inspiration which conceives of an incarnate soul leaving the body in its flight for communion with God is not in accordance with the fundamentals of Hebrew psychology. Neither does the invasive divine spirit annul or displace the conscious faculties of the mind, but rather stimulates the whole personality to a deeper and more illuminating conception of God. It is thus in so far as it affects the nature of inspiration that Hölscher's reconstruction of the psychical experience of the canonical prophets is unsatisfactory; for on his presentation of the matter the prophetic consciousness is so overwhelmed by external influences that apprehension of the divine communication is itself inevitably obscured. It is likewise difficult to reconcile any view of divine inspiration with Haldar's theory of prophetic ecstasy. For if the prophets had to use alcohol and such drugs to induce the ecstatic state, they were necessarily in such a condition of mental disintegration as to be incapable of intelligible communication with God.[1] A view which appears to be more in conformity with Hebrew mode of thought is that which regards the process of inspiration, not as one of mental dissolution or absorption with the Divine, but as one in which the prophet becomes vividly aware of the illumination which has its source in God.[2]

But while on the basis of certain biblical material we may attempt some reconstruction of the prophetic consciousness we cannot thereby claim to evaluate the moral and spiritual content of the prophetic utterance. For other individuals in Israel exhibited all the externals of psychic phenomena characteristic of the true prophet. In the time of Ahab a prophet with 'a lying spirit' appeared no different from one motivated by the genuine spirit of God (I Kgs. 22 : 20-23). And the problem of 'false prophecy' was one of the most serious which confronted the great prophets. Throughout their ministry they were opposed and rivalled by individuals

---

[1] *Op. cit.*, p. 109.
[2] Cf. Harold Knight, *op. cit.*, p. 93. So Robertson Smith, 'The characteristic of the true prophet is that he retains his consciousness and self-control under revelation, *The Old Testament in the Jewish Church*, 2nd edn., 1895, p. 289.

who earned their livelihood as professional prophets (Jer. 14 : 18). Whatever their origin and training these figures laid claim to oracular powers and so gave utterance to words which were accepted as inspired and authentic. [1]

Thus it was that the false prophets of Jeremiah's day exhibited all the external characteristics of inspired prophecy. Yahweh 'did not send' these prophets 'yet they ran': he 'did not speak to them, yet they prophesied' (23 : 21). By prefacing their remarks with 'Thus saith Yahweh' they succeeded in deceiving the people and in prophesying lies (23 : 25-26). Jeremiah was himself convinced that true prophecy differed from false as wheat from chaff (vs. 28) but that difference was not apparent to the eye of sense. He was certain that Hananiah was not 'sent' by Yahweh and that he made the 'people trust in a lie' (28 : 15) but he could appeal to neither sign nor logic to establish his point. His own enemies referred to him as a 'madman' (29 : 31); and there was nothing in his speech or demeanour to distinguish him from the prophets he himself so vehemently condemned. Indeed the question of determining true and false prophecy seems to have been a particular issue shortly before Jeremiah began his ministry. [2] For when Deuteronomy was composed it was commonly asked 'How may we know the word which the Lord has not spoken'? (18 : 21). In this particular context a false prophet may be exposed if his words did not

---

[1] Skinner regarded these prophets as 'the degenerate survivors of a phase of prophecy which had once played an influential and honourable part in the history of the national religion, *op. cit.*, p. 186. Knight, however, expressed the view that the men to whom the great prophets were opposed were not the charismatic *nebiim* but the ecstatic-priest prophets who were attached to the sanctuaries of Canaan, *op. cit.*, pp. 80-81.

[2] On the view that he was not called to the prophetic office till after the death of Josiah in 609, see the present writer, *The Exilic Age*, London, 1957, pp. 34-42.

materialise (vs. 22). In chapter 13 : 1 f., however, we find that the utterances of a false prophet may issue in fulfilment, thereby establishing for him a claim to inspired prophecy. Complicated by such considerations the question of the essentials of true prophecy is therefore a difficult though important one. [1]

Of the canonical Prophets Jeremiah is perhaps the most helpful in enabling us to discuss, if not to solve, this problem; but as Skinner has remarked 'He has no *psychological* test by which true prophecy can be distinguished from false'. [2] The basis of his message was rather a personal intuitive knowledge of the mind and purpose of God. [3] On being called by Yahweh he was commissioned with the words, 'Whatever I command you, you shall speak' (1 : 7). Unlike the false prophets he 'stood in the council of Yahweh' and perceived and heard 'his word' (23 : 18). He is sent by Yahweh and the false prophets are not (23 : 21; 28 : 15); and while they 'speak visions of their own minds' he is conscious of a word 'from the mouth of Yahweh' (23 : 16). Impelled by nothing more than 'the deceit of their own heart' (23 : 26) these prophets 'take their tongues and utter an oracle' (23 : 31), but the words which issue from Jeremiah's 'lips' have their source in God himself. [4] Far from having to affect an authoritative voice or to borrow his words (28 : 30) Jeremiah cannot

---

[1] See here, Gottfried Quell, *Wahre und falsche Propheten*, 1952, pp. 9-43.

[2] *Op. cit.*, p. 194.

[3] 'Jeremiah's conviction was not the conclusion of a syllogism but the result of a religious experience', S. H. Blank, *Of a Truth the Lord Hath sent me* (The Goldensen Lecture for 1955, The Hebrew Union College Press), p. 8.

[4] Cf. further 5 : 30-31 where Jeremiah regards the conduct of the false prophets as 'an appalling and horrible thing'. See also Micah 3 : 5 and Ezek. 13 : 3 f. for a similar condemnation of these prophets.

resist the word of God which compels expression through him:

> 'If I say, I will not mention him, or speak any more in his name,
> there is in my heart as it were a burning fire shut up in my
>   bones,
> and I am weary with holding it in, and I cannot' (20 : 9).

His rivals may indeed profess a knowledge of dreams and visions, but Jeremiah was convinced that the genuine word of God would be ultimately recognised by its inherent truth: 'Let the prophet who has a dream tell the dream, but let him who has my word speak my word faithfully' (23 : 28). It was the certainty of this conviction which on a later occasion prompted him to say: 'The Lord sent me to prophesy against this house and this city all the words you have heard ... But as for me, behold, I am in your hands. Do with me as seems good and right to you. Only know for certain that if you put me to death, you will bring innocent blood upon yourselves and upon this city and its inhabitants, for in truth the Lord sent me to speak all these words in your ears' (26 : 12-15). Dominating his prophetic mission, then, was his absolute certainty that he was uttering the word of Yahweh. 'The Lord made it known to me and I knew' (11 : 18) was how he himself expressed it. But the consciousness which underlies this certitude is scarcely susceptible of analysis. It is an intuitive apprehension of the word of God aptly referred to by Jeremiah as 'fire' and as 'a hammer which breaks the rock in pieces' (23 : 29); and Amos gives expression to the same incommunicable spiritual conviction when he says:

> 'The lion has roared; who will not fear?
> The Lord God has spoken; who can but prophesy?' (3 : 8).

Similarly, in mentioning the overpowering 'hand of Yahweh' both Isaiah (8 : 11) and Ezekiel (1 : 3) refer to experiences which defy more precise description. It was sufficient for them to know that they were speaking under divine compulsion and not from the visions of their own heart. [1] And this intuitive certainty of the mind and will of God is of the essence of true prophecy. In thus presenting as their credentials the familiar 'Thus saith Yahweh' the prophets were but constantly affirming that 'no prophecy ever came by the impulse of man, but men moved by the Holy Spirit spoke from God' (2 Peter 1 : 21).

The question how the Spirit moved men and why in consequence they spoke from God does not, however, admit of psychological analysis; for it is clear that inspiration and the religious certitude which it engenders are in themselves phenomena which are ultimately irreducible. Hence the limits of psychology in the study of prophetic inspiration are becoming increasingly recognised. In a 'Postscript' to a study which claimed his attention for many years Sigmund Mowinckel confessed: 'I am no longer primarily interested in unravelling the processes of the prophet's spiritual experiences, in discussing how far the factors hold good in general, which caused the experience in particular cases to take on an ecstatic character, to assume the form of visions, auditions etc. etc. . . .'. [2] More recently in a work entirely devoted to examining the pertinence of psychology to Old Testament prophecy W. C. Klein remarked: 'It is futile in the extreme to treat this as an exclusively psychological question', [3] and he concluded his study of the question with

---

[1] Cf. here R. B. Y. Scott: 'The supreme moment when a man knew that God had commissioned him as a prophet . . . was an experience which coloured all his subsequent ministry and gave authority to his utterances', *The Interpreter's Bible*, 5, 1956, p. 155a.

[2] J.B.L., 56, 1937, p. 264.

[3] *Op. cit.*, p. 85. So J. P. Hyatt is of the opinion that the psychological 'approach to understanding the prophets is of little value. They must be

the comment, 'There are limits . . . to psychology and the most important things lie beyond them' (p. 87).

The secrets of the prophetic consciousness must, then, it seems, elude investigation and the process of spiritual inspiration resist exact definition. Yet however we conceive of prophetic inspiration it is unlikely that it was confined to any one mode of illumination, but that it was as manifold as that suggested by the author of the Epistle to the Hebrews when he wrote: 'In many and various ways God spoke of old to our fathers by the prophets' (1 : 1). Thus it is that vision, dream and symbol may all, in their season, have contributed to the mediation of God's word to his prophets. Nor would such media necessarily detract from the content of divine revelation; for if God reveals himself through humanity it can scarcely be other than by such means as are themselves factors of the human personality.[1] Of an age that will experience the universal outpouring of his own spirit Yahweh is himself represented as saying:

'Your sons and your daughters shall prophesy,
Your old men shall dream dreams,
and your young men shall see visions' (Joel 2 : 28).[2]

But however God chose to reveal himself in Old Testament times it is through his servants the prophets that his words are most clearly and authoritatively transmitted to us.

---

evaluated by theological rather than psychological standards', *Prophetic Religion*, 1947, p. 8.

[1] 'The word of the Lord came through the common things of the common days', W. A. Irwin, *The Old Testament: Keystone of Human Culture*, 1952, p. 94.

[2] So numbers 12:6, where Yahweh is regarded as saying, 'Hear my words: if there is a prophet among you, I the Lord make myself known to him in a vision, I speak with him in dreams'.

CHAPTER TWO

THE ORIGINALITY OF THE PROPHETS

The conviction with which the prophets spoke poses the immediate question of the basis and authority of their teaching. Were they but appealing for a stricter adherence to principles inherent in Yawhistic tradition, or are they to be regarded primarily as enunciating truths which were novel to the Israelite thought of their day? Scholarship has not spoken with unanimity on this question. S. A. Cook was of the opinion that 'The prophets . . . point backward not to a forgotten Mosaism which they revived, but to an older and cruder religion which they transformed'.[1] The substance of this contention becomes clearer from a remark he made elsewhere: 'Yahwism, one might almost say, was, apart from its name, a Canaanite religion which was profoundly spiritualised and ethicised, and it owed its permanent value both to the prophets and to influences . . . from the desert'.[2] Again, emphasising the independence of the prophetic approach to the problems of their day W. C. Graham wrote: 'Fundamentally . . . the prophets are thinkers, philosophers, men . . . whose intellectual activities constituted the controlling factor in their psychology, and whose intellectual pre-eminence can only be appreciated, not from the vantage point of the culture of a later age and of another place, but from that of the culture which was dominant

---

[1] *The Old Testament: A Reinterpretation*, 1936, p. 168.
[2] *The Truth of the Bible*, 1938, p. 63.

when and where they lived'. [1] With reference to the source
of the prophetic revelation W. A. Irwin expressed himself
in somewhat similar terms: 'It is apparent that the source
and origin of the prophets' knowledge of God, lay in their
own human endowment of thought and feeling. They
pondered deeply, devoutly and long on the issues of their
days, and they were profoundly concerned about them; out
of such activity there came to them the convictions which
they have set down for us as revelations of the will of God'. [2]
But while such scholars emphasise the original element in
the teaching of the prophets, recent writers as a whole
tend to stress the extent of their indebtedness to tradition.
Thus according to W. J. Phythian-Adams the prophets
'never saw themselves as sent to proclaim a new vision *or*
a new conception of God: they came, as messengers with
strict and definite orders, to recall revolting Israel to Yahweh
who had chosen it'. [3] A. C. Welch similarly thought that the
prophets 'were continually recalling their hearers to the
memory of events which both interpreted alike, and of
convictions which were the common property of all Israel
... Men who worked along these lines were not creating
a new thing, and they who constantly appealed to the past,
never supposed they were'. [4] So according to N. W. Porteous
the prophets 'were inheritors and not the creators of a
religious tradition': they indeed 'laid posterity under their
debt but they were themselves debtors for the heritage
which they augmented ...'. [5] G. E. Mendenhall likewise

---

[1] *The Prophets and Israel's Culture*, 1934, p. 45.

[2] 'Revelation in the Old Testament' in *The Study of the Bible Today
and Tomorrow* (ed. H. R. Willoughby), 1947, p. 258.

[3] *The Call of Israel*, 1934, p. 23.

[4] *Prophet and Priest in Old Israel*, 1936, pp. 148-149.

[5] 'Prophecy' in *Record and Revelation* (ed. H. Wheeler Robinson) 1938,
p. 217. Cf. also his article 'The Basis of the Ethical Teaching of the

sees little originality in their work: their messages are rather 'essentially indictments of Israel for breach of covenant'. [1] Again, while admitting that Amos was 'a man on fire with zeal for a revival of religion and of social morality', W. F. Albright, nevertheless, added 'but he was no religious innovator, much less the earliest monotheistic teacher'. [2] Referring to the literary activity of the critical years before the fall of Jerusalem he further wrote: 'Under such circumstances spirits turn with nostalgia to the past and endeavour to recapture the vital element underlying former prosperity and stability. So the men of Judah turned back to Mosaic tradition, endeavouring to recover it as fully as possible and especially to reorganise the religion of the state on as pure a Mosaic basis as possible'. [3] Similarly, in discussing the origin of Israel's faith, G. E. Wright remarked, 'There can be no doubt that the fundamental elements of this faith were established *early* in Israel's history, which means that we are led to Sinai and to the work of Moses, like unto whom there did not arise a prophet in Israel'. [4] Resuming this theme on a later page (70) Wright contended, 'Things basically or entirely new were not added by the prophets, except as new events made necessary a deeper understanding of the implications of the covenant'. Equally convinced that the covenant derives from Moses, P. E. Brown, again, remarked: 'The rest of the Old Testament might be consi-

---

Prophets' in *Studies in Old Testament Prophecy* (ed. H. H. Rowley), 1950, pp. 143-156.

[1] *Law and Covenant in Israel and the Ancient Near East*, 1955, p. 19.

[2] *From the Stone Age to Christianity*, 1940, p. 239.

[3] *Op. cit.*, p. 241.

[4] *The Old Testament against its Environment*, 1950, p. 29. So H. M. Orlinsky speaks of 'the New Covenant' made by Moses which 'replaced the older, individual covenants between God and the Patriarchal leaders', *Ancient Israel*, 1954, p. 40.

dered as a commentary upon Israel's effort to keep the covenant'. [1]

But despite the confidence with which such scholars speak, the extent to which the prophets were indebted to tradition remains a doubtful issue. Nor indeed is the connection of the covenant with Moses an established principle of Old Testament exegesis. Eduard Meyer traced the origin of the covenant to the Canaanite deity El Berith of Shechem (Jud. 9 : 4, 46; Josh. 24 : 25), [2] and C. A. Simpson has similarly argued that it was here the Elohist writer became acquainted with the notion. [3] Wellhausen, however, associated the origin of the Israelite covenant with the promulgation of the Deuteronomic law: 'After the solemn and far-reaching act by which Josiah introduced this law, the notion of covenant-making between Jehovah and Israel appears to have occupied the central position in religious thought.' [4] W. A. Irwin agrees in substance with this contention, [5] while R. H. Pfeiffer confessed his inability 'to discover any reference to the divine covenant with Israel in passages which are earlier than 621'. [6] Explaining the 'origin of the doctrine of Israel's election through the covenant as a brilliant intuition of the author of the Book found in the Temple in 621' he says: 'Aware of the sharp contrast between the ardent religious nationalism of the J document, in which Jehovah supports Israel whether right or wrong, and the threat of Amos, who unequivocally

---

[1] *Interpretation*, 9, 1953, p. 35.

[2] *Die Israeliten und ihre Nachbarstämme*, 1906, pp. 546 f.

[3] *The Early Traditions of Israel*, 1948, p. 647.

[4] J. Wellhausen, *Prolegomena to the History of Israel* (Eng. trans.), 1885, p. 418.

[5] *The Intellectual Adventure of Ancient Man* (ed-. H. and H. A. Frankfort), 1946, p. 328.

[6] 'Facts and Faith in Biblical History', *J.B.L.*, 70, 1951, p. 2, n. 3.

declared that Jehovah would destroy Israel for its sins, and
being unwilling to relinquish either patriotism or divine
punitive justice, he was forced to combine them. Israel's
election through the covenant was his admirable synthesis
of apparently irreconcilable notions: for on the one hand
the choice of Israel among all nations satisfied the utmost
national pride, and on the other, according to the terms of
the covenant this election was conditional upon the fulfilment
of the divine commands' (p. 4). Martin Noth even regards
the tradition of Sinai as itself a late inclusion in the material
from which the Pentateuch was compiled and adds that 'an
essential part of this Sinai tradition that was developed
later on ... was the story ... of the establishment of a
permanent relationship between God and the people in the
form of a covenant'. [1] It is true that Ludwig Koehler has
attached considerable importance to the covenant, [2] while
Walter Eichrodt not only attributes it to Moses, but accords
it a fundamental place in his presentation of the theology
of the Old Testament. [3] James Muilenburg recently suggested that Exodus 19 : 3-6, a passage which ccnnects the
covenant with Moses, belongs to the Elohistic document of
the eighth century and concludes 'What we have in Exod.
19 : 3-6 is a special covenantal *Gattung*, and it is scarcely
too much to say that it is *in nuce* the *fons et origo* of the many
covenantal pericopes which appear throughout the Old
Testament'. [4] The relevant material of this passage in Exodus

---

[1] *The History of Israel* (Eng. trans. from the 2nd German edn.), 1958,
p. 126.

[2] *Old Testament Theology* (Eng. trans. from the 3rd German edn.),
1957, pp. 64 ff.

[3] *Theologie des Alten Testament*, 1, 1933, pp. 6 ff.

[4] 'The Form and Structure of the Covenantal Formulations', *V.T.* 9,
1959, pp. 351-352. Many scholars, of course, have attributed this
passage to J; e.g., S. R. Driver, *Intro. to the Lit. of the Old Test.*, 9th edn.,
1913, p. 31.

is that of verses 5-6 and reads thus: 'Now therefore, if you
will obey my voice and keep my covenant, you shall be my
own possession among all peoples; for all the earth is mine,
and you shall be to me a kingdom of priests and a holy
nation . . .'. It is, however, doubtful if this can be regarded
as of Elohistic provenance. The concept of Israel as Yahweh's
'own possession' is a commonplace in Deuteronomy (7 : 6;
14 : 2; 26 : 18) and also appears later in Leviticus (25 : 23).
The idea of Israel as ' a holy nation' is again basic to the
Holiness Code (*e.g.*, Lev. 19 : 2; 20 : 7, 24, 26), while the
presentation of Israel as 'a kingdom of priests' can scarcely
be earlier than Leviticus Chapter 21 where we read that
members of the Aaronic priesthood 'shall be holy to their
God' (vs. 6). If, then, Exodus 19 : 3-6 is the underlying
pattern of the many covenants which appear in the Old
Testament we can hardly argue with any confidence for their
antiquity. G. E. Mendenhall, again, claims that in view of
the heterogenous nature of the Israelite tribes only a covenant
relationship could serve as the basis of solidarity, and he has
therefore no hesitation in speaking of a 'Mosaic Covenant'. [1]
But in the Song of Deborah (Jud. 5), which is probably as
early as the twelfth century, there is no suggestion that the
Israelite tribes who did not join in the struggle against
Sisera (vv. 15-17) failed in loyalty to a federation effected
by covenantal terms. Neither is there any hint that Israel's
relationship with Yahweh was conceived of in terms of a
covenant: Israel is simply referred to as 'the people of

---

[1] *Op. cit.*, pp. 25, 40. Cf. also page 5 where we read that 'the federation
of tribes can be understood and explained only on the assumption that
it is a conscious continuation and re-adaptation of an earlier tradition
which goes back to the time of Moses. The covenant at Sinai was the
formal means by which the semi-nomadic clans, recently emerged
from state slavery in Egypt, were bound together in a religious and
political community'.

Yahweh' (vv. 11, 13). Wheeler Robinson, moreover, reminds us that the importance of the covenant 'is of formal expression rather than of independent idea' [1], while in a study of the election traditions of Israel Kurt Galling points out that the covenant itself does not rest on an act of redemption but is rather the confirmation of such an act. [2]

But whatever the origin and nature of the covenant we may doubt if the term was used by the eighth-century prophets to express God's relationship with Israel. In the records of such prophets we find only two references in which it might be thought to be used in this sense: namely Hosea 6 : 7 and 8 : 1. These passages are, however, of questionable authenticity. [3] In 6 : 7 we read:

> But at Adam they transgressed the covenant,
> there they dwelt faithlessly with me.

The Hebrew text of the verse is unfortunately uncertain and the meaning consequently doubtful. But on any reading [4] it seems to have little relevance to the material which precedes and follows, and altogether we may doubt its originality. The text of 8 : 1 is:

> Set the trumpet to your lips,
> for a vulture is over the house of the Lord,
> because they have broken my covenant,
> and transgressed my law.

Israel's sins are here described in summary fashion such as the breaking of the covenant and transgression of the law, although this is not characteristic of the prophet. Elsewhere he dwells on the nation's sins in detail (.e.g, 2 : 1 ff.; 4 : 1 ff.; 5 : 4, 11), while in verse two of this chapter he specifically

---

[1] *Inspiration and Revelation in the Old Testament*, p. 153.
[2] *Die Erwählungstraditionen Israels*, 1928, p. 37.
[3] Cf., e.g., Wellhausen, *op. cit.*, p. 418.
[4] Cf., e.g., Kittel's *Biblia Hebraica*, 3, *ad. loc.*

mentions certain shortcomings. Moreover, the concept of a vulture hovering over Yahweh's people is sufficient reason for setting a trumpet to the lips. It is the prophet's poetic presentation of the punishment which is shortly to overtake Israel, and of which she may now be publicly reminded. The notion of the breaking of law and covenant seems, on the other hand, to be but an editor's explanation of this symbolic reference to coming doom. Acceptance of both of these passages as original would, however, constitute but slight evidence that Hosea was indebted to the doctrine of the covenant, for they could as equally refer to divine law as to a Sinaitic covenant with Yahweh. [1] And although the term appears frequently in the Books of Jeremiah and Ezekiel we do not find it in contexts associated with the most distinctive character of their teaching.

Further, in view of the problem inherent in the recovery of the figure of Moses it is doubtful if we can assess the extent of his influence on the prophets. Covenants are indeed associated with his name in certain passages in the Book of Exodus (*e.g.*, 24 : 7-8; 34 : 10, 27), but the identity and contents of such covenants are by no means clear. Uncertainty, moreover, attaches to the date of these passages when we recognise that they are in contexts which are for the most part Deuteronomically revised editions of earlier Semitic laws. [2] Again, the Deuteronomist who wrote that there was 'none like' Moses 'for all the signs and wonders . . . and for all the mighty power and all the great and terrible deeds which' he 'wrought' (Dt. 34: 10-12) exerted, doubtless, an editorial influence on material relating to the work of Moses. [3] The hand of the Priestly writer is likewise evident

---

[1] Cf. Pfeiffer, *J. B. L.*, 70, 1951, p. 2, n. 3.
[2] See Pfeiffer, *Introduction to the Old Testament*, 1941, pp. 211 ff.
[3] Cf., e.g., 2 Sam. 7: 8-18 where the Deuteronomic editor represents

in Exodus 24 : 16-18, a passage descriptive of God's speaking
with Moses out of a cloud, while throughout the Book of
Leviticus the same writer represents Moses as the mouth-
piece of Yahweh (e.g., Lev. 1 : 1; 4 : 1; 5 : 1; 6 : 1).
However, then, we interpret the Pentateuchal documents it
must be admitted with Noth that the question of the role
which Moses filled historically is 'extraordinarily difficult
to answer.' [1] Noth himself is of the opinion that his original
role is to be placed within the framework of the deliverance
from Egypt during the phase of preparations for the entry
to Canaan. [2] Stating that the earliest tradition does not
specifically connect him with the Sinaitic theme, Noth
suggests 'that Moses had no historical connection with the
event which took place on Sinai'. [3] Indeed 'to describe him
as the "founder of a religion", or even to speak of a "Mosaic
religion" is quite misleading and incompatible with the
Moses tradition as it was developed later on'. [4] Thus, while
some scholars may take a more positive view of our Pentateuchal records, [5] we may doubt the validity of assigning a
determinative place to Moses in the structure and development of Israelite thought. In consequence the question
of Mosaic influence on the teaching of the prophets can
scarcely be approached with confidence.

But however we conceive of the events at Sinai there is
little evidence that they constituted the dominant element

David in as favourable a light as he is portrayed by the Chronicler
(I Chron. 28).

[1] *Op. cit.*, p. 134.
[5] *Op. cit.*, p.135, n.1.
[3] *Op. cit.*, p. 135.
[4] *Op. cit.*, p. 135, n.2.
[5] Cf., e.g., John Bright, *Early Israel in Recent History Writing*, 1956,
pp. 79-126, both for a criticism of Noth's views and for a more conser-
vative attitude to the biblical records.

in Israelite tradition. It is rather the Exodus from Egypt and related acts which appear to occupy the foremost place in the traditions of Israel. [1] As early as the tenth century we hear Jeroboam I appealing to the traditional sentiments of the people when he exclaimed, 'Behold your gods, O Israel, who brought you up out of the land of Egypt' (I Kgs. 12 : 28). Deliverance from Egypt is again the main theme of the ancient creed embedded in the present text of Deuteronomy 26 : 5-9: 'A wandering Aramean was my father; and he went down into Egypt and sojourned there ... And the Egyptians treated us harshly, and afflicted us, and laid upon us hard bondage ... and the Lord brought us up out of Egypt with a mighty hand ... and he brought us into this place and gave us this land ...'. [2] Elsewhere in Deuteronomy we find that the observance of divine commands is but the expression of gratitude for this deliverance: 'When your son asks you in time to come, What is the meaning of the testimonies and the statutes ... which the Lord our God has commanded you? then you shall say to your son, We were Pharaoh's slaves ... and the Lord brought us out of Egypt ... and the Lord showed signs and wonders, great and grievous, against Egypt ... and he brought us out from there, that he might ... give us the land which he swore to give to our fathers' (Dt. 6 : 20-23). [3]

Of more interest to us, however, is the fact that we also find references to Israel's deliverance from Egypt in the writings of the great prophets. [4] Amos supplements his statement that Yahweh brought 'up Israel from the land of Egypt' (9 : 7) with a reference to Yahweh's unique associa-

---

[1] Cf. here G. E. Wright, *God Who Acts*, 1952, pp. 70 f.

[2] Cf. here G. Von Rad, *Studies in Deuteronomy* (Eng. trans., Studies in Biblical Theology, 9), 1953, p. 23.

[3] Cf. also Dt. 32 : 10; Ps. 114 : 1.

[4] Cf. Wheeler Robinson, *op. cit.*, pp. 151-152.

tion with her (3 : 2). Hosea conceives of Yahweh saying, 'When Israel was a child, I loved him, and out of Egypt I called my son' (11 : 1; cf. also 13 : 1), while in Micah we find Yahweh appealing for Israel's faithfulness on the grounds that he 'brought' her 'up from the land of Egypt', and redeemed her 'from the house of bondage' (6 : 4). Jeremiah has likewise the events of the Exodus in mind when he represents Yahweh as saying:

> 'I remember the devotion of your youth,
> your love as a bride,
> how you followed me in the wilderness,
> in a land not sown' (2 : 2).

It was Israel's departure from the simplicity and loyalty of those days that led to her sinfulness:

> 'They did not say, Where is the Lord
> who brought us up from the land of Egypt
> who led us in the wilderness . . .' (2 : 6).

Ezekiel too knows of the tradition of Israel's connection with Egypt: 'Thus says the Lord God: On the day when I chose Israel . . . making myself known to them in the land of Egypt, I swore to them . . . that I would bring them out of the land of Egypt into a land that I had searched out for them . . .' (20 : 5-6). Similarly, it is doubtless a knowledge of the events of the Exodus which is the basis of Deutero-Isaiah's statement that Yahweh

> 'Makes a way in the sea, a path in the mighty waters,
> who brings forth chariot and horse, army and warrior'
> (43 : 16-17).

It will further be observed that the prophets conceive of Yahweh's connection with Israel in terms of human relationships rather than that of a covenant. Thus, Hosea represents this relationship as that of a marriage (2 : 13-14) and also as a father's love towards his son (11 : 1), while

Isaiah refers to the sons whom Yahweh 'reared and brought up' (1 : 2). Jeremiah speaks of Israel as Yahweh's bride (2 : 2; 3 : 20) and again of Yahweh as Israel's father (3 :19). Ezekiel portrays Yahweh's association with Israel as that of a foster parent who rescued a child abandoned in the wilderness (ch. 16), while in Deutero-Isaiah too we find a reference to Yahweh as Israel's husband (54 : 5). Through such relationships Israel was enabled to 'know' Yahweh; and hence it is unfaithfulness to this knowledge of God, rather than to a covenant with him, that is at the root of the prophets' denunciation of Israel. [1] Isaiah (1 : 3) complains that although an ox recognises its master 'Israel does not know' Yahweh. Advocating that Israel should 'press on to know the Lord' Hosea (6 : 3) condemns her for insincerely confessing 'My God, we Israel know thee' (8 : 2). Yahweh has likewise 'a controversy with the' people because

'There is no faithfulness or kindness
and no knowledge of God in the land' (4 : 1).

God primarily demands from man 'steadfast love' and 'knowledge' of himself (6 : 6) but 'lack of knowledge' leads to rejection from privileged association with him. [2] Indeed emphasis on the knowledge of God is so characteristic of the prophetic teaching that in the idealistic future envisaged by Jeremiah and Ezekiel Yahweh will impart a know-

---

[1] H. M. Orlinsky, however, writes: 'To the prophets ... every act of injustice on the part of one Israelite to another, or of one group against another, was an act of transgression against the Covenant', *op. cit.*, p. 152. So in a context in which he equates the law with that of Moses he further comments: 'It was this emphasis on the spirit of the law which at once provoked the prophets to their greatest denunciations and exhortations and at the same time brought them into conflict with the privileged members of their society' (p. 154).

[2] So the late editor of Hosea 11 : 2 was aware of the principle that Yahweh's recognition of Judah depended on her faithfulness to him: 'Judah is still known by God, and is faithful to the Holy One'.

ledge of himself both to those who are estranged from him, [1]
and to those who had not yet come to know him. [2] Again,
it is in the context of proclaiming the unique properties of
God that Deutero-Isaiah says:

> 'They have no knowledge
> who carry about their wooden idols,
> and keep on praying to a God that cannot save' (45 : 20).

A few verses in the prophetic literature further imply that
certain religious and moral standards were accepted by the
Israelites from early times. Thus reproving Israel for her
waywardness Jeremiah counsels:

> 'Stand by the roads and look
> and ask for the ancient paths,
> where the good way is; and walk in it,
> and find rest for your souls' (6 : 16).

Again we hear the complaint,

> 'My people have forgotten me,
> they burn incense to false gods;
> they have stumbled in their ways
> in the ancient roads . . .' (18 : 15)

In Isaiah 30 : 10-11 we find a similar condemnation of those
'who say to the seers, "See not"; and to the prophets,
"Prophesy not to us what is right; speak to us smooth
things, prophesy illusions, leave the way, turn aside from the
path" . . .' We have little information as to the guardians and
mediators of these standards, but passages in Amos
(2 : 11-12) and Hosea (12 : 10) represent certain 'prophets'
as mediators between Yahweh and the Israelites. Who these
prophets were it is not easy to say, but if the references
are authentic, they could conceivably be figures of the stature
of Elijah and Micaiah. [3]

---

[1] E.g., Jer. 24 : 7; Ezek. 28: 24; 36: 11.
[2] E.g., Ezek. 36 : 23; 38 : 23. Cf. also Jer. 31 : 34.
[3] Cf. here R. S. Cripps, *op. cit.*, p. 145.

But while the prophets seem to have referred to certain elements in Israelite tradition there is much in their teaching which cannot be regarded as deriving from tradition. And having regard to the circumstances of their call and their close personal relationship with God, it can hardly be doubted that they were themselves direct channels of divine revelation. For men who were privileged to stand 'in the council of Yahweh' and who were thus enabled 'to perceive and to hear his word' (Jer. 23 : 18) were scarcely dependent on tradition for the source and authority of their message. 'Whatever I command you, you shall speak' was the assurance of God to Jeremiah (1 : 7), and he henceforth claims to speak 'from the mouth of Yahweh' (23 : 16). It was the 'word' of Yahweh which in consequence was the sole authoritative basis of the prophetic pronouncements. Isaiah believed that when Yahweh speaks both heaven and earth are alike constrained to give attention (1 : 2), while his indictment of the people begins with the phrase 'Hear the word of the Lord' (1 : 10). When Amos left his sheep on the mountains of Tekoa and travelled to Bethel to prophesy, it was not because he claimed a particular aptitude to expound the contents of traditional dogma: it was rather because Yahweh, who said 'Go prophesy to my people Israel' (7 : 15), revealed 'his secret to his servants the prophets' (3 : 7). Indeed the message of Amos was regarded as being so contrary to accepted opinion that his visit was interpreted as an attempt to undermine the ruling authority (7 : 10). Nor is it likely that the prophet would have undertaken so dangerous a mission had he not been fortified in the knowledge that the source of his message was Yahweh whose call he found irresistible (3 : 8). Jeremiah too quoted Yahweh as the source of his authority. His first recorded appearance was in response to Yahweh's command, 'Go and proclaim in the hearing of Jerusalem' (2 : 1), while his revolutionary temple address was delivered at Yahweh's request that he should 'stand in the gate of the Lord's house and say, Hear the word of the Lord, all ye men of Judah' (7 : 1-2). Nor was it by appealing to tradition that he more than once incurred the opposition of his audience: it was rather by his faithful mediation of the 'word of Yahweh' which he, himself, was powerless to suppress (20 : 7). Ezekiel's condemnation of the religious practices of his countrymen was, again, dictated by 'the word of Yahweh', (6 : 1 f.), while his startling delineation of the origin and history of the Hebrews, likewise prompted by Yahweh (16 : 1 ff.), was scarcely in accordance with that represented in tradition.

But inasmuch as this 'word' had its source in God it was regarded as an entity in itself and, therefore, as detachable from the personality of the prophet through whom it found expression. Hence it is justly claimed that an 'important aspect of the prophet's function consists in the liberation of a word of God, which becomes objectively powerful far beyond the personal range of the prophet's activity'. [1] Charged thus with an independent dynamic it was conceived by Jeremiah not only as a raging 'fire' within his own bones (20 : 9), but as consuming people as fire consumes wood (5 : 14). Possessing a character of its own it actually performs functions by itself. According to Deutero-Isaiah it is one of the most effective agents in the achievement of the divine purpose; for Yahweh himself says, the

'word that goes forth from my mouth . . .
shall not return to me empty,
but it shall accomplish that which I purpose,
and prosper in the thing for which I sent it' (55 : 11).

Nor is the effect of this word confined to one age or place.

---

[1] Wheeler Robinson, *op. cit.*, p. 170.

The natural order is but ephemeral and transient 'but the word of . . . God will stand for ever' (Is. 40 : 8).

A consideration of the source of the message of the prophets cannot, moreover, be indifferent to the requirements of the particular circumstances in which they were called to their task. From the eighth century the political structure, not only of Palestine, but of the ancient Near East as a whole was changing. Israel was rapidly becoming subject to the threat of invading armies, marching under the tutelage of their national gods.[1] Confronted by overwhelming forces the Hebrews could place but little confidence in their own strength. Yet if they were to be fortified in their religion it must necessarily be through a conception of Yahweh which differed considerably from traditional belief. Tradition related that Yahweh afflicted the Pharaoh with plagues till eventually he was compelled to release the Israelites from bondage (Exod. chs. 7-12). But although under the protection of their Deity, they were forced to take a devious route through the wilderness (Exod. 13 : 17-18) and were denied a passage through the territory of Moab (Num. 20 : 14-21). The God Yahweh who had compassion on the Israelites in Egypt became their national God on their entry to Canaan (*e.g.*, 1 Sam. 5 : 7-11), while on establishing themselves in the land he became more exclusively regarded as 'the God of Israel' (Jud. 5 : 3-5; 1 Kgs 18 : 36; 2 Kgs 1 : 3; 10 : 31). When, however, the resurgence of Assyrian power threatened to disrupt their national life it was inevitable that the question of the sovereignty of their national God should arise. Hence it is doubtful if on the traditional view the Judeans of the day could have effectively answered the question of the Assyrian Rabshakeh: 'Has any of the

---

[1] Cf., e.g., *A.N.E.T.*, p. 277 and p. 284b, where both Shalmaneser III and Sargon II attribute success to their gods.

gods of the nations ever delivered his land out of the hand of the king of Assyria? Where are the gods of Hamath and Arpad? Where are the gods of Sepharvaim, Hena, and Ivvah? Have they delivered Samaria out of my hand? Who among all the gods of the countries have delivered their countries out of my hand, that Yahweh should deliver Jerusalem out of my hand?' (2 Kgs. 18 : 33-35). It would seem probable that Rabshakeh was but representing the view of the ordinary Israelite when he implied that Yahweh was no more powerful against the Assyrian armies than the gods of Hamath, Arpad and other peoples. We are thus not surprised to read that 'the people were silent and answered him not a word' (vs. 36); and although an editor adds that their silence was due to the command of Hezekiah it is significant that the king himself 'rent his clothes . . ., covered himself with sackcloth', and sent officials to discuss the matter with the prophet Isaiah (2 Kgs. 19:1-2).

In virtue of his privilege of immediate knowledge of the nature and will of Yahweh Isaiah alone was able to offer a word of assurance in this hour of crisis. Knowing that Assyria was but an instrument in the hand of Yahweh (Is. 10 : 5 f.) he regarded the presence of her soldiers before Jerusalem as a mere incident in a series of events which Yahweh had initiated and directed for his own purpose. Therefore, as he previously assured Ahaz that the Syro-Ephraimite attack on Jerusalem would prove unsuccessful (Is. 7 : 1-7), so now he reported Yahweh as saying: 'Do not be afraid because of the words that you have heard . . . Behold, I will put a spirit in him so that he shall hear a rumour and return to his own land' (2 Kgs. 19 : 6-7).

In presenting a view of God adequate to the challenge of his age Jeremiah had again to contend strongly with the presuppositions of tradition. Recognising God's hand

in the movements of the nations he interpreted Nebuchadrezzar's triumph at Carchemish as fraught with the most
far-reaching consequences for the people of Judah; and as
events unfolded themselves he became increasingly aware
of the inevitable destruction of the state and temple. But
when he attempted to warn his countrymen of such developments he met with the most hostile opposition (26 : 1 ff.).
For, a people who regarded themselves as 'called' by the
'name' of Yahweh and as entitled to his protection (14 : 9)
would not readily accept that their national life was drawing
to a close. The intimation was naturally most disquieting to
those who claimed to represent the traditional religion and
institutions of the land. It is thus not surprising to find that
the false prophets and priests were conspicuous in shouting
'This man deserves sentence of death, because he has prophesied against this city' (26 : 11). When eventually many of the
Judeans were deported to Babylon it was the consciousness of
severance from traditional life that hindered acceptance of
their situation. But in the knowledge that it was Yahweh's
will that the exiles should remain in Babylon (24 : 4-7),
Jeremiah urged that they should establish their homes
there and become worthy Babylonian citizens (29 : 1-7). The
exiles, however, not only regarded it as their inalienable
right to live in the land of Yahweh, but they were accustomed
to worship him through the medium of sacrifice and temple.
The complexity of their situation was, moreover, increased
by the inherence in their traditions of the notion that Yahweh
could not be worshipped outside the boundaries of his
own land;[1] and the recently published Deuteronomic
Law restricting sacrifice to the temple in Jerusalem (Dt.
12 : 5 f.) but served to confirm such views. Expressive,

---

[1] Cf. I Sam. 26 : 19; 2 Kgs 5 : 17.

therefore, of their sense of alienation from God was their cry, 'How can we sing Yahweh's songs in a strange land?' (Ps. 137 : 4).

It was consequently in response to the spiritual needs of the exiles that Jeremiah elaborated his own views of God. Fundamental to his theology was the assumption that Yahweh was independent of territorial boundaries and was indifferent to the ceremonial of temple ritual. The state of Judah may fall and the temple services may come to an end but Yahweh could be worshipped wherever the exiles earnestly sought him: 'You will . . . come and pray to me, and I will hear you. You will seek me and find me; when you seek me with all your heart, I will be found, saith Yahweh' (29 : 12-14).

Similarly, in his ministry in Babylon Ezekiel was directly concerned with the misleading effects of traditional dogma on the exiles. Incorporated in their traditions was the belief that Yahweh visited 'the iniquity of the fathers upon the children to the third and fourth generation' (Exod. 20 : 5; Num. 14 : 18). However this view may be justified from the standpoint of national solidarity and the welfare of the community it could have but an unfortunate affect on the scattered groups of exiles living in Babylonia. Yet so fundamental had the belief become that it now found expression in the proverb: 'The fathers have eaten sour grapes, and the children's teeth are set on edge' (Ezek. 18 : 2). The exiles, accordingly, interpreted their circumstances as being but the inevitable consequence of the transgressions of their forbears. Thus frustrated, they considered it pointless to follow the paths of righteousness and futile to seek the consolations of religion. Life seemed without either purpose or hope; and at length in utter despair they cried, 'Our transgressions and our sins are upon us, and we waste away

because of them; how then can we live?' (33 : 10). Labouring under such misconceptions they were naturally led to question the justice of God; for a God who was thought of as punishing the children for the sins of the fathers could not be regarded as a just God. It was therefore with some conviction that they exclaimed 'The way of Yahweh is not just' (18 : 29).

If, then, the exiles were not to become entirely indifferent in their allegiance to Yahweh they must conceive of him in radically different terms. This was the nature of the task awaiting Ezekiel. Declaring that 'all souls' belonged to God (18 : 4) he demonstrated the falsity of the assumption that Yahweh punished the children for the sins of the fathers. Yahweh was concerned with the individual and judged him on his own merits irrespective of the conduct of his father. Contrary to popular opinion the principle underlying divine retribution was that 'the righteousness of the righteous shall be upon himself, and the wickedness of the wicked shall be upon himself' (18 : 20). Consequently, if a man observed the standards of Yahweh 'he shall not die for his father's iniquity; he shall surely live' (18 : 17). There can, therefore, be no substance in the charge that Yahweh is unjust. The basis of his rewards and punishments is rather to be inferred from his statement: 'O house of Israel, I will judge each of you according to his ways' (33 : 10).

Such considerations indicate, then, that the great creative prophets were but little indebted to traditional Israelite belief for the content of their message. It is true that, with the object of reminding Israel of her privileged association with Yahweh, they occasionally pointed to tradition; but there is no evidence of their doing so in times of acute national and religious crises. Indeed such occasions disclosed the limited nature of traditional theology; and it was, therefore, in order to reveal himself more fully to his people that Yahweh called and commissioned his prophets. Their primary task was to declare what was directly revealed to them by Yahweh (*e.g.*, Amos 3 : 7-8; Jer. 1 : 7; Ezek. 3 : 10-17), while the opposition they experienced from the interested representatives of traditional beliefs and institutions (*e.g.*, Jer. 1 : 18-19) sufficiently testifies to the novelty of their teaching. Nor in all the struggles of their difficult task did they attempt to justify their statements by reference to traditional dogma. [1] They did not, like the priests, appeal to the authority of official status or to a law which they claimed to propound. [2] Rather, convinced of the inspired source of their message their sole claim to authority was 'Thus saith Yahweh'.

---

[1] Cf. W. A. Irwin, 'The prophet received his messages ... not out of law or tradition, but through his own individual experience in which he heard the Lord speaking to himself. Accordingly, he stood before king, priest, and people and, on his own unsupported conviction that he as a person possessed invaluable truths denied to all others, hurled his denunciations and directions in opposition to accepted standards and conduct'. *The Old Testament: Keystone to Human Culture*, p. 206. Cf. here also the suggestive remarks of I. I. Mattuck, *The Thought of the Prophets*, 1953, pp. 36-37.

[2] Cf., e.g., Jer. 2 : 8; 8 : 8; 14 : 18.

CHAPTER THREE

BASIC PROPHETIC PRINCIPLES

Confident that their commission and inspiration derived from Yahweh the canonical prophets were fearless in their denunciation of the religious and social conditions of their time. In many respects the religion of their fellow Israelites was scarcely recognisable from contemporary Canaanite practice. The vast majority of the people sacrificed to Baal and freely participated in the gross and sensual practices associated with the local shrines (Hos. 4 : 13-14). Baal was even thought of as the god of fertility; and grain, oil, and other produce of the earth were consequently attributed to him. Unmindful of the ethical nature and demands of Yahweh the nation as a whole countenanced a social code which was completely void of moral content; yet their attitude was one of self-satisfied complacency, believing that as Yahweh was in their 'midst' no evil could befall them (Mic. 3 : 11). Regarding Yahweh as a national God whose function was to protect his own people, the Israelites still adhered to the notion of an earlier day that Yahweh's sphere of activity was exclusively confined to the territory of Israel (cf. I Sam. 26 : 19 : 2 Kgs. 5 : 17). In this respect they were doubtless influenced by the beliefs of neighbouring peoples. For they observed that Baal was worshipped by the Canaanites (cf. I Kgs. 18 : 20-29), Rimmon by the Syrians (2 Kgs. 5 : 18), Chemosh by the Moabites (I Kgs. 11 : 33) and Milcom by the Ammonites (I Kgs. 11 : 33). And considering that many of the Israelites also worshipped these gods (1 Kgs. 11 : 33) they can scarcely have conceived of Yahweh as differing significantly from them. King Ahaz indeed regarded the martial qualities of 'the gods of Damascus which had defeated him' as comparable, if not superior, to Yahweh (2 Chron. 28 : 23; cf. also 2 Kgs 16 : 10 f.).

But although the Israelites regarded Yahweh as their national God they were still dubious as to the power he wielded even in their own land. On entering Canaan they were attracted by such deities as Baal Berith (Jud. 8 : 33; 9 : 4), while the great national god of the land was Baal whose primary function was the advancement of growth and fertility. It was, therefore, natural that Israel too should attribute her subsistence to his bounty and say:

> 'I will go after my lovers, who give me my bread and my water,
> my wool and my flax, my oil and my drink' (Hos. 2 : 5).

It was accordingly one of the essential tasks of the prophets to dispose of this commonly accepted belief and to emphasize that Yahweh was Lord of the whole realm of nature and its produce. With reference then to Israel's ignorance and sin Hosea represents Yahweh as saying:

> 'And she did not know that it was I who gave her
> the grain, the wine and the oil, and who
> lavished upon her silver and gold which they used for Baal.
> Therefore I will take back my grain in its time,
> and my wine in its season;
> and I will take away my wool and my flax' (2 : 8-9).

Yahweh thus not only provided Israel with wool and oil, but was also responsible for the mineral products of the earth. In like manner 'the beasts of the field, and the birds of the air, and even the fish of the sea' (4 : 3) are subject to his commands.

Amos likewise speaks of Yahweh's power to withhold

or send rain with its consequent affect on the cereal and
vintage crops:

'And I also withheld the rain from you
when there were yet three months to the harvest;
I would send rain upon one city,
and send no rain upon another city;
one field would be rained upon,
and the field on which it did not rain withered ...
I smote you with blight and mildew;
I laid waste your gardens and your vineyards;
your fig trees and your olive trees the locust devoured' (4 : 7-9).

But Amos further implies that in addition to exercising
control over nature and its products Yahweh is also the
ultimate cause of all events and activity:

'Do two walk together, unless they have made an appoint-
ment?
Does a lion roar in the forest, when he has no prey?
Does a young lion cry out from his den,
If he has taken nothing?
Does a bird fall in a snare on the earth,
when there is no trap for it?
Does a snare spring up from the ground,
when it has taken nothing?
Is a trumpet blown in a city,
and the people are not afraid?
Does evil befall a city,
unless the Lord has done it?' (3 : 3-6) [1].

---

[1] Commenting on this passage Pfeiffer aptly remarked: 'Lacking the
Aristotelian terms "cause and effect" Amos succeeds in showing, by a
series of images ... that every effect has a cause', *Intro. to the Old Test.*
p. 584. Further references to God's creative activity appear in 4 : 13;
5 : 8-9; and 9 : 5 f., but it is doubtful if these passages derive from
Amos himself. Cf. here F. Horst, 'Die Doxologien im Amosbuch',
Z.A.W., *N.F.* 6, 1929, pp. 45-54 for a statement on their date and
purpose. R. Gordis, however, argues that the entire Book apart from
9 : 13-15 is from the hand of Amos, *H.T.R.*, 33, 1940, pp. 239-251.

Jeremiah also assumes that the natural order is dependent upon God. Thus the wasting of pastures and the ruination of cities is but the expression of Yahweh's anger for the wilful neglect of his law (9 : 12-13), while the illimitable tracts of sand which bound and control the sea point to further evidence of Yahweh's power over nature (5 : 22). It is Yahweh too

> 'who gives the rain in its season,
> the autumn rain and the spring rain,
> and keeps . . . the weeks appointed for the harvest' (5 : 24).

Such statements do not merely represent the theological formulation of Jeremiah's own views: they were rather uttered with the object of enlightening the people of his time. Yet even late in his career the Judeans were still unconvinced of Yahweh's ability to provide the necessities of life. Confronting him on one occasion they exclaimed in defiant mood: 'As for the word which you have spoken to us in the name of Yahweh, we will not listen to you. But we will do everything that we have vowed, burn incense to the queen of heaven and pour out libations to her, as we did, both we and our fathers, our kings and our princes, in the cities of Judah and in the streets of Jerusalem; for then we had plenty of food, and prospered, and saw no evil. But since we left off burning incense to the queen of heaven and pouring out libations to her, we have lacked everything and have been consumed by the sword and by famine'. (44 : 16-18). Jeremiah's teaching on the divine providence and bounty was designed therefore, like that of his predecessors, to meet the false conceptions of Yahweh entertained by so many of his contemporaries.

It is, however, in the writings of Deutero-Isaiah that we find the most profound prophetic expression of God's sovereignty over nature. Such is Yahweh's power that he

can create at will those elements that are necessary for the
sustenance of his people.

> 'When the poor and needy seek water, and there is none,
> and their tongue is parched with thirst,
> I Yahweh will answer them,
> I the God of Israel will not forsake them.
> I will open rivers on the bare heights,
> and fountains in the midst of the valleys' (41 : 17-18).

Even more significant still is the fact that the bare, forbidding,
wilderness changes its appearance at his command. Hence
to the exiles who are contemplating the difficult journey
homewards his assurance is:

> 'I will make the wilderness a pool of water,
> and the dry land springs of water.
> I will put in the wilderness the cedar,
> the acacia, the myrtle and the olive;
> I will set in the desert the cypress,
> the plane and the pine together' (41 : 18-19).

But in addition to creating the firmament and the heavenly
planets, it is Yahweh also

> 'who spread forth the earth and what comes from it,
> who gives breath to the people upon it
> and spirit to those who walk in it' (42 : 5).

Another misconception of the Israelites was their assumption that Yahweh was obliged to protect and sustain them
irrespective of their religious and moral conduct. By the
time of Amos it was believed that in the event of national
crisis Yahweh would appear and deliver his people. This
manifestation of the divine was known as the 'Day of
Yahweh', a term which is probably to be associated with
'the day of Yahweh's manifestation in the festal cult at the
New Year Festival'. [1] On that particular Day in the Festival

---

[1] So S. Mowinckel, *He That Cometh* (Eng. trans. of *Han som Kommer*

Yahweh was thought to come and promise deliverance from
the enemy and to assure peace and prosperity in the coming
year. It was for such a day of assurance that the Israelites
as a whole now yearned, but Amos ironically retorts

'Woe to you who desire the day of the Lord
Why would you have the day of the Lord?
It is darkness and not light . . .
and gloom with no brightness in it' (5 : 18 f.).

Thus, contrary to the popular hope that Yahweh would
appear and sustain his people, the prophet declares that in so
far as Yahweh manifests himself at all it will be in dis-
comfiting the arrogant and apostate. Amos further implies
that although Israel was 'known' by Yahweh there were
other nations whom he might easily have chosen: the
Israelites were indeed called but this was in fact admission
to a privilege which incurred an obligation to service and
obedience (3 : 2).

Hosea too explains Israel's call in terms of divine love and
grace (11 : 1), while Isaiah refers to the care and nurture
which Yahweh bestowed on her (1 : 2). Concerned with the
same problem as his predecessors, Jeremiah likewise attempted to dispose of the view that Israel had a special claim to
Yahweh's protection. In their distress the people clamour
for God's salvation and say:

'O thou hope of Israel, its saviour in time of trouble,
why shouldst thou be like a stranger in the land,
like a wayfarer who turns aside to tarry for a night?
Why shouldst thou be like a man confused,
like a mighty man who cannot save?
Yet thou, O lord art in the midst of us,
and we are called by thy name; leave us not' (14 : 8-9).

by G. W. Anderson, 1956), p. 132. On the meaning of the Day of
Yahweh and the question of a prophetic eschatology see Appendix,
below, pp. 202 ff.

Jeremiah, however, replies that their plight is a direct consequence of their own sins:

> 'Thus says the Lord concerning this people:
> They have loved to wander thus,
> they have not restrained their feet;
> therefore the Lord does not accept them,
> now he will remember their iniquity
> and punish their sins' (14 : 10).

There are thus no grounds for assuming that Yahweh has a national obligation to the people of his choice. The continuance of his favour depended on allegiance to his demands, but

> 'long ago you broke your yoke and burst your bonds;
> and you said, I will not serve . . .
> Yet I planted you a choice vine, wholly of pure seed.
> How then have you turned degenerate
> and become a wild vine?' (2 : 20-21).

This is in fact what Israel has become. Despite the protection and bounty Yahweh has accorded her she now says

> 'to a tree, You are my father,
> and to a stone, You gave me birth'.

Yet as if by a natural right they turn to Yahweh 'in the time of their trouble' and say 'Arise and save us' (2 : 27). But to their surprise his retort now is,

> 'Where are your gods that you made for yourself?
> Let them arise, if they can save you,
> in your time of trouble' (2 : 28).

Ezekiel is more emphatic still on the true nature of the relationship between Yahweh and Israel. Even on the assumption that Yahweh was a national God, Israel could not claim his protection. For Israel herself could not be regarded as a nation composed of homogeneous elements. 'Your origin and your birth are of the land of the Canaanites:

your father was an Amorite, and your mother a Hittite'
(16 : 3). Abhorred even from the day of her birth 'no eye
pitied' her. 'And when I passed by you . . . I said . . . Live
and grow up like a plant of the field . . . I plighted my
troth to you . . . and you became mine . . . And your renown
went forth among the nations because of your beauty, for
it was perfect through the splendour which I had bestowed
upon you, says the Lord God' (vv. 5-14). Hence any relationship that subsisted between Israel and Yahweh rested
entirely on Yahweh's initiative in approaching and defending
her when she was but an insignificant outcast among the
nations of the world.

The prophets were further concerned to present Yahweh's
relationship with Israel in terms of morality. Indeed the
ethical standards they required constituted the most serious
difference between them and the people of their day. For
fundamental to all their teaching was the notion that Yahweh
was a God of Righteousness. It was this property of his
nature which ultimately underlay both his love and his
wrath for Israel. Yahweh could only act according to
that which is Right, and his Righteousness was, therefore,
a law of his Being. The Israelites expected their national
god to protect them in all circumstances, thinking it was
only 'right' and 'natural' that he should. But the prophets
insisted that Yahweh's acts were ethically conditioned and
that therefore it was 'as "right" that Israel should suffer
for her shortcomings as that she should be rewarded for her
piety'. [1] Adherence to that which is right, honourable and
just is, then, necessarily enjoined upon man. One of the
complaints of Yahweh in the time of Amos was that 'they do
not know how to do right' who practise 'violence and

---

[1] S. A. Cook, *The Truth of the Bible*, p. 35.

robbery' (3 : 10). Hence many of the utterances of Amos are directed against the ethical standards which prevailed in his day. [1] The claims of justice and truthfulness were ignored and those who attempted to observe them became the object of scorn and oppression:

> 'They hate him who reproves in the gate,
> and they abhor him who speaks the truth' (5 : 10).

One of the most deplorable features of the social structure was the ruthless exploitation of the poor. Victims of economic circumstances they had perforce to borrow their bread from the rich, but only to suffer unduly from their status as debtors. Exorbitant exactions further diminished their resources, while on the other hand the prosperity of the rich increased with a consequent indulgence in stately homes and pleasant vineyards (5 : 11). Nor was such dishonesty and oppression confined to private dealings. It also obtained in public life, and particularly in the courts of law where it was customary to

> 'sell the righteous for silver
> and the needy for a pair of shoes' (2 : 6).

Intent on the prosecution of illicit gain avaricious merchants ask

> 'When will the new moon be over, that we may sell grain?
> And the sabbath, that we may offer wheat for sale,
> that we may make the ephah small and the shekel great,
> and deal deceitfully with false balances . . .
> and sell the refuse of the wheat?' (8 : 5-6).

---

[1] Cf. here H. W. Hertzberg's study of the ethical significance of the Hebrew word *mishpat* ('judgment') as used by the prophets, *Z.A.W.*, 40, 1922, pp. 274-287, and vol. 41, 1923, pp. 22-41. Cf. also J. A. Bollier, '*The Righteousness of God*', *Interpretation*, 8, 1954, pp. 404-409, who, however, claims that the righteousness demanded by the prophets refers to the terms of the Covenantal agreement with Yahweh.

Thus it is that certain sections of the people enjoy the luxury of ivory bedsteads and comfortable couches, and dine on choice lambs and stall-fed calves. They drink wine by the bowlful and anoint themselves with the most precious oils, but are, alas, completely indifferent to the moral degradation of the nation (6 : 4-6).

But Amos is not exceptional in his delineation of the social and religious standards of the Israelites. His contemporary, Hosea, was equally vehement in his denunciation of Israelite society, while the ritual of the cult of Baal receives even greater condemnation at his hands. [1] Yahweh was Israel's 'first husband' (2 : 7) but she forsook him for Baal mainly owing to the false belief that it is he who provided her daily subsistence (2 : 5 f.). In deference to the claims of Baal 'for grain and wine they gash themselves' and 'rebel' against Yahweh (7 : 14), and the more their substance increased the more altars they built (10 : 1). It is, then, against a background of widespread disregard for the ideals of Yahweh that Hosea says:

> 'There is no faithfulness or kindness,
> and no knowledge of God in the land;
> there is swearing, lying, killing, stealing . . .
> they break all bounds and murder follows murder' (4 :1-2).

Drunken orgies stupify the people (4 : 11) who are thus rendered even less capable of resisting the sensual appeal of the local sanctuaries (4 : 14) [2]. Void of understanding they

> 'inquire of a thing of wood,
> and their staff gives them oracles.
> For a spirit of harlotry has led them astray,

---

[1] See H. G. May 'The Fertility Cult in Hosea', *A.I.S.L.*, 48, 1932, pp. 73-98.

[2] 'The fertility cult was a religion of the senses, an aesthetic cult. It was literally a religion of wine, women, and song', May, *ibid.*, p. 93.

and they have left their God to play the harlot.
They sacrifice on the tops of the mountains,
and make offerings upon the hills,
under oak, poplar, and terebinth,
because their shade is good' (4 : 12-13).

Indulging themselves in the most gross extravagances the
heads of the nation did little to restrain the licentiousness
of the populace (5 : 1). The priests, who should be the
advocates of the highest religious principles, not only failed
in their duty, but by their actual examples encouraged the
practice of vice:

'They feed on the sin of my people;
they are greedy for their iniquity.
And it shall be like people, like priest' (4 : 8-9).

Hence all members of the community are reduced to the
same level of degradation and apostasy. But in view of the
grace Yahweh has bestowed on Israel he cannot condone
such conduct and consequently

'will punish them for their ways,
and requite them for their deeds' (4 : 9).

It has been said that 'Amos bases religion on morality,
while Hosea deduces morality from religion'. [1] It is true that
the principle of divine righteousness was fundamental to the
teaching of Amos, while influenced by the conception of
Yahweh's close relationship with Israel Hosea implied that
there can be no morality which is not inspired by sincere
religion. [2] Yet even with Hosea morality is scarcely a secondary consideration. One of his criticisms of Israel's preoccupation with Canaanite religion was its effect on her

---

[1] W. Robertson Smith, *The Prophets of Israel*, p. 163.
[2] So S. A. Cook remarked, 'The two supplement each other . "All's
love yet all's law": either by itself is incomplete', *The Old Testament:
A Reinterpretation*, p. 175.

moral standards (4 : 17-18). Falsehood was so characteristic of the people that

> 'They utter mere words;
> with empty oaths they make covenants;
> so judgment springs up like poisonous weeds' (10 : 4).

This indifference to truth and integrity justifies the statement that Israel has become

> 'a trader in whose hands are false balances,
> he loves to oppress.
> Ephraim has said, Ah, but I am rich,
> I have gained wealth for myself' (12 : 7-8).

Yahweh, however, significantly retorts:

> 'But all his riches can never offset
> the guilt he has incurred' (vs. 7).

Hence it is that 'Samaria shall bear her guilt because she has rebelled against her God' (13 : 16). Similarly, the calf-god of Beth-aven which was so much the object of Israel's attention will itself be destroyed:

> 'Its people shall mourn for it,
> and its idolatrous priests shall wail over it,
> over its glory which has departed from it' (10 : 5).

Isaiah's indictment of Israel is based on similar grounds. Despite her privileged association with Yahweh she has become indifferent to him.

> 'Sons have I reared and brought up,
> but they have rebelled against me.
> The ox knows its owner, and the ass its master's crib;
> but Israel does not know,
> my people does not understand' (1 : 2-3).

Instead of acknowledging their gratitude to Yahweh and observing his moral requirements the Israelites are a

> 'sinful nation, a people laden with iniquity,
> offspring of evildoers, sons who deal corruptly.

They have forsaken Yahweh . . .
they are utterly estranged' (1 : 4).

Attracted by the music and ritual of the feasts at the local sanctuaries they become so drunken with wine that

'they do not regard the deeds of the Lord
or see the work of his hands' (5 : 11-12).

Abandonment of Yahweh and his religious ideals inevitably leads to a declension in moral standards and so 'every one loves a bribe and runs after gifts' (1 : 23), while it is common practice to

'acquit the guilty for a bribe,
and deprive the innocent of his right' (5 : 23).

Moral values are subverted by 'those who call evil good and good evil' (5 : 20), and in place of 'justice' there is 'bloodshed' and for 'righteousness' a pitiful 'cry' (5 : 7).

Unfaithfulness to the standards of Yahweh is likewise the burden of Micah's invective. The social disorders of his time are such that

'The godly man has perished from the earth,
and there is none upright among men;
they all lie in wait for blood,
and each hunts his brother with a net.
Their hands are upon what is evil,
to do it diligently' (7 : 2-3).

Constantly occupied with schemes for increasing their wealth, the rich 'covet fields and seize them . . . houses and take them away' (2 : 2). Wicked and fraudulent dealings characterise the commerce of the day with the resultant accumulation of dishonest gains. Consequently it is with some indignation that Yahweh asks:

'Shall I acquit the man with wicked scales
and with a bag of deceitful weights?' (6 : 11).

Such conduct is not, however, exceptional; for the nation as a whole is guilty of immoral dealings. Even

> 'the prince and the judge ask for a bribe,
> and the great man utters the evil desire of his soul . . .
> The best of them is like a brier,
> The most upright of them a thorn hedge' (7 : 3-4).

The priests and prophets too are only concerned with the financial rewards of their profession (3 : 11), while professing a nominal allegiance to Yahweh all alike say

> 'Is not the Lord in the midst of us?
> No evil shall come upon us' (3 : 11).

But in claiming the protection of Yahweh without regard to their own conduct they entirely overlook his moral demands. Such a claim will find little acceptance before him. His judgment rather is,

> 'Behold, against this family I am devising evil' (2 : 3).

The moral nature of Yahweh and his demands for right-eousness from Israel is similarly an element in the teaching of both Jeremiah and Ezekiel,[1] but in the writings of Deutero-Isaiah we find a more varied interpretation of the concept of divine Righteousness. Here 'Righteousness' is used not only to denote honourable relations between man and man, but in a variety of ways to express the character and nature of God. It is thus in accordance with Yahweh's being that 'in righteousness' a word has gone forth from his mouth to reveal his purpose to mankind (45 : 23), while he is 'a righteous God and a Saviour' (45 : 21) because in his omniscient power he was able to declare things from of old and determine the future from the beginning of time. When, again, Yahweh says that he 'aroused' Cyrus 'in right-eousness' he infers that he did so in accordance with

---

[1] So e.g., Jer. 9 : 24; 12 : 1; 17 : 9-10; Ezek. 18 : 20 f.

his definite purpose, for only Yahweh could call Cyrus and
sustain him in the mission he was destined to accomplish. [1]
The gods and idols of the nations could neither prophesy
nor conceive of such an event and therefore it could not be
said of any of them 'He is right' (41 : 26). It can be predicated
of Yahweh, because in bringing to fulfilment thoughts long
conceived he is but expressing his divine nature. Yahweh
created the heavens and the earth for the purpose of
habitation: 'he did not create it a chaos', nor did he expect
his people to seek him 'in a land of darkness'. It was because
of such purposeful activity that he can say,

> 'I Yahweh speak the truth, I declare what is right' (45 : 19).

There are, moreover, certain passages in which the term
'Righteousness' is expressive of God's purpose for mankind
as a whole and is therefore used in the sense of deliverance
and salvation. Thus in 46 : 13 we read:

> 'I bring near my righteousness (צדקתי,) [2]
> it is not far off, and my salvation will not tarry'.

The same thought is evident in chapter 51 where Yahweh
says:

> 'Hearken to me, you who pursue deliverance (צדק),
> you who seek the Lord . . .
> My deliverance (צדקי) draws near speedily,
> my salvation has gone forth,
> and my arms will rule the peoples' (vv. 1-5).

Again in a passage which appeals to nature itself to manifest
the divine power on earth we read:

> 'Shower, O heavens, from above,
> and let the skies rain down righteousness;
> let the earth open, that salvation may sprout forth,

---

[1] Cf. James Muilenburg who says, 'The meaning here is "with a
purpose firm and sure" ', *The Interpreter's Bible*, 5, 1956, p. 527.
[2] The *R.S.V.* here translates 'deliverance'.

and let it cause righteousness to spring up also;
I the Lord have created it' (45 : 8).

But although nature is of divine creation it is unstable and
transient, and in contrast to its changing, evanescent character we have Yahweh's own assurance that his righteousness
will endure beyond the realms of space and time (51 : 6).

God's righteousness, then, is but the expression of his
character and purpose, and it was in conformity with this
purpose that he says of Israel: 'I have called you in righteousness, I have taken you by the hand and kept you' (42 : 6). He
'took' her 'from the ends of the earth, and called' her
'from its farthest corners' (41 : 9) that she 'might declare'
his 'praise' to the world (43 : 21). But she proved unworthy
of her calling. Her allegiance to Yahweh was at most nominal; for though she may 'swear by the name of the Lord
and confess the God of Israel' it was 'not in truth or right'
(48 : 1).

The prophets were indeed so emphatic on the question
of Yahweh's righteousness that they were critical of the
moral standards obtaining even amongst nations other
than Israel. Nathan reproved David for arranging the
murder of Uriah (2 Sam. 11) and Elijah could rebuke Ahab
for his covetous possession of Naboth's vineyard (1 Kgs. 21),
but Amos declared that Yahweh was also concerned with the
moral actions of neighbouring peoples. In eloquent language he declaims against the atrocities committed by the
Syrians:

'Thus says Yahweh:
For three transgressions of Damascus,
and for four, I will not revoke the punishment;
because they have threshed Gilead
with threshing sledges of iron.
So I will send a fire upon the house of Hazael,
and it shall devour the strongholds of Benhadad' (1 : 3-4).

He similarly condemns the Philistines for their practice of selling entire populations into slavery (1 : 6).[1] So, the Ammonites will suffer for the brutal treatment of their women captives (1 : 13), while Moab will be punished for the gruesome habit of desecrating the bones of the dead (2 : 1).[2]

Contemptuous of the ethical standards of Egypt and Assyria, Hosea could but scorn Israel's association with them. Yahweh's indictment of her accordingly is:

> 'Ephraim is like a dove, silly and without sense,
> calling to Egypt, going to Assyria.
> As they go, I will spread over them my net;
> I will bring them down like birds of the air;
> I will chastise them for their wicked deeds' (7 : 11-12).

Isaiah's censures of Judah's intrigues with Egypt were likewise made on the grounds that in so acting she was but further tainting herself with sin:

> 'Woe to the rebellious children, says the Lord,
> who carry out a plan, but not mine;
> and who make a league, but not of my spirit,
> that they may add sin to sin;
> who set out to go down to Egypt,
> without asking for my counsel,
> to take refuge in the protection of Pharaoh,
> and to seek shelter in the shadow of Egypt.
> Therefore shall the protection of Pharaoh
> turn to your shame . . .

---

[1] The same accusation is made against Tyre in verse 9, and it is instructive to compare Joel 3 : 4: 'What are you to me, O Tyre and Sidon, and all the regions of Philistia? . . . You have sold the people of Judah and Jerusalem to the Greeks, removing them far from their own border'. See also the comments of R. S. Cripps, *The Book of Amos*, p. 124.

[2] Further oracles against Tyre (1 : 9-10), Judah (2 : 4-5) and other states appear in this context but they are probably later additions to the text.

> every one comes to shame
> through a people that cannot profit them,
> that brings neither help nor profit,
> but shame and disgrace' (30 : 1-5).

Jeremiah too was aware of the injurious affect of social and political relations with Egypt and Assyria. It is thus in the hope of dissuading her from such a course that he makes the following appeal:

> 'And now what do you gain by going to Egypt,
> to drink the waters of the Nile?
> Or what do you gain by going to Assyria,
> to drink the waters of the Euphrates?
> Your wickedness will chasten you,
> and your apostasy will reprove you.
> Know and see that it is evil and bitter
> for you to forsake the Lord your God' (2 : 18-19).

The foregoing considerations enable us, then, to discern the basic principles underlying the teaching of the prophets. Fundamental to their conception of Yahweh was the notion of his unqualified uniqueness. It was he and not Baal who was responsible for the fruits of the earth and who, moreover, exercised control over the wide realms of nature. Even more significant was their apprehension of the ethical nature of God and their consequent emphasis on the moral basis of his relationship with man. Israel may profess the most punctilious religious observances, but a religion which was indifferent to moral values cannot claim to have its source in God.

CHAPTER FOUR

THE PROPHETIC ATTITUDE TO THE CULT

The emphasis of the great prophets on the ethical nature of God leads us to a consideration of their attitude to the cult. Although this question has attracted much attention since the days of Wellhausen it is one on which the findings of scholars have rarely concurred. Claiming that the prophetic dislike of ritual incurred also an opposition to priestly religion Wellhausen himself wrote: 'If the Priestly Code makes the cultus the principal thing, that appears to amount to a systematic decline into a heathenism which the prophets incessantly combated and yet were unable to eradicate'. [1] This view, so ably propounded by Wellhausen, was reflected in the writings of subsequent scholars, and in an article on the Religion of Israel E. Kautzsch expressed himself thus: 'The gulf between the religion of the prophets . . . and that of the Priest's Code has been described as one that cannot be bridged. That there is, in fact, a deep gulf between the two, and that this shows itself in P in the shape of a falling away from the pure level reached by the Prophets, are truths that need be denied all the less, seeing that the teaching of Jesus attached itself to the Prophets, and would have the law interpreted only in their sense and spirit.' [2] In more modern times G. Hölscher likewise maintained that Amos 'fought against the existing Yahweh cult, and indeed not merely

---

[1] J. Wellhausen, *Prolegomena to the History of Israel*, Eng. trans. 1885, p. 423.

[2] *H.D.B.*, Extra Volume (5), 1906, p. 723a.

against individual Canaanite ethics or immoralities, but on principle, against the cult as such: Yahweh abhorred sacrifice and festivals, he accepts no cult but righteousness ...'. [1] So with regard to Hosea he similarly commented, 'He wishes to know nothing of the cult: Yahweh has pleasure in the love and knowledge of God, not in sacrifices'. [2] Again, in opposing the notion that the prophetic repudiation of sacrifice was relative rather than absolute Skinner remarked, 'It seems clear, however, that the prophetic principle goes deeper than that. Not only is sacrifice of no avail as a substitute for righteous conduct, but a perfect religious relationship is possible without sacrifice at all'. [3] Commenting on Jeremiah 7 : 21 f. he further observed, 'The error here rebuked is not simply the practical abuse of sacrificial ritual by men who sought thus to compound for their moral delinquencies; it is the notion that Yahweh had ever instituted sacrifice at all. The whole system, and all laws prescribing it, are declared to lie outside the revelation on which the national religion of Israel was based'. [4] Representing a similar viewpoint J. E. McFadyen also wrote: 'If the prophets mean what they say, they were unquestionably the implacable opponents of the cult: and if it is argued that so bold a challenge of the ritual in which they had been brought up is inconceivable, it may be answered that with men of their insight and calibre, it is precisely the inconceivable that is possible'. [5] Reminiscent of Wellhausen again are the words of R. H. Kennett: 'When ... we turn from the Pentateuch to the utterances of the great prophets of the

---

[1] *Geschichte der israelitischen und jüdischen Religion*, 1922, p. 104.
[2] *Ibid.*, p. 106.
[3] *Prophecy and Religion*, p. 181.
[4] *Ibid.*, p. 182.
[5] *The People and the Book* (ed. A. S. Peake), 1925, p. 210.

eighth and seventh centuries B.C., we find a remarkable difference. Here *sacrifice*, so far from being taken for granted, is *absolutely repudiated*'.[1] I. G. Matthews was equally definite in his judgment. Referring to the attitude of the eighth century prophets to the sacrificial religion of their day he said, 'To these prophets . . . the whole show was nothing less than damnable. They were scathing in their criticism and absolute in their insistence that such abominable rites had never been instituted, and could not be countenanced, by Yahweh'.[2] Similarly according to H. P. Hyatt, 'The opposition of the prophets to the whole sacrificial and ritualistic system and practices of their day seems to have been absolute, and they thought it should be abolished as an offence against the God of Israel'.[3]

But while such scholars regard the prophetic condemnation of sacrifice as absolute, many past and present writers would not share this view. Adopting a more cautious approach to the question, Robertson Smith observed, 'When the prophets positively condemn the worship of their contemporaries, they do so because it is associated with immorality . . . This does not prove that they have any objection to sacrifice and ritual in the abstract'.[4] It was likewise the opinion of J. M. Powis Smith that 'A religion without ritual would have been practically inconceivable to the Hebrew mind' and he thus thinks of Amos, Isaiah and Jeremiah as according 'a certain place to ritual'.[5] A. C. Welch similarly regarded as 'open to grave objection' the view

---

[1] *The Church of Israel* (ed. S. A. Cook) 1933, p. 120.
[2] *The Religious Pilgrimage of Israel*, 1947, p. 125.
[3] *Prophetic Religion*, 1947, p. 127. So also, J. A. Bewer, *The Book of Jeremiah*, vol. I., 1951, p. 33.
[4] *The Old Testament in the Jewish Church*, 2nd edn., 1892, p. 295.
[5] *The Moral Life of the Hebrews*, 1932, pp. 80 f.

that the prophets condemned 'the sacrificial system *per se*'. [1]
In a course of lectures entitled 'Sacrifices in Ancient Israel'
W. O. E. Oesterley was also concerned to show that the
prophetic condemnation of sacrifice applied only to such
sacrifices as were unworthily offered by an impenitent
people. [2] Wheeler Robinson too maintained that the prophets
'were attacking a false and non-moral reliance upon' sacrifices 'rather than the expression of true worship through a
eucharistic gift'. [3] Again, while believing that the prophets
were primarily concerned with moral and spiritual issues
John Paterson still declared that 'neither Amos nor Isaiah
nor Jeremiah would deny a place to sacrifice'. [4] Finally,
after examining the relevant references of the pre-exilic
prophets to sacrifice H. H. Rowley concluded: 'In all these
passages there is no reason to suppose that the prophets
condemned the cultus as such, but only the cultus that was
regarded as an end in itself'. [5] So in an article on 'Ritual and
the Hebrew Prophets' he later wrote: 'If the prophets had
really meant that sacrifice under all circumstances was evil,
they would not have needed to bring condemnation of the
lives of men into association with their sacrifices ... We
ought not therefore to go beyond our text, and to be content
to say that these prophets declared that the religious observances of their day were meaningless in the eyes of God
because they were the observances of men whose lives
were an affront to him'. [6]

---

[1] *Prophet and Priest in Old Israel*, 1936, p. 21.
[2] *Sacrifices in Ancient Israel*, 1937, pp. 191-213.
[3] *Inspiration and Revelation in the Old Testament*, p. 226.
[4] *The Goodley Fellowship of the Prophets*, 1948, p. 27.
[5] *B. J.R.L.*, 29, 1945-46, pp. 347-348.
[6] *J.S.S.*, 1, 1955, p. 343. Cf. further G. E. Wright, *The Challenge of Israel's Faith*, 1946, p. 57; B. D. Eerdmans, *The Religion of Israel*, Eng. trans. 1947, pp. 140 f.

We have thus some indication of the divergence of opinion which has obtained amongst scholars on the attitude of the great prophets to the cult. On the whole, however, there appears to be a tendency on the part of modern writers to interpret the prophetic polemics against sacrifice and ritual as pertaining only to sacrifice which was offered by those people who were otherwise given to sin and apostasy. [1] This tendency is in itself influenced by the advocacy of the view that the Hebrew prophets were closely connected with the cult, and that in consequence there was not that antagonism between prophet and priest which was formerly held. Indeed it could be said that this view has been gaining ground since Sigmund Mowinckel's interpretation of certain prophetic elements in the Psalter. Hermann Gunkel had earlier recognised much material in the Psalter as being prophetic in nature, and attributed it to the direct influence of the prophetic teaching. [2] Mowinckel, however, contended that the presence of such material could be accounted for only on the theory that it was composed by prophets who were themselves members of the sanctuary personnel. [3] Mowinckel's views not only proved influential in the subsequent study of the Psalter, but were regarded as particularly suggestive in the investigation of the place of the prophet in the ancient Israelite community. Following the lead of Mowinckel, Hubert Junker suggested that it was the prophets who were responsible for the development of Hebrew religious poetry. Nor was their contribution to the

---

[1] Cf. here R. S. Cripps, *The Book of Amos*, (1955 edn.), pp. xxviii ff.

[2] E.g., 'The Poetry of the Psalms' in *Old Testament Essays* (Papers read before the Society for Old Testament Study at Oxford, 1927, and published by C. Griffin and Co., 1927), pp. 137 f.; *What Remains of the Old Testament*, Eng. trans. by A. K. Dallas, 1928, pp. 84, 96 ff.

[3] *Psalmenstudien III. Kultprophetie und prophetische Psalmen*, 1922, e.g., pp. 1-29.

worship of their day confined to such compositions, for, according to Junker, they also participated in the singing and dancing which were a feature of the ritual observed in the sanctuary. [1] Developing this argument somewhat further J. Pedersen represented the prophets not only as taking part in the temple worship, but as actually constituting 'a stable part of the staff of the temple'. [2]

It will not, of course, be denied that there were some prophets in Israel who had an intimate association with the sanctuaries. It is recorded that Samuel the prophet blessed the sacrifice at a 'high place' (I Sam. 9 : 9-12) and built an altar to the Lord at Ramah (I Sam. 7 : 16). The prophetic functions of Elijah are emphasised in certain passages (*e.g.*, 1 Kgs. 17 : 1, 14) but he also officiates at an altar on Mount Carmel (1 Kgs. 18 : 20-35). We again read of 'a band of prophets coming down from the high places' (1 Sam. 10 : 5) and of 'the sons of the prophets' who dwelt at the sanctuary of Bethel, while we note too that similar prophets were connected with the sanctuaries of Jericho (2 Kgs. 2 : 5) and Gilgal (2 Kgs. 4 : 38). In the time of Jeremiah we hear of priests and prophets alike being present in the temple (Jer. 26 : 7) while Hananiah, one of the most notorious of the false prophets, regularly frequented its precincts (Jer. 28 : 1 ff.). It would further appear that at this time a priest not only exercised authority over the personnel of the temple, but over any prophet who prophesied there (Jer. 29 : 26).

But, while such passages indicate that certain prophets had an association with the sanctuary, it is questionable if we can draw a similar conclusion with regard to the canonical

---

[1] *Prophet und Seher in Israel*, 1927, pp. 14 ff.

[2] *Israel III-IV*, 1940, pp. 116-117. Cf. also A. R. Johnson's monograph, *The Cultic Prophet in Ancient Israel*, 1944, pp. 6 f and 25 f.

prophets. Indeed the important question of the relationship of these cultic figures to the great creative prophets remains. There were certainly occasions when the classical prophets condemned these official prophets in common with the priests. Thus Hosea represents Yahweh as saying:

> 'For with you is my contention, O priest.
> You shall stumble by day,
> the prophet also shall stumble with you by night' (4 : 4-5).

Similarly in Isaiah we read that

> 'the priest and the prophet reel with strong drink,
> they are confused with wine,
> they stagger with strong drink; they err in vision,
> they stumble in giving judgment' (28 : 7).

Many such allusions further appear in the Book of Jeremiah. In 5 : 31 we find that

> 'the prophets prophesy falsely,
> and the priests rule at their direction',

while according to 14 : 18

> 'both prophet and priest ply their trade
> through the land, and have no knowledge'.

The prophets of Samaria are of ignoble character (23 : 13), but they are not alone in their infamy, for

> 'in the prophets of Jerusalem
> I have seen a horrible thing:
> they commit adultery and walk in lies;
> they strengthen the hands of evildoers,
> so that no one turns from his wickedness;
> all of them have become like Sodom to me,
> and its inhabitants like Gomorrah' (23 : 14).

In yet another context Yahweh says, 'When one of this people, or a prophet, or a priest asks you, What is the burden of the Lord? you shall say to them, You are the burden,

and I will cast you off . . .' (23 : 33). A similar condemnation
of such prophets appears also in the Book of Ezekiel: 'Thus
says the Lord God, Woe to the foolish prophets who
follow their own spirit, and have seen nothing! Your
prophets have been like foxes among ruins, O Israel . . .
They have spoken falsehood and divined a lie; they say,
"Says the Lord", when the Lord has not sent them . . .
Have you not seen a delusive vision, and uttered a lying
divination, whenever you have said, "Says the Lord",
although I have not spoken?' (13 : 3-7).

Such language scarcely indicates that the canonical
prophets had much in common with these men or that they
showed any approval of the ethics of their profession. Yet
some writers assume that there is but little difference, if any,
between the professional prophets and the great classical
figures. Regarding it as 'axiomatic . . . that the *nabi* . . . is
a cult functionary' Haldar declares that 'one must not put
too much emphasis on the pronouncements in the prophetical
"books" which seem to be directed against the cult'. [1]
Indeed the notion that the canonical prophets were
themselves cult officials has not been without its advocates.
Ivan Engnell has argued that the term *noqed* which is used
of Amos (I : 1) means a cultic official, [2] while he later
contends that this word 'shows that Amos in some way
had a connection with a class of persons linked with the
temple. Tekoa must have been a "branch" of the temple in
Jerusalem. Bearing in mind the way in which in ancient
times the whole of economic and political life too was
centralised at the sanctuary, his position as at the same time
"shepherd" and member of a group of temple personnel of

---

[1] *Associations of Cult Prophets among the Ancient Semites*, p. 113.
[2] *Studies in Divine Kingship in the Ancient Near East*, 1943, p. 87.

some sort may be easily comprehended'. [1] Again, Haldar claims that because Amos was one of the shepherds of Tekoa and called himself a *boqer* (herdsman) he must 'have belonged to the cult staff'. [2] Haldar's reason for this conclusion does not, however, command unhesitating assent. On an earlier page (79) he notes that in Ugaritic texts the leader of a guild of divination officials is called 'chief of the priests and chief of the shepherds'. From this he apparently assumes that because Amos is represented as one of the 'shepherds' of Tekoa he must also have been an official of the sanctuary there. But this is an inference which can claim but little support from the Book of Amos itself; for in the records there preserved Amos before his call was nothing more than an ordinary shepherd. [3] Again, on the supposition that the word *sod* refers to a cultic assembly in Genesis 49 : 6 Haldar infers that it must have the same meaning in Jeremiah 23 : 22 where Yahweh speaks of the prophets standing in his 'council'. He consequently draws the conclusion that 'like Isaiah and Ezekiel, Jeremiah obviously belongs to the temple staff'. [4]

It is true that certain references in the prophetical literature connect some of the canonical prophets with the temple. According to chapter 6 of the Book of Isaiah that prophet experienced his inaugural vision in the temple. But, as the present writer has argued elsewhere, [5] the authenticity of

---

[1] *Svenskt Bibliskt Uppslagsverk*, 1, 1948, col. 59 f. (I owe this translation from the Swedish to my colleague, Mr. D. R. Ap-Thomas).

[2] *Op. cit.*, p. 112.

[3] Cf. here the cogent remarks of N. W. Porteous in *E.T.*, 62, 1950-51, p. 8b.

[4] *Op. cit.*, p. 121.

[5] 'The Call and Mission of Isaiah', *J.N.E.S.*, 18, 1959, pp. 38-42. Cf. also M. M. Kaplan, 'Isaiah 6 : 1-11', *J.B.L.*, 45, 1926, pp. 251-259, who was concerned to show that instead of being a description of Isaiah's

this chapter is not beyond question. Apart from this material there is little else in the Book which associates Isaiah with the temple. It is, therefore, doubtful if Pedersen is justified in writing: 'The intimate connection of Isaiah's experience with the sanctuary is no chance feature; it is, on the contrary, characteristic of the activities of the prophets'. [1]

We further note that the superscription of the Book of Jeremiah refers to the prophet as 'the son of Hilkiah, of the priests who were in Anathoth in the land of Benjamin'. Meek has indeed contended that these words are only a gloss, [2] but their originality could only mean that Jeremiah was a descendant of a priestly family who lived at Anathoth. We would look in vain in the Book for definite evidence identifying him as a member of the temple staff. He appears in the temple on the occasion of his sensational address, recorded in chapters 7 and 26, but this was hardly in the capacity of a temple official; it was rather in obedience to the word of God which commanded him, 'Stand in the gate of the Lord's house and proclaim there his word . . .' (vs. 2). The opposition which on this occasion Jeremiah experienced from the temple officials ill accords with the view that he had much in common with them. On the contrary we are told that the 'priests and the prophets . . . laid hold of him, saying, You shall die . . .' (26 : 7-8). Had Jeremiah been a member of the same staff as these priests and prophets he would hardly have been so treated. The incident can only be explained on the assumption that, far from being a cultic colleague of such people, Jeremiah had little sympathy with

---

call to prophesy, chapter 6 reflects the sense of despair which came over him in the course of his career.

[1] *Israel III-IV*, p. 115.

[2] 'Was Jeremiah a Priest?', *The Expositor*, 8th series, March 1923, No. 147, pp. 215-222.

their interests, as indeed his words on this occasion amply testify (26 : 6).

Nor does the evidence suggest that Ezekiel the prophet had any closer association with the temple. In chapter 1 : 3 we read that 'the word of the Lord came to Ezekiel the priest, the son of Buzi, in the land of the Chaldeans'. The intrusive nature of this material is, however, evident from the fact that it is in the form of reported speech, whereas that which immediately precedes and follows is in direct speech. [1] But retention of the passage would mean no more than that prior to his call by Yahweh Ezekiel had been a priest; and since he spent his prophetic career in exile further association with the temple would have been impossible. There is little, therefore, to substantiate Haldar's contention that Ezekiel was a regular member of the temple personnel. [2]

But, while there is no evidence to indicate that the great canonical prophets were cult officials, there are certain passages in their writings which enable us to discuss their attitude to the cult. In a well-known chapter of the Book of Amos Yahweh says:

'I hate, I despise your feasts,
and I take no delight in your solemn assemblies.
Even though you offer me your burnt offerings
and cereal offerings, I will not accept them,
and the peace offerings of your fatted beasts
I will not look upon.
Take away from me the noise of your songs;
to the melody of your harps I will not listen.
But let justice roll down like waters,
and righteousness like an overflowing stream' (5 : 21-24).

---

[1] Cf. the present writer, 'The "Thirtieth" Year in Ezekiel I : 1', *V.T.*, 1959, 3, pp. 326 f.

[2] 'Jeremiah and Ezekiel are clearly described as members of the temple staff', *op. cit.*, p. 112.

Some scholars have argued that Amos is not so much condemning sacrifice here as emphasising the prior claims of God to the moral obedience of his people. [1] It is, of course, true that the prophet speaks of 'your feasts' and 'your burnt offerings' and hence it may be doubted if we are justified in drawing the general conclusion that all sacrifices are objectionable to God. This is not, however, the only reference of Amos to the cult. Elsewhere he says:

> 'Come to Bethel, and transgress;
> to Gilgal, and multiply transgression;
> bring your sacrifices every morning,
> your tithes every three days;
> offer a sacrifice of thanksgiving of that which is leavened,
> and proclaim freewill offerings, publish them;
> for so you love to do, O people of Israel' (4 : 4-5).

The Deuteronomic Law limiting sacrifice to a single altar at Jerusalem was unknown at this time. Hence it is not the act of sacrificing at shrines like Bethel and Gilgal which in itself is condemned here. The transgressions referred to may indeed pertain to the immoral practices associated with the Canaanite shrines (cf. Amos 2 : 7-8), and sacrifice offered under such circumstances would naturally not be acceptable to Yahweh. Yet when in another context the prophet represents Yahweh as saying, 'Seek me and live', he significantly adds

> 'but do not seek Bethel,
> and do not enter into Gilgal
> or cross over to Beersheba . . .' (5 : 5).

These were ancient and well-known sanctuaries at which the Israelites were accustomed to worship [2], but is is clear

---

[1] So, e.g., Oesterley, *op. cit.*, p. 193; H. H. Rowley, *B.J.R.L.*, 29, 1945-46, p. 341.

[2] Cf., e.g., Amos 7 : 13; I Sam. 11 : 15; Gen. 23 : 8; 2 Kgs. 23 : 8.

that Amos does not here regard them as contributing anything to man's approach to God.

Again, according to Amos, Yahweh asks, 'Did you bring to me sacrifices and offerings the forty years in the wilderness, O house of Israel?' (5 : 25). These words seem to imply that there were no sacrifices offered during the period of wandering in the wilderness and, further, suggest that Amos did not know of the directions relating to sacrifice attributed to Moses in the Book of Exodus (e.g., 10 : 9; 12 : 21; 13 : 11-12; 20 : 24; 34 : 18, 25-26). The exegetical difficulties of the passage accordingly become apparent. H. H. Rowley is of the opinion that 'there is no reason whatever to suppose that Mosaic Yahwism was entirely non-sacrificial, and every reason to accept the tradition, itself older than the time of Amos, that it was sacrificial'. Nor does this scholar see any necessary conflict between the material of Exodus and the words of the prophet. He accordingly writes: '. . . if Amos's meaning is that sacrifices that are not the organ of the spirit are meaningless and an offence to God, then he was not talking patent nonsense. For then he meant: "Was it mere sacrifices and offerings, sacrifices and offerings that were an end in themselves and not the expression of your loyalty of spirit, that you offered in the wilderness days?" ' [1]. With regard to the question posed by Amos Oesterley similarly wrote: 'it is not a negative answer that is implied, but an affirmative one, and . . . the meaning is this: Did not your forefathers offer me sacrifices which were acceptable because they were offered in faithfulness and sincerity?'. [2] So according to C. Lattey 'The answer to be expected is "no", but a relative "no"; not a blank denial that sacrifice was ever offered to Jehovah in the

[1] B.J.R.L., 29, 1945-46, pp. 341-342.
[2] Op. cit., p. 195.

wilderness, but a denial that the sacrifices were the kind acceptable to Jehovah'. [1] On the other hand, noting the agricultural nature of the sacrifices and festivals mentioned in the Decalogue embedded in Exodus 34, some scholars have observed that such ceremonies presuppose a period of settled residence in the land of Canaan. [2] R. H. Pfeiffer maintains that this Decalogue is dependent on an old Ritual Decalogue of Canaanite origin and argues that 'the influence of the ritual decalogue on all later Pentateuchal codifications cannot be overestimated'. [3] Originating at Shechem it was adopted by the Israelites before the time of Saul and edited and supplemented in the Deuteronomic Code shortly before 621 and again in Exodus 34 about 550, while it was likewise 'brought up to date in the Holiness Code and in the various strata of the Priestly Code'. [4] The prescriptions for building altars which we find in Exodus 20 : 24-26 and the instructions relating to sacrifice in Exodus 13 : 11-16 are similarly dependent on this old Decalogue. [5] Moses is, however, represented as enjoining sacrifice in Exodus 5 : 3 and 10 : 9, passages which are thought to belong to the J document. But even if such passages are of J provenance they can scarcely be older than the ninth century and, accordingly, may but reflect the norm of Israelite worship practised at that time. Amos may not therefore have regarded such traditions as reliable representations of Israelite worship during the wilderness period. [6]

---

[1] 'The Prophets and Sacrifice', *J.T.S.*, 42, 1941, p. 164.

[2] E.g., T. H. Robinson, *Prophecy and the Prophets in Ancient Israel*, 2nd edn., 1953, p. 15.

[3] *Introduction to the Old Testament*, p. 221-222.

[4] *Op. cit.*, p. 222.

[5] *Op. cit.*, p. 221.

[6] 'There is no doubt' said Skinner 'that Amos shared the view of Hosea that the desert sojourn was the ideal period in Israel's history;

Moreover, Amos was not alone among the great prophets in doubting the divine ordering of sacrifice. Jeremiah too raised a questioning voice, and seems to have known nothing of the role attributed to Moses in Exodus 5 : 3 and 10 : 9. [1] Otherwise he could hardly have said: 'For in the day that I brought them out of the land of Egypt, I did not speak to your fathers or command them concerning burnt offerings and sacrifices. But this command I gave them, Obey my voice, and I will be your God, and you shall be my people' (7 : 22-23). [2] Thus, whatever sacrifice may have been observed in the wilderness period it is here expressly stated that God gave no commands concerning it. Yahweh did indeed issue commands regarding his will, but their fulfilment did not depend on the offering of sacrifice to him. As Skinner observed, Jeremiah was not concerned to justify the prevalent belief that sacrifice was divinely ordained. On the contrary 'His conviction of its non-essential character is the outcome of his prophetic knowledge of God, and is so strong that he is prepared to defy all traditional opinion, and affirm that it could never have been

---

and the obvious inference is that if Yahwe could be properly served without sacrifice then, He could be still', *op. cit.*, p. 181.

[1] Lattey, however, comments here: 'It would certainly require a bold spirit to assert that, as late as Jeremiah, a prophet could deny that God had ever commanded sacrifices; and it would raise grave problems in the interpretation of Jeremiah himself'. So on the same page he writes: '. . . sacrifices are included among the good things promised. Thus in Jer. 17 : 26 men are to bring from all over Palestine "Burnt-offerings and sacrifices and grain offerings and frankincense . . . unto Jehovah's house". And again in 33 : 18: "and to the Levitical priests there shall never fail a man before me to offer burnt-offerings and to send up oblations and sacrifice" ', *loc. cit.*, p. 163. It is doubtful, however, if these passages derive from Jeremiah himself. See, e.g., J. P. Hyatt, *The Interpreter's Bible*, 5, pp. 958-959, 1956.

[2] Although probably in editorial form the Jeremianic content of the passage is nevertheless clear.

commanded by God who had revealed himself to Moses.' [1]

We have seen in the previous chapter that Hosea had an abhorrence of the cult of Baal. But while, like Jeremiah, he maintained that Israel's sojourn in the wilderness was marked by commendable innocence, he condemns her when she participates in the idolatry of other nations:

> 'Like grapes in the wilderness, I found Israel.
> Like the first fruit on the fig trees, in its first season,
> I saw your fathers.
> But they came to Baal-peor,
> and they consecrated themselves to Baal,
> and became detestable like the thing they loved' (9 : 10) [2].

His polemic against the local shrines is no doubt roused by the immorality prevalent there. Hence Israel's visit to the sanctuary of Gilgal prompts the comment,

> 'Every evil of theirs is in Gilgal;
> there I began to hate them' (9 : 15).

Association at such places has so evil an influence on Israel that 'they have become to him altars for sinning' (8 : 11). To people accustomed to this conduct the laws of God can only 'be regarded as a strange thing' (8 : 12).

But, while it may be argued that Hosea's denunciation of sacrifice primarily sprang from his aversion to Baal-worship, he also expresses criticism of sacrifice when it is made to Yahweh:

> 'They love sacrifice;
> they sacrifice flesh and eat it;
> but the Lord has no delight in them' (8 : 13).

Though such sacrifice is offered to God it is not acceptable. So in another passage in Hosea Yahweh says:

---

[1] *Op. cit.*, pp. 182-183.

[2] Cf. Num. 25 : 1 f. where Israel on her way to Canaan associates with the Moabite deity Baal-peor.

'I desire steadfast love and not sacrifice,
the knowledge of God, rather than burnt offerings' (6 : 6).

It has, of course, been claimed that the reference to Yahweh's dislike of sacrifice here is to be regarded in a comparative rather than in an absolute sense. Thus H. H. Rowley suggests that on the principles of Hebrew poetic parallelism the reference 'means that God's demand for *hesed* is more fundamental than the demand for sacrifice',[1] while C. Lattey considered the verse from the point of view of a 'relative negation'.[2] Yet whatever conclusion we reach on this issue it is significant that man may possess both steadfast love and the knowledge of God without recourse to sacrifice or burnt offerings.

In the records of Isaiah too we find a lengthy passage relating to sacrifice as it was offered in the temple of his day:

'What to me is the multitude of your sacrifices?
says the Lord;
I have had enough of burnt offerings of rams
and the fat of fed beasts;
I do not delight in the blood of bulls
or of lambs, or of he-goats.
When you come to appear before me,
who requires of you this trampling of my courts?
Bring no more vain offerings;
incense is an abomination to me.
New moon and sabbath and the calling of assemblies-
I cannot endure iniquity and solemn assembly.
Your new moons and your appointed feasts my soul hates;
they have become a burden to me,

---

[1] *B.J.R.L.*, *loc. cit.*, p. 340.

[2] *Loc. cit.*, p. 160. Kautzsch on the other hand remarked, 'it is perfectly futile to read out of Hos. 6 : 6 anything else than a categorical rejection of sacrifice', *loc. cit.*, p. 685 b. So with regard to verse 6 b R. H. Kennett thought that ' a more precise translation would be "the knowledge of God *as distinct from* burnt offerings" ', *op.cit.*, p. 121, note 3.

I am weary of bearing them.
When you spread forth your hands,
I will hide my eyes from you;
even though you make many prayers, I will not listen;
your hands are full of blood.
Wash yourselves; make yourselves clean;
remove the evil of your doings from before my eyes;
cease to do evil, learn to do good;
seek justice, correct oppression' (1 : 11-17).

This would seem to be a description of sacrifice as witnessed by the prophet himself. And as such it finds little acceptance in the eyes of God. Burnt offerings, incense and appointed feasts are alike burdensome to him. Of the 'vain offerings' and ceremonial acts with which the people appear before him he asks, 'who requires of you this trampling of my courts?'. It is through no demand of his. Thus, when in this ceremonial approach the people spread forth their hands he will hide his face from them; to their many prayers he will not listen. On the other hand the words 'cease to do evil, learn to do good' imply that the people in question were accustomed to doing evil rather than good; and elsewhere Isaiah speaks of a 'sinful nation, a people laden with iniquity' (1 : 4). Yet it is not clear that in the passage before us sacrifice is condemned because it is offered by a sinful and impenitent assembly.

In the Book of Micah we find yet another reference to sacrifice:

'With what shall I come before the Lord,
and bow myself before God on high?
Shall I come before him with burnt offerings,
with calves a year old?
Will the Lord be pleased with thousands of rams,
with ten thousands of rivers of oil?
Shall I give my first-born for my transgression,
the fruit of my body for the sin of my soul?

He has showed you, O man, what is good;
and what does the Lord require of you
but to do justice, and to love kindness,
and to walk humbly with your God?' (6 : 6-8).

Although doubts on the authorship of this passage have
long been expressed [1] its teaching on sacrifice accords with
what we find in the records of the other classical prophets. [2]
As in Isaiah we observe that burnt offerings, rams, and oil
find little acceptance in the divine presence. God does not
require sacrifice. His only demands relate to justice and mercy
towards mankind, and obedience and humility towards
himself. Even if it is claimed that the author has in mind
here the sacrifices which are offered by those whose lives are
full of iniquity, and who in consequence are insincere in their
approach to the altar, [3] there is still no indication that sacrifice
was instituted by God or that it would find any favour
before him even if accompanied by a contrite heart.

There remains to mention a passage which appears in the
pages of the Second-Isaiah:

You did not call upon me, O Jacob;
but you have been weary of me, O Israel.
You have not brought me your sheep for burnt offerings,
or honoured me with your sacrifices.
I have not burdened you with offerings,
or wearied you with frankincense.
You have not bought me sweet cane with money,
or satisfied me with the fat of your sacrifices.
But you have burdened me with your sins,
you have wearied me with your iniquities' (43 : 22-24).

It can scarcely be thought that Yahweh is here demanding
sacrifices, for sacrificial worship was impracticable in the

---

[1] See J. M. Powis Smith, *Micah, I.C.C.,* (2nd impression 1928), p. 124.
[2] Wheeler Robinson aptly calls it 'the best epitome of the prophetic
teaching', *Inspiration and Revelation in the Old Testament,* p. 83.
[3] As, e.g., is maintained by Powis Smith, *op. cit.,* p. 126.

exile. The prophet is rather referring to Israel's idolatrous
tendencies, and the passage is thus in effect a satire on the
nature of her past association with Yahweh. For although
Israel indulged in lavish sacrifices and burnt offerings she
did not do so for the honour of Yahweh. He did not, indeed,
make any such demands, but it is significant that he was not
the recipient of sweet cane or the fat of sacrifices. [1] The only
constant and conspicuous feature of Israel's association
with him was the sin she so blatantly committed in his
sight.

Our survey of the foregoing passages now raises the
question: Were the great canonical prophets opposed on
principle to sacrifice? It may be doubted if the evidence is
such as to give a definite answer to this question, because
the relevant material is to a large extent in contexts in which
sacrifice is offered by an indifferent and sinful people. Yet
it is clear that such references as we have to sacrifice are of
a condemnatory nature; and irrespective of the disposition
of the offerer nowhere in the words of the great prophets
is it regarded as a medium of communion with God. As
G. B. Gray observed: 'in repudiating the popular theory of
sacrifice as gifts, the prophets . . . do not call the people back
to a theory of sacrifice as a means of communion with God;
there is not the slightest suggestion in any of their sayings
that they were aware that any such idea had ever been held
and was now abandoned or disregarded, or that they thought
that such an idea ought now to be imposed upon sacrifice'. [2]
So when Isaiah said that Yahweh does 'not delight in the
blood of bulls or of lambs' and when he quotes Yahweh as

---

[1] It is noteworthy that the LXX version of 'or satisfied me with
the fat of your sacrifices' is: 'neither have I *desired* the fat of your sacrifices'.

[2] *Sacrifice in the Old Testament*, 1925, p. 43.

saying 'When you come to appear before me, who requires
of you this trampling of my courts?' it is difficult to believe
that he considered sacrifice and ritual as divinely ordained.
Again, when we read in Micah 'With what shall I come
before the Lord and bow myself before God on high?' we
can scarcely assume from the context that Yahweh would
'be pleased with thousands of rams, with ten thousands of
rivers of oil'. In his temple address Jeremiah also would
seem to have been critical of formal worship. It is true that
many of those who attended on this occasion led sinful lives
and therefore their presence in the temple could only be
regarded as hypocrisy. Well might Yahweh, himself, exclaim
'What right has my beloved in my house when she has done
vile deeds? Can vows and sacrificial flesh avert your doom?'
(11 : 15). Such doom could, moreover, be averted if the
assembly were to turn from their sin, for Yahweh says,
'Amend your ways and your doings, and I will let you dwell
in this place' (7 : 3). Yet it is doubtful if we can deduce
from this that Jeremiah would have regarded sacrifice as a
means of grace if offered by a virtuous people. He was at
pains to emphasise that there were no divine commands
concerning it (7 : 20 f.), and he would scarcely have done this
if sacrifice in itself found favour with God. [1]

Doubts have, of course, been expressed if the prophets
could have contemplated the entire abolition of sacrifice in
favour of a religion independent of the cult. [2] Since the
temple was built by Solomon it was representative of the

---

[1] Cf. the remark of Kautzsch: 'No wresting of the text can alter the
fact that Jeremiah is as little acquainted as the prophets before him with
a law-book which issued in God's name statutes as to sacrifice', *loc.
cit.*, p. 686 b.

[2] See, e.g., Oesterley, *op. cit.*, p. 191; Powis Smith, *The Moral Life of
the Hebrews*, p. 80.

national worship of the Israelites; and in view of its elaborate furnishings (I Kgs. 7) it is doubtful if any non-cultic worship was practised within its precincts. The view, then, that the great prophets advocated a form of worship which was free of cultic accessories postulates an almost immeasurable gulf between them and their fellow Hebrews. Yet however closely they identified themselves with the national issues of their day there can be little doubt that the prophets represented a religious ideal which was far removed from the religion of the populace. We must remember with S. H. Hooke, himself one of the most distinguished writers of the Myth and Ritual School, that the religious environment of the prophets had inherited much from Canaanite culture. [1] A prominent feature of this culture was that ritual was regarded as a means of influencing the deity, who, however, was neither conceived of as a moral being nor as the source of an ethical standard. The prophets, on the other hand, thought of Yahweh as a personal God 'whose activity in the universe is neither arbitrary nor controlled by the potency of ritual' but is based solely on moral grounds (p. 108). 'Such a conception', concluded Professor Hooke, 'cut at the root of the whole pattern of the ancient religious life. It was impossible that a God who could be described in the magnificent words of Amos as "he that formeth the mountains and createth the wind, and declareth unto man what is his thought..." should be conceived of as a dying and rising god, as a god who could be compelled by incantations, or persuaded by offerings, to do what men desired...' (p. 109). Again, although it may be objected that the advocacy of a non-cultic worship would have been an impracticable ideal, it can scarcely be denied that on the question of

---

[1] *The Siege Perilous*, 1956, pp. 104 ff.

man's approach to God the prophets were idealists. Jeremiah certainly conceived of a worship which was independent of temple and cult; for not only did he declare that Yahweh would destroy the temple, but that he could be worshipped wherever the heart of man sought him in sincerity (29 : 12 f.). Ezekiel declared that it was by repentance and righteous acts that man acquires 'a new heart and a new spirit' (18 : 31), while according to Deutero-Isaiah 'the people in whose heart is' Yahweh's law are those 'who know righteousness' (51 : 7). There is some substance in Montefiore's remark that of the pure worship desired by the prophets 'We are able to tell what it would not have been, rather than what it would'. [1] Yet if their own relationship with God is to be any indication, then, it seems that they conceived of a fellowship with him which was immediate and independent of cult and ceremony. [2]

Attempts have been made to interpret the attitude of the classical prophets to the cult from the viewpoint of the post-exilic writers and editors. Thus with reference to the compilation, editing, and subsequent canonisation of the pre-exilic writings H. H. Rowley asks: 'Why, then, should the oracles of the pre-exilic prophets have been not only edited, but accorded ... recognition and esteem by circles to which their supposedly non-cultic religion ought to have

---

[1] C. G. Montefiore, *Origin and Growth of Religion*, 2nd edn., 1893, p. 127.

[2] Commenting on the question whether Amos thought in terms of the reform rather than the abolition of the sacrificial system W. A. L. Elmslie wrote: 'He would have said to his contemporaries that he meant exactly what he said; and to us that, if our eyes had seen what his eyes beheld, we would have no doubt that to consign the whole ... business to the nethermost pit was the first step towards discovering spiritually sensible ways and means of adoring Him who must be worshipped in spirit and in truth', *How Came our Faith*, 1948, p. 261.

been anathema?'. [1] It is sufficient to observe here, however, that the oracles of the pre-exilic prophets were collected and edited because, like the material incorporated in the Pentateuchal and historical books, they were regarded as part of Israel's literary and religious heritage and accorded a rightful place in the canon of scripture. A similar question was posed by N. W. Porteous: 'If it be the case', he asks, 'that the prophetic movement had been in irreconcilable opposition to the cult, how are we to explain the remarkable circumstance that the men of the post-exilic period, recognising, as they did, that the prophet's forecast of judgment to come had been justified by events, nevertheless in the time of reconstruction turned to the very thing which the prophets had so bitterly condemned, and the still more remarkable circumstance that this "pagan" cult proved the means of preserving the Jewish faith?'. [2] But the importance attaching to ritual in the post-exilic age does not find its explanation in the assumption that the writers and legislators of the period were consciously adopting a precedence set by the pre-exilic prophets. It is to be found rather in the fact that the hopes of the Jews of the Return found expression not only in the building of the temple, but in the worship connected with it. The golden age of prophecy had passed and, conscious of their declining powers, the prophets of the day identified themselves with the hopes and aspirations of the populace. [3] As T. H. Robinson remarked, 'It is difficult to imagine a greater contrast than that which appears between the Prophet of Isaiah 40-55 and Haggai. There is no longer a really spiritual message. Even the denunciations of sin and

---

[1] *B.J.R.L.*, 29, 1945-46, p. 335.
[2] *E.T.*, 62, 1950-51, p. 4b.
[3] Cf., e.g., Hag. 1 : 3 f.; Zech. 1 : 16; Ezra 5 : 1-2; 6 : 14.

corruption which had marked the utterances of the pre-exilic prophets are wanting, and the prophet seems to have included stone and timber amongst the essentials of his spiritual and religious ideal'.[1] Again, referring to the interest in ritual manifested by the post-exilic prophets, he argued that while the pre-exilic prophets 'would never for an instant have endorsed the contention that ritual of any kind was amongst the absolute demands of Yahweh ... the post-exilic Prophets were in the line of the development of Judaism, rather than in the full stream of the revelation of God'.[2] Thus it was that, henceforth, the temple and its worship became the focus of the national as well as the religious life of the Jews. At the end of the Book of Zechariah we read that in the happy age of the future 'Every one that survives of all the nations that have come against Jerusalem shall go up year after year to worship the King, the Lord of hosts ... And the pots in the house of the Lord shall be as bowls before the altar; and every pot in Jerusalem and Judah shall be sacred to the Lord of hosts, so that all who sacrifice may come and take of them and boil the flesh of the sacrifice in them' (14 : 16-21). Similarly in Isaiah 60 we find that a restored temple will be the most significant feature of the newly built city of Zion. The city itself will receive the wealth and homage of the nations (vs. 11), but the aromatic cedars of Lebanon will 'beautify the place of my sanctuary' (vs. 13).

With regard to the fact that within the collection of oracles which formed the Minor Prophets are the Books of Amos, Hosea and Micah in common with writings like Haggai, Zechariah and Malachi Professor Rowley observes: 'No explanation is offered of the strange supposition that the

---

[1] *Prophecy and the Prophets in Ancient Israel*, p. 177.
[2] *Op. cit.*, p. 194.

same circles should cherish these collections, without apparently realising how inconsistent they were'. [1] But consistency of view or of content was never the criterion by which the material of the Old Testament was collected and preserved. Otherwise we would not have the differences of viewpoint and other discrepancies which abound not only in the Pentateuch but throughout much of the Old Testament. The post-exilic writer, or compiler, of Chronicles must have been aware of the accounts of David and Solomon presented in the earlier documents, yet he chose to represent them in very different terms from those in which they were there portrayed. According to 2 Samuel 7 : 13 and 1 Kings 5 : 5 the building of the temple was no more than a divine promise in the time of David, but from the standpoint of one who was concerned 'to depict the marvels of the Temple ritual and the magnificent organisations of the clergy' [2] the Chronicler represents David not only as organising the temple personnel, but as having made elaborate preparations for the structure of the building itself (I Chron. chs. 22-29). Similarly, Solomon (II Chron. chs. 4-5) is represented as having an interest in cultic matters far in advance of what we read in I Kings (ch. 6) [3]. This inconsistency of presentation did not, however, prevent the Jews of a later age from preserving the material of Samuel and Kings in common with the work of the Chronicler.

Professor Rowley further raises the question of the relationship of the Deuteronomic Code to the prophetic teaching. It is true, as he remarks, that though this Code is commonly regarded as based on the teaching of the eighth-century

---

[1] *B.J.R.L.*, 29, 1945-46, p. 335.

[2] R. H. Pfeiffer, *Intro. to the Old Test.*, p. 807.

[3] That these passages in Kings derive from a Deuteronomic hand does not, of course, affect the question of their priority to the Chronicler.

prophets it 'knows no hostility to the sacrifices of the cultus'. [1] He then contends, 'If, *ex hypothesi*, the Book of Deuteronomy reflects the teaching of the eighth-century prophets, it might be supposed that its authors would have understood those teachings, and that, therefore, its recognition of the legitimate place of a purified and regulated sacrificial cultus, not as the sole expression of religious loyalty, but validated by the expression of the fundamental loyalty of spirit to Yahweh in the reflection of His will in all life, reflects the like recognition by the eighth-century prophets'. [2] It must, however, be remembered that, though influenced by the moral pronouncements of the prophets, Deuteronomy did not entirely embody the ideals of their teaching. In the circumstances this would not have been practicable, and we may doubt if it were the object of the author to do so. As Pfeiffer commented, 'At the time when the nation, faced by a choice between the old religion of the cult and the new one of conduct, a man inspired by the prophet's ideals but simultaneously well aware of the current trend and of practicable possibilities, effected a compromise between the two antagonistic religions . . . He realised that an agreement between priests and prophets . . . could only be effected by mutual concessions' [3]. Thus, according to Deuteronomy 12 : 5-7 sacrifice and the eating of sacrificial flesh is limited to one altar, but, doubtless due to the humanity of the prophetic utterances, we find a subsequent

---

[1] *B.J.R.L.*, 29, 1945-46, p. 336.
[2] *Ibid.*
[3] *Intro. to the Old Test.*, pp. 179-180. So I. G. Matthews refers to the Book of Deuteronomy as 'a co-operative venture of priest and prophet', *The Religious Pilgrimage of Israel*, p. 149. Those scholars, however, who place Deuteronomy in the post-exilic age regard it as essentially a priestly work. See, e.g., G. Hölscher, 'Komposition und Ursprung des Deuteronomiums', *Z.A.W.*, 40, 1922, pp. 161-255.

clause enabling those who live some distance from the central
shrine to slaughter their own animals and eat their flesh
provided that the blood is not eaten (12 : 15-24). We
again read that a tithe of produce and cattle is to be presented
yearly to Yahweh at the central sanctuary, but we also hear
of the concession that those who live far from this place
may convert the tithe into money and on arriving at the
sanctuary purchase some suitable offering there (Dt.
14 : 22-26). The influence of the prophetic teaching is
likewise discernible in the injunction that the judges of the
land should judge righteously, that justice should not be
perverted and that bribes should not be accepted (Dt.
16 : 18-20), but we also read that it is the priests at the
central sanctuary, together with a secular judge, who
constitute the supreme court of appeal and that 'the man
who acts presumptuously by not obeying the priest who
stands to minister there . . . shall die' (Dt. 17 : 8; 12).
Deuteronomy is, therefore, as much a priestly as a prophetic
document. It is essentially a compromise, and its sanctioning
of even a regulated cult does not necessarily suggest that the
prophets themselves would have approved of such a course.
For, while we have abundant instances of the prophets
condemning the activities associated with the cult, we have
no evidence that they regarded the sacrifices of their day
as the medium of an ethical and spiritual religion.

It is, moreover, significant that, despite the emphasis on
ritual in the period of the Return, the essence of the teaching
of the great prophets survived in some measure. In a few
of the post-exilic writers the thought still obtains that
sacrifice and ritual find little acceptance in the eyes of God.
Indeed, according to Isaiah 66 : 1-3 no earthly edifice is
capable of expressing the worship of a God whose throne is
heaven itself. Animal slaughter and sacrifice are unworthy

of man's attention, while offerings of cereal and frankincense
are distasteful and idolatrous:

'Thus says the Lord:
Heaven is my throne and the earth is my footstool;
what is the house which you would build for me,
and what is the place of my rest?
All these things my hand has made,
and so all these things are mine . . .
He who slaughters an ox is like him who kills a man;
He who sacrifices a lamb, like him who breaks a dog's neck;
he who presents a cereal offering,
like him who offers swine's blood;
he who makes a memorial offering of frankincense,
like him who blesses an idol . . .'.

A passage in Psalm 50 again represents Yahweh as saying:

'I do not reprove you for your sacrifices;
your burnt offerings are continually before me.
I will accept no bull from your house,
nor he-goat from your folds.
For every beast of the forest is mine,
the cattle on a thousand hills . . .
If I were hungry I would not tell you;
for the world and all that is in it is mine.
Do I eat the flesh of bulls,
or drink the blood of goats? . . .' (vv. 8 : 13).

God who is himself the creator of the earth, and Lord of
all beasts and birds does not want sacrificial offerings from
man. Hence, although burnt offerings are continually before
him, he will accept neither bull nor he-goat. On the other
hand he significantly says:

'He who brings thanksgiving as his sacrifice honours me;
to him who orders his way aright
I will show the salvation of God' (vs. 23).

Sincere thanksgiving towards God is thus not only in itself
favourably countenanced, but when accompanied by right-

eous conduct effects man's salvation. In the last resource burnt offerings and sacrifices are no means of communing with God, and consequently have no place in the scheme of divine salvation. They neither do justice to the spiritual and personal nature of God nor adequately express the penitence of soul which finds forgiveness with him. It was thus, fully aware of the inadequacies of the ceremonial approach to God, that another Psalmist wrote:

'thou hast no delight in sacrifice;
were I to give a burnt offering,
thou wouldst not be pleased.
The sacrifice acceptable to God is a broken heart;
a broken and contrite heart,
O God, thou wilt not despise' (51 : 16-17).

Finally, it is noteworthy that this thought also finds expression in the Epistle to the Hebrews, where we read: 'It is impossible that the blood of bulls and goats should take away sins. Consequently, when Christ came into the world, he said, "Sacrifices and offerings thou hast not desired ... in burnt offerings and sin offerings thou hast taken no pleasure"' (10 : 4 : 6).

CHAPTER FIVE

THE MEDIATORS OF MONOTHEISM

The sovereignty of God in nature and history is one of the most distinctive elements in the thought of the prophets. And as there is no evidence that this property of Yahweh was emphasised before their time so it might be said that they were the first to conceive of him in terms of monotheism. It has of course been claimed that monotheism was a feature of Israelite religion long before the rise of the prophets, and some scholars would even be prepared to recognise a monotheistic trend in the beliefs of the Patriarchs. Thus connecting the Patriarchs with the Amarna Age, C. H. Gordon claims to find a 'universal God' in the pages of Genesis and says, 'We are therefore led to the conclusion that the significant monotheistic development of the Amarna Age was not the ephemeral religion of Akhenaton but the lasting one of Abraham'.[1] Similarly, while doubting if we may credit the Patriarchs with a belief in the existence of one God, H. M. Orlinsky is of the opinion that 'In a sense they may be said to have practised — but without defining—monotheism'.[2] More serious attempts have, however, been made to attribute monotheism to Moses. In his presentation of the Theology of the Old Testament Hermann Schultz spoke of the omnipotent and creative properties of the God of Moses,[3] while Paul Volz felt justified in discussing the reli-

[1] 'The Patriarchal Narratives', *J.N.E.S.*, 13, 1954, p. 58.
[2] *Ancient Israel*, p. 28.
[2] *Old Testament Theology* (2nd English edn.), vol. 1, 1898, p. 130.

gious beliefs of Moses in terms of advanced monotheism. [1]
Again, in a chapter entitled 'Moses, the founder of Monotheistic Religion' C. H. Cornill wrote: 'In all religions there
have been monotheistic tendencies, currents and attempts,
but only in the religion of Israel had monotheism become
a power, and indeed a power determining the entire religion;
and this is the work and merit of Moses'. [2]

It is mainly due to the influence of W. F. Albright that
in recent years many writers have inclined to the view that
the religious beliefs of Moses may legitimately be regarded
as monotheistic. In answer to the question 'Was Moses a
monotheist?' Albright himself declared: 'If by "monotheism" is meant a thinker with views specifically like
those of Philo Judaeus or of Rabbi Aqiba, of St. Paul or
St. Augustine . . . of St. Thomas or Calvin . . . Moses was
not one. If, on the other hand, the term "monotheist"
means one who teaches the existence of only one God, the
creator of everything, the source of justice, who is equally
powerful in Egypt, in the desert, and in Palestine, who has
no sexuality and no mythology, who is human in form but
cannot be seen by human eye and cannot be represented in
any form—then the founder of Yahwism was certainly a
monotheist'. [3] Admitting that monotheism was not logically
articulated in early Israel John Bright, however, remarked,
'Yet in that Mosaic religion ascribed all power in creation
and in the universe to one God, in that it not only ruled

---

[1] 'Der Gott des Mose' in *Old Testament Essays* (1927), pp. 29-36.
[2] *The Culture of Ancient Religion*, London 1914, p. 63. On the question
of early Israelite monotheism, see further the surveys of W. L. Wardle,
'The Origins of Hebrew Monotheism', *Z.A.W.*, N.F., 2, 1925, pp.
193-209, and H. H. Rowley, 'The Antiquity of Israelite Monotheism',
E.T., 61, 1949-50, pp. 333-338.
[3] *From the Stone Age to Christianity*, p. 207. Cf. also his conception of
monotheism in *Archaeology and the Religion of Israel*, 1953 p. 116.

other gods out of Israel but also deprived them of any
function in the universe and rendered them nonentities, it
seems ... that the term monotheism is justified'. [1] F. James
similarly regarded Moses as having mediated to Israel 'a
practical monotheism, out of which the later theoretical
monotheism of a Second Isaiah grew', [2] while more recently
Yehezekiel Kaufmann spoke 'of the monotheistic revolution
which occurred at Israel's birth as a nation in the days of
Moses'. [3]

Albright's view of Mosaic religion is largely based on the
meaning of the word *Yahweh* (יהוה). He interprets this as
'He causes to be'; and assuming that the phrase אהיה אשר
אהיה ('I am who I am') of Exodus 3 : 14 should be transposed
into the causative form '*Yahweh asher yihweh*', he translates
'He causes to be what comes into Existence'. [4] But, although
this ontological interpretation of the word *Yahweh* is representative of the opinion of most scholars of the past, [5]
some have hesitated to accept it and today many other
derivations are proposed. Kautzsch objected to the interpretation of *Yahweh* as creator on the grounds that it 'would
ill agree with Hebrew usage, which employs the name of
Yahweh chiefly with reference to revelations of God to
his people, or the conduct of the people toward their national
God, whereas the cosmic working of God is connected
with other divine names'. [6] G. R. Driver, again, contended

---

[1] *Interpretation*, 5, 1951, p. 7. Bright states here that 'his position is
that of his teacher, W. F. Albright', n. 9. So G. E. Wright, in discussing
the time when the concept of God as creator appeared in Israel, declared
himself inclined to the views of Albright, *The Old Testament against its
Environment*, p. 29, n. 35.

[2] *Personalities of the Old Testament*, 1939, p. 32.

[3] 'The Bible and Mythological Polytheism', *J.B.L.*, 70, 1951, p. 193.

[4] *From the Stone Age to Christianity*, p. 198.

[5] See *B.D.B.*, p. 218.

[6] *E.B.*, 3, 1902, col. 3323.

that while there may be some justification for 'the biblical
explanation of *Yahweh* as predicating being 'it does not
mean 'bringing into being'. [1] Regarding the word as coming
from a root (*hawa*) 'to blow' Wellhausen thought that it was
applied to the God of Israel because he was conceived of
as a storm god, [2] and this interpretation was also adopted
by Hempel [3] and later favoured by Meek. [4] More recently
Julian Obermann approached the question in the light of
inscriptions deriving from ancient Phoenicia. [5] On the
analogy of forms appearing in this material he regards
Yahweh as 'a causative participle of the underlying root
hwy' and thinks that its primary meaning is that of Sustainer,
Maintainer, or Establisher. [6] Like Obermann, J. Bowman
also claims that the root *hwy* underlies the word *Yahweh*
and on the evidence of a Ugaritic text argues that it means
'he declares' or 'he speaks'. [7] lt is, therefore, clear that there
is some divergence of opinion as to the etymological connotation of *Yahweh* and that, accordingly, we are scarcely
justified in basing any theological assumptions on the
name itself.

Furthermore, it is doubtful if Albright can claim historical
textual support for his interpretation in the phrase אהיה
אשר אהיה ('I am who I am') of Exodus 3 : 14. Lods found
difficulty in accepting the existential meaning of these
words on the grounds that if this had been 'the intention

---

[1] 'The Original Form of the name "Yahweh" ', *Z.A.W.*, N.F. 5,
1928, p. 24, n. 1.

[2] *Israelitische und judische Geschichte*, 6th edn., 1907, p. 25, n. 1.

[3] J. Hempel, *Gott und Mensch im Alten Testament*, 1936, pp. 27 f. and
38 f.

[4] *Hebrew Origins*, 2nd edn., 1950, pp. 95 and 103 f.

[5] 'The Divine Name YHWH in the light of Recent Discoveries',
J.B.L., 68, 1949, pp. 301-323.

[6] Page 308; so also p. 320.

[7] 'Yahweh The Speaker', *J.N.E.S.*, 3, 1944, pp. 1-8.

of the author he would have used the correct construction: "I am he who is", the more so that the word "is" (*yihyeh*) was much more akin than "am" (*ehyeh*) to the name Yahweh which he was explaining.'[1] W. R. Arnold has contended that the presence of this phrase is due to a glossator who tried to explain the form אהיה (*ehyeh*) later in the verse where we read 'I AM has sent me to you': this form, says Arnold, was itself employed in order 'to prevent the utterance of the ineffable name' in the passage in which God reveals himself to Moses.[2] It may, however, be argued that not only is this phrase a gloss, but that the whole of verse 14 is itself the work of an interpolator. For whatever the origin and date of the context it would in itself be complete without the material of verse 14. The information Moses seeks of God in verse 13 is naturally and adequately supplied in verse 15. Thus verse 13 reads: 'Then Moses said to God, If I come to the people of Israel and say to them, The God of your fathers has sent me to you, and they ask me, What is his name? what shall I say to them?[3] A direct and full answer to this question appears in verse 15 where God says to Moses, 'Say this to the people of Israel, The Lord, the God of your Fathers, the God of Abraham, the God of

---

[1] *Israel*, p. 322. The third person singular form of the verb would be all the more likely when we remember with Driver that 'there is considerable evidence that the prefix of the imperfect was *ya* . . .', *ibid.*

[2] 'The Divine Name in Exodus 3 : 14', *J.B.L.*, 24, 1905, pp. 133 f. See also Pfeiffer, *Intro. to the Old Testament*, p. 95.

[3] There is of course nothing inherently improbable in the story that Moses sought to discover the name of the God he encountered in the wilderness. According to the Babylonian 'Doctrine of the Name' nothing exists unless it has a name (see George Contenau, *Everyday Life in Babylonia and Assyria*, Eng. trans. 1954, p. 160). The Babylonian epic *Enuma Elish* conceived of primeval chaos at a time
'When no gods whatever had been brought into being,
Uncalled by name, their destinies undetermined' (Tablet I, lines 7-8 as translated in *A.N.E.T.*, p. 61a.

Isaac, and the God of Jacob, has sent me to you: this is my name . . .'. Moreover, in view of the fact that in his question in verse 13 Moses refers to the Israelite deity in terms of the Patriarchal God we should expect some attempt to identify that God with Yahweh in the answer which follows. Verse 14, however, merely states: 'God said to Moses, I am who I am. And he said, Say this to the people of Israel, I Am has sent me to you'. It cannot then be regarded as naturally following the preceding verse, while, on the other hand, in identifying Yahweh with the God of the Fathers the material of verse 15 represents a much more harmonious sequence. Again, it is doubtful if this existential conception of Yahweh would have had any significance for the Hebrews of an early period; nor, indeed, have we any evidence that it obtained in Israel before the teaching of Deutero-Isaiah.

It must further be recognised that in view of the nature of the biblical material pertaining to Moses we cannot determine with any certainty what he himself believed and taught; for although purporting to recount the events of the Mosaic period much of this material derives from a later age when it was the tendency to idealise the figures of the past and to ascribe to them beliefs and doctrines which have little historical reality. [1] Emerging, however, from the text are certain indications which scarcely admit of the view that Mosaic religion was monotheistic. While we read that

---

[1] Cf. Lods here: 'The narratives of the Pentateuch relating to the most distinctive period of the national religion have been, even more than the rest, recast, idealized and enlarged in the course of centuries, as each successive generation of historians referred back to the founder those principles, laws or institutions which they considered essential to the national religion . . . Owing to the lack of contemporary documents it is very hard to say with certainty who Moses was and what he did', *Israel*, pp. 308-309.

Yahweh 'made sport of the Egyptians' (Exod. 10 : 2) his jurisdiction was not normally regarded as extending over Egypt. In Exodus 3 : 8 he is represented as descending to Egypt to deliver the Israelite people, but apart from such acts as this he has no sovereignty over the land. Yahweh is localised at Sinai (Exod. 19 : 21), and his national status is indicated by the fact that he is specifically called 'the God of the Hebrews' (Exod. 7 : 16; 9 : 1, 13). Again, even if against the judgment of many scholars we grant the Mosaic authorship of the first Commandment we have here but a plea for the worship of Yahweh to the exclusion of other gods.[1] The statement in Exodus 18 : 11 that 'Yahweh is greater than all gods' implies the existence of other gods, while in other passages relating to Mosaic times we find mention of sacrifices to heathen gods (e.g., Exod. 34 : 15-16; Num. 25 : 2).

It will moreover be observed that throughout the Book of Exodus somewhat primitive notions are associated with Yahweh. He dwells on Mount Sinai amid thunder and lightning, and man approaches only at the peril of death (19 : 20 f.). He is represented as inhabiting the ark from which in some magical manner he holds converse with the people of Israel (25 : 8, 10, 21-22).[2] We read in 20 : 24 that sacrifice may be offered to Yahweh at any altar, but if an altar is to be constructed it must not be built of hewn stones (20 : 25). This prohibition derives no doubt from the primitive belief that the dressing of the stone would disturb the indwelling god who would forthwith leave his abode.[3] The conception of Yahweh as going forth to

---

[1] See here T. J. Meek, op. cit., p. 192, who regards this as 'henotheism'.

[2] According to Lods the 'ark was a sacred coffer similar to those in which the Egyptian gods were carried', op. cit., p. 427.

[3] Oesterley and Robinson, Hebrew Religion, 2nd edn., 1944, p. 48.

battle on behalf of his people (Exod. 14 : 14, 25; 15 : 3) is, again, similar to what we hear of Chemosh of Moab or Asshur of Assyria. [1] Thus, although Yahweh is the God who revealed himself to Moses, he is represented in terms which identify him exclusively with the nation of Israel and which in some respects are reminiscent of the naturalistic conceptions of deity obtaining in the ancient Semitic world.

This is not, however, to underestimate the work of Moses. Following his encounter with Yahweh it was his mission to declare to the Israelites that henceforth they were to accept Yahweh as their God who would in turn protect them from their enemies (e.g., Exod. 3 : 6-12). Hence, although Yahweh was the only God for Israel he was not necessarily the only God of the nations. But as Meek observed 'monotheism to be monotheism must transcend national limitations; it must be supernational'. [2] By the nature of the case this could not have been a feature of Mosaic religion, for the Israelites of the period were following a tribal existence and consequently their God was little more than a tribal God. [3] Thus, whatever the intensity of his religious experience, the views of God entertained by Moses can scarcely be termed monotheism; and indeed to attribute it to him is to misinterpret his place in the history and religion of Israel. [4]

Nor do we find any significant advance in Israel's conception of God in the period that followed the settlement in

---

[1] See Moabite Stone, lines 14 f., *A.N.E.T.*, p. 320a, and the Annals of Shalmaneser III, *A.N.E.T.*, p. 277.

[2] 'Monotheism and the Religion of Israel', *J.B.L.*, 61, 1932, p. 35.

[3] 'Modes of theological thought never establish themselves as disembodied ideologies. They develop along with and inside of corresponding institutional structures', W. C. Graham, *American Scholar*, 7, 1938, p. 423.

[4] As Wellhausen remarked, 'For Moses to have given to the Israelites an "enlightened conception of God" would have been to have given them a stone instead of bread', *Prolegomena to the History of Israel*, p. 437.

Canaan. In the Song of Deborah Yahweh is the God of Israel who still had associations with the southern desert where the mountains quaked before him (Jud. 5 : 3-5). The belief that each people had its own god likewise appears in Judges chapter 11 where Jephthah remarks that as the Israelites retain the spoils which their God Yahweh acquires on their behalf, so the people of Moab are entitled to that which Chemosh secures for them.[1] The power of Chemosh in his own land is again recognised by the Hebrew writer who relates that despite initial successes the invading armies of Israel suffered defeat at the hands of the Moabites when the king of Moab offered his eldest son in sacrifice (2 Kgs. 3 : 24-27). An Israelite king, lying ill on his bed, entertained such faith in the predictive powers of the god of Ekron that he sent messengers to consult him about the possibility of his recovery; and although he is censured by Elijah for this act of unfaithfulness to Yahweh, Elijah's words indicate that even he, himself, recognised the existence of the Phili- stine God: 'Is it because there is no God in Israel that you are going to inquire of Baal-zebub, the god of Ekron?' (2 Kgs. 1 : 1-3). Elijah's contest with the prophets of Baal on Mount Carmel shows, likewise, that while Baal was less powerful than Yahweh there was no doubt as to his existence (1 Kgs. 18 : 20 ff.). Yahweh's limitation to the land of Israel is, moreover, implied by David when, with reference to his exile in Philistia, he says: 'They have driven me out this day that I should have no share in the heritage of

---

[1] The context suggests that Jephthah is addressing the king of the Ammonites here, but as Chemosh is mentioned elsewhere in the Old Testament as the God of Moab (Num. 21 : 29; 1 Kgs 11 : 7, 33) it is likely that 'Moabites' should be read for 'Ammonites' throughout this apparently composite text. Cf. G. F. Moore, *The Book of Judges*, *I.C.C.*, 1903, pp. 294 f. and C. F. Burney, *The Book of Judges*, 1920, pp. 299 ff.

Yahweh, saying, Go, serve other gods' (I Sam. 26 : 19). [1]
Such considerations suggest, then, that in the period of the
Judges and of the early monarchy there was no definite
trend towards monotheism in the religious beliefs of the
Hebrews.

It is not till we come to the thought of the eighth-century
prophets that we find evident dissatisfaction with the conception of Yahweh as a national God and hence an attempt
to conceive of him in more comprehensive terms. Hitherto
the Israelites had lived in comparative peace and isolation
within their own borders and were but rarely concerned
with events which were happening elsewhere in the world
of their day. In the middle of the eighth century, however,
the power of Assyria appeared on the horizon and threatened
to overwhelm the whole of Syria-Palestine. Israel was thus
confronted with a movement of world history on a scale
which she never previously experienced. A century earlier
the combined efforts of the western states had, at the battle of
Karkar, effectively checked Assyrian expansion, but now
under the able generalship of Tiglath-Pileser III the Assyrian
armies constituted a formidable force. It was, moreover,
the boastful claim of the Assyrian gods that it was at their
behest the Assyrian armies were on the march. [2] This was
in fact an indication to the western peoples that the gods of
the Assyrians were more powerful than their own gods, while
to the Israelites too it can only have seemed that Asshur
had more forces at his command than Yahweh. The limitations of their national God became manifestly apparent

---

[1] Cf. also 1 Kgs. 20 : 23, where it is implied that the Israelite 'gods'
were confined to the hills.

[2] It is 'upon the command of Ashur' that Adad-Nirari III receives
tribute from defeated peoples, *A.N.E.T.*, p. 282 a. So Tiglath-Pileser
III makes an expedition against Arabia because she 'acted against an
oath (sworn) by Shamash', *A.N.E.T.*, p. 282 b.

and hence their traditional conception of him utterly inadequate to sustain them in the critical developments to which
they were now exposed.

It was thus when, for the first time in her history, Israel
stood in danger of being overwhelmed by an invading army
that Amos appeared on the scene.[1] Far from regarding
Yahweh as helpless before the events now impending he
interpreted them as but Yahweh's judgment on Israel's
sins. Incensed by the indifference to moral and religious
standards which characterised the prosperous reign of
Jeroboam II his words to Amaziah, the priest, at Bethel
were:

> 'Jeroboam shall die by the sword,
> and Israel must go into exile away from his land' (7 : 11).

Complacent and satisfied with Israel's conduct, Amaziah
objected to such words of censure (7 : 12), but Amos
replied:

> 'Your sons and your daughters shall fall by the sword,
> and your land shall be parceled out by line;
> you yourself shall die in an unclean land,
> And Israel shall surely go into exile . . .' (7 : 17).

Nor is there any doubt as to the instrument of such humiliation, for Yahweh's word is,

> 'Behold, I will raise up against you a nation . . .
> and they shall oppress you from the entrance of Hamath
> to the Brook of the Arabah' (6 : 14).

Having accepted Yahweh as her national God Israel was,
nonetheless, unfaithful to his demands; and in an oracle
aptly conveyed to Amos through the vision of a plumbline
Yahweh declares that, unable to condone her iniquities any

---

[1] R. S. Cripps, *op. cit.*, p. xxiii, places the call of Amos in the year
'742-741, or at the earliest 744-743, that is, within Jeroboam's lifetime
and after the rise of Tiglath-Pileser III'. See further, below pp. 207 f.

longer, he will judge her in accordance with his standards
of moral rectitude:

'Behold, I am setting a plumb line
in the midst of my people Israel;
I will never again pass by them;
the high places of Isaac shall be made desolate,
and the sanctuaries of Israel shall be laid waste' (7 : 8-9).

The people who are indifferent to the moral ruin of the nation
'shall be the first' to go into exile (6 : 7), and because of
the pride and presumption of the rulers of Samaria Yahweh
'will deliver up the city and all that is in it' (6 : 8). Such
will be the violence of the destruction (6 : 11) and the
confusion of the scene (8 : 8) that it will be futile to offer
resistance:

'Flight shall perish from the swift,
and the strong shall not retain his strength,
nor shall the mighty save his life;
he who handles the bow shall not stand,
and he who is swift of foot shall not save himself,
nor shall he who rides the horse save his life' (2 : 14-15).

But, awful and devastating as these events will be, it is
Yahweh who will bring them to pass; for in accordance
with the views of Amos Yahweh may use non-Israelite
nations to further his moral purposes. Contrary to the
beliefs of the day he implies that Yahweh has a knowledge
of 'all the families of the earth' (3 : 2), and, far from conce-
ding that Yahweh manifests an exclusive interest in Israel,
he declares:

'Are you not like the Ethiopians to me,
O people of Israel, says Yahweh.
Did I not bring up Israel from the land of Egypt,
and the Philistines from Caphtor
and the Syrians from Kir?' (9 : 7).

To the Israelites of the eighth century this utterance was

startling in the sweep of its manifold implications. For it revealed that in the eyes of Yahweh they were no different from the Ethiopians of Africa, and that as he brought themselves out of Egypt so he brought the Philistines from the isles of the Mediterranean and the Arameans from the distant East. [1] Thus the Philistines who had been the traditional enemies of Israel, and the Syrians who had more than once oppressed her (I Kgs. 20 : 26; 2 Kgs. 13 : 3, 22), owed their origin and history to Yahweh himself. But an inference more far-reaching still was that as these peoples were ultimately dependent on Yahweh for their existence, so their gods too must be inferior to him. In exposing, then, the inadequacy of the notion that Yahweh was the national God of Israel, and in declaring that on the contrary his sovereignty extended to other peoples, the teaching of Amos represents the first significant advance in Hebrew theological thought. [2]

The resurgence of Assyrian power was likewise the signal for Hosea's call to prophesy. [3] Less concerned than Amos

---

[1] It is usual to identify Caphtor with Crete. For a statement connecting the original home of the Philistines with Caria and Lycia, however, see R. S. Cripps, *op. cit.*, p. 263. But whatever the locality of Kir it is here in Amos represented as the place from which the Arameans migrated. In Isaiah 22 : 6 it is mentioned in proximity to Elam and is probably to be associated with that region. In 2 Kings 16 : 9 we read that Tiglath-Pileser III took the people of Damscus captive to Kir and so at that time it must have been within the limits of the Assyrian empire.

[2] Regarding Amos as only 'a universalist in a sense' J. Morgenstern, nevertheless, wrote: 'It suffices that he should have been the pioneer of this new doctrine, this new interpretation of life and new concept of deity, so fraught with significance for the religious thought and destiny of mankind. Viewed from this angle Amos was truly one of the greatest, not only of the prophets of Israel, but also of the creative religious thinkers of all human history', 'The Historical Antecedents of Amos', *H.U.C.A.*, 15, 1940, p. 290.

[3] See W. R. Harper, *Hosea*, *I.C.C.*, 1905, p. cxli, who inclined to the view that Hosea was called to his office somewhere round the year

with events external to Israel he, nevertheless, regarded the consequences of Assyrian domination as being in accord with the divine will. Israel will come to an end but it is Yahweh who has ordained her doom. Thus, commanding the prophet to call his eldest son 'Jezreel', Yahweh says: 'for yet a little while, and I will punish the house of Jehu for the blood of Jezreel, and I will put an end to the kingdom of the house of Israel' (1 : 4). Israel's fall will be accompanied by such violence and devastation as could be caused only by the ruthlessness of a hostile army (8 : 14); and there can have been no doubt in Hosea's mind as to the agency of such destruction. For the dominance of Assyria and the conquests she has already made indicated only too clearly to him the course of future events:

> 'They shall return to the land of Egypt,
> and Assyria shall be their king,
> because they have refused to return to me.
> The sword shall rage against their cities,
> consume the bars of their gates,
> and devour them in their fortresses' (11 : 5-6).

In the utterances of Isaiah we find, however, a more developed expression of the prophetic theme that Yahweh's hand is discernible in the significant events of the day. Amos and Hosea had already recognised that the western advance of Assyria would inevitably engulf the state of Israel but Isaiah was able to discern its relevance for Judah as early as the year 734-733. [1] At that time both Rezin of Damascus

---

743 B.C. See also N. Snaith, *Mercy and Sacrifice: a Study of the Book of Hosea*, 1953, pp. 14 f. who would place both Amos and Hosea close to 745 and suggests that Hosea may even have been a year or so earlier than Amos.

[1] For the probability that Isaiah entered on his mission at this period see the present writer, 'The Call and Mission of Isaiah', *J.N.E.S.*, 18, 1, 1959, pp. 38 f.

and Pekah of Israel invaded Judean territory (2 Kgs. 15 : 37; 16 : 5), but calculating on Assyrian intervention Isaiah assured the panic-stricken Ahaz that

'it shall not stand,
and it shall not come to pass' (7 : 7).

But it is evident that Ahaz interpreted the Syrian invasion of his land as indicative of the superiority of the Syrian gods over Yahweh, and consequently he appealed to Assyria for help. Moreover, while paying homage to Tiglath-Pileser in Damascus he so admired the altar there that he decided to have an altar of similar dimensions erected in Jerusalem (2 Kgs. 16 : 10 f.). We are told in 2 Kings (16 : 12-13) that Ahaz himself officiated at this new altar, while the Chronicler reports him as saying; 'Because the gods of the kings of Syria helped them, I will sacrifice to them that they may help me' (2 Chron. 28 : 23). It is thus clear that the Judean king considered the God of Israel helpless in the face of such critical international developments and, despite the counsel of Isaiah, sought other means of averting the danger which appeared so imminent.

The accuracy of Isaiah's judgment was vindicated by the issue of events. By 732 the Assyrian armies had not only completed the conquest of Syria, but had devastated much of northern Israel.[1] But while popular opinion regarded such events as outside the domain of Yahweh, Isaiah proclaimed that they were proceeding in accordance with the divine purpose. For it was Yahweh who had empowered and sustained the Assyrians in their unparalleled feats of conquest: it was indeed none other than he who lent substance to the proud Assyrian boast,

'Are not my commanders all kings?
Is not Calno like Carchemish?

---

[1] See W. F. Albright, *The Biblical Period*, p. 40; *A.N.E.T.*, p. 283.

Is not Hamath like Arpad?
Is not Samaria like Damascus?' (10 : 8-9).

Isaiah's words could only seem strange to a Judean audience
of that day, but their novelty was equalled by the further
declaration that the Assyrian power was only an avenging
instrument in the hand of God:

'Ah, Assyria, the rod of my anger, the staff of my fury,
Against a godless nation I send him,
and against the people of my wrath I command him,
to take spoil and seize plunder,
and to tread them down like the mire of the streets.
But he does not so intend,
and his mind does not so think;
but it is in his mind to destroy,
and to cut off nations not a few' (10 : 5-7).

Assyria's campaign will not, then, be confined to the peoples
of Syria and Palestine. In pursuit of her destined course she
must also defeat the designs of Egypt. For Egypt had been
meddling in Palestinian affairs and was now inciting Ashdod
to resist Assyrian authority. [1] But even Ashdod will say of
Egypt: 'Behold, this is what has happened to those in whom
we hoped and to whom we fled for help to be delivered
from the king of Assyria! And we, how shall we escape?'
(20 : 6). Elsewhere the prophet reveals in some detail the
true nature of Egypt:

'For Egypt's help is worthless and empty,
therefore I have called her
Rahab who sits still' (30 : 7).

Since the days of their bondage the Hebrews regarded
Egypt as a formidable people whose ability was in excess of
ordinary mortals, but in the eyes of Isaiah

---

[1] See here D. J. Wiseman, *Documents from Old Testament Times* (ed.
D. Winton Thomas), pp. 59 f.

'The Egyptians are men, and not God;
and their horses are flesh, and not spirit.
When Yahweh stretches out his hand
the helper will stumble,
and he who is helped will fall,
and they will all perish together' (31 : 3).

Yet Assyria which has been so active in the service of
Yahweh will in turn be humbled at his hands. In 701 the
Assyrians surrounded the walls of Jerusalem, but trusting
in the strength of Yahweh Hezekiah exhorted his subjects
to resist (2 Kgs 18 : 31). Scorning the notion that Yahweh
could protect them the Rabshakeh arrogantly asked, 'Who
among all the gods of the countries have delivered their
countries out of my hand, that Yahweh should deliver
Jerusalem out of my hand?' (2 Kgs. 18 : 35). Confronted
by such words even Hezekiah lost confidence, but Isaiah
assured him that in the providence of God the Assyrians
would be compelled to return to their own land without
inflicting any injury on Judah (2 Kgs. 19 : 6-7).

Thus throughout the critical years which marked Judean
history from the Syro-Ephraimite war to the appearance
of Assyrian forces before the gates of Jerusalem, Isaiah
exercised a ministry in which he declared that Yahweh's
hand was the decisive factor in all the events of the period.
This proclamation of God's sovereignty over the nations,
and of his protection for those who unconditionally trust
in him, introduced, then, a new and significant element into
Israelite religious thought.

The notion that Yahweh's hand may be seen in the movements of the nations is again evident in the prophecies of
Jeremiah. Called to the prophetic office at a more critical
moment of Israelite history than his predecessors it was
necessarily a fundamental tenet of his teaching. Descending

from the steppe-lands of the north, the Scythians and Medes were harassing the Assyrian frontiers, and despite her imperial greatness, Assyria herself was about to vanish from the historical scene. Egypt too, save for petty intrigues, had ceased to be an effective political force. The Chaldeans were emerging from the marshes of southern Babylonia and were about to establish the last Semitic empire in the ancient world. In Palestine the Josianic reforms were interpreted as a measure of national independence and Josiah contemplated the extension of his kingdom northwards.[1] When therefore in 609 Necho was passing through Megiddo to aid the Assyrians in their final efforts against the combined forces of the Scythians and Chaldeans, Josiah did not hesitate to challenge his passage.[2] He was, however, killed in this encounter, and though immediately succeeded by his son Jehoahaz the Egyptians later elevated Jehoiakim to the throne of Judah. It was probably at this disruptive juncture of Judean history that Jeremiah was called to his work,[3] although the most onerous period of his ministry fell within the years which immediately followed the battle of Carchemish in 605. Heedless of his warnings, the Judean people pursued their own irreligious ways but Jeremiah's prophetic eye discerned that sooner or later the victors at Carchemish must turn their gaze towards the west. Indeed, it is probable that soon after 605 Nebuchadrezzar appeared in Judah and

---

[1] 2 Kgs 23 : 15. See also Albright *op. cit.*, pp. 44-45.

[2] It is now thought that Josiah's motive in attacking Necho was to prevent him effecting a junction with the Assyrian troops. An anti-Assyrian movement seems to have been contemplated on a wide scale by states once subject to Assyria. Cf. here A. Malamat, 'The Last Wars of the Kingdom of Judah', *J.N.E.S.*, 9, 1950, pp. 218-227.

[3] For a statement of the view that Jeremiah did not begin his ministry till after the death of Josiah see the present writer, *The Exilic Age*, pp. 34-42 and the literature cited there.

demanded the submission of Jehoiakim. [1] Interpreting this
as in accordance with Yahweh's will Jeremiah urged his
countrymen to acknowledge the sovereignty of Babylon,
but instead they countenanced the hope that help would
be forthcoming from Egypt. Disapproving of such a policy
Jeremiah accordingly comments:

> 'How lightly you gad about, changing your way.
> You shall be put to shame by Egypt
> as you were put to shame by Assyria.
> From it too you will come away
> with your hands upon your head,
> for Yahweh has rejected those in whom you trust,
> and you will not prosper by them' (2 : 36-37).

As Isaiah regarded Assyria the avenging agent of Yahweh,
so now Jeremiah similarly conceives of the Chaldeans.
Referring to them as the 'foe from the north' he interprets
their appearance in Judah as God's judgment on a sinful
people: 'Out of the north evil shall break forth upon all
the inhabitants of the land, For, lo, I am calling all the tribes
of the kingdoms of the north, says Yahweh; and they shall
come and every one shall set his throne at the entrance of the
gates of Jerusalem, against all its walls round about, and
against all the cities of Judah. And I will utter my judgments
against them for all their wickedness in forsaking me'
(1 : 14-16). The Judeans, however, persisted in their refusal
to submit to Babylon and at length, in 597, [2] the armies of
Nebuchadrezzar invaded their land and carried many of
them captive to Babylonia. But despite this Judah still hoped
to exert her independence, and to this end favourably

---

[1] Cf. D. J. Wiseman, *Chronicles of Chaldean Kings* (625-556 *B.C.*),
1946, pp. 26, 30, who argues that Jehoiakim submitted to Nebuchadrezzar as early as 605.

[2] Wiseman, *Chronicles of Chaldean Kings* (625-556 *B.C.*), p. 33.

received a deputation from neighbouring states advocating resistance against Babylon (27 : 2 f.). Perceiving the futility of this course Jeremiah promptly declared that it was not only Yahweh's will that Nebuchadrezzar should rule over Judah, but that these other rebellious nations should also submit to him. Symbolically placing a wooden yoke on his neck he forthwith delivers the charge of Yahweh: 'I have given all these lands into the hand of Nebuchadrezzar, the king of Babylon, my servant . . . But if any nation or kingdom will not serve this Nebuchadrezzar king of Babylon, and put its neck under the yoke of the king of Babylon, I will punish that nation with the sword, with famine and with pestilence . . .' (27 : 6-8). And to Zedekiah his message is of similar purport: 'bring your necks under the yoke of the King of Babylon, and serve him and his people, and live. Why will you and your people die by the sword . . . as Yahweh has spoken concerning any nation which will not serve the king of Babylon?' (27 : 12-13). In accordance with their practice of engendering an unjustified optimism amongst the people, the false prophets were, however, proclaiming that within two years the exile would end (28 : 1 f.), and now one of them, Hananiah, seizing the yoke from Jeremiah, broke it declaring that Yahweh would so break the power of Babylon (28 : 10-11). But, convinced that Yahweh's purpose would not be frustrated, Jeremiah replaced the wooden yoke by an iron one (28 : 12) and hears Yahweh say: 'Go, tell Hananiah . . . You have broken wooden bars, but I will make in their place bars of iron' (28 : 13). Yahweh's purpose is therefore irrevocable: submission to the Chaldeans is his will; and this course alone will save both the land and the people from destruction (38 : 17 f.). But it was in vain that Jeremiah pleaded with his countrymen. Yielding to the demands of some of his subjects, Zedekiah withheld tribute from Nebuchadrezzar; and the Babylonian forces were again forced to take the field. During the course of the final onslaught against Jerusalem Egypt attempted to intervene,[1] but her efforts proved unavailing for Yahweh had already decreed: 'Behold, Pharaoh's army which came to help you is about to return to Egypt, to its own land. And the Chaldeans shall come back and fight against this city; they shall take it and burn it with fire' (37 : 7-8). Nor will the resistance offered by the Judeans themselves accomplish much; for however valiantly they may fight Yahweh is himself on the side of the Chaldeans. 'Behold, I will turn back the weapons of war which are in your hands and with which you are fighting against the king of Babylon and against the Chaldeans who are besieging you outside the walls ... I myself will fight against you with outstretched hand and strong arm, in anger and in fury' (21 : 4-5). Surrender is the way of life but resistance is the way of death (21 : 8): 'He who stays in this city shall die by the sword ... but he who goes out and surrenders to the Chaldeans ... shall live and shall have his life' (21 : 9).

The role of the Chaldeans is not, however, confined to destroying Jerusalem. As the 'servant' of Yahweh Nebuchadrezzar will also execute judgment on the surrounding nations and so forward the divine purpose. Thus, far from being limited to the land of Israel, Yahweh chooses the greatest military leader of the day and commissions him to his service.

It is, then, in accordance with this more comprehensive

---

[1] Jer. 37 : 5. The Lachish Letters pertaining to the years immediately preceding the fall of Jerusalem mention a Judean 'commander of the army ... on his way to Egypt', apparently for aid against the invading Babylonians. See D. Winton Thomas, *Documents from Old Testament Times*, pp. 214 f.

conception of God that Jeremiah advised the exiles to settle in Babylonia and to establish their homes there. For although Yahweh was popularly regarded as the national God of Israel with neither interest nor influence in foreign lands it was in fact possible to feel his presence in Babylon. (29 : 11 f.). Yahweh is independent of either temple or nation and may be found wherever he is earnestly sought. It is he who in reality is the sovereign God of Babylon, and it is therefore his will that it should prosper and that the exiles should contribute to the common good (29 : 7). Nor should the exiles think that their transportation to foreign soil was an indication of divine displeasure: on the contrary, Yahweh has said, 'I will regard as good the exiles from Judah, whom I have sent away from this place to the land of the Chaldeans' (24 : 5).

In conformity with this view of Yahweh Jeremiah regards the gods of the nations as mere 'worthlessness' (2 : 5) and as 'broken cisterns that can hold no water' (2 : 13). So in censuring those who worship gods made from trees and stones he scornfully remarks, 'Let them arise, if they can save you in your time of trouble' (2 : 28), while, again, Israel cannot expect Yahweh's pardon because she has 'sworn by those who are no gods' (5 : 7). In contrast Yahweh is a God of wide dominions whose hand may be seen even in the international struggles of the time. Nor would any less exalted view of God have been adequate to the task to which Jeremiah was called. For Yahweh must either be regarded as cognisant of the movements and even the intrigues of the day, or else it must be granted that as the mere national God of Israel he was powerless before them. Hence Israel must accept the crisis she was experiencing as not only in accordance with Yahweh's will, but as evidence of his interest in her spiritual advancement. And although we can scarcely claim that in presenting such a view of God Jeremiah uses the language of inductive monotheism, yet it is clear that for him Yahweh was the only God of the world of his experience and that he may be found by Israel in Babylonia as well as in Judah.

The assumption that the sovereignty of Yahweh extended over nations other than Israel was likewise basic to the teaching of Ezekiel. Deported to Babylon in 597 he received his prophetic call some three years later.[1] Local military revolts in Babylon at this time contributed to a restlessness among the exiles, who, encouraged by the false prophets, hoped for an early return to Judah. When, moreover, Psammetichus II succeeded to the Egyptian throne in 594 his accession was greeted by many of the western states as the moment for a concerted revolt against Babylon. Ezekiel, however, declared that such designs would be rendered ineffective by Yahweh. Nor would the Judeans be advised to make ill-advised alliances, for events had proved that those states which had formerly sought the support of Judah readily rejoiced at her fall. Despite pledges that may have been given to the contrary, Ammon was jubilant when Nebuchadrezzar eventually destroyed Jerusalem. But Ezekiel contended that the destruction of Jerusalem was no indication of Yahweh's defeat in battle. It was rather part of an extensive campaign of destruction designed to overtake the western nations, and in which Ammon herself was inevitably involved: 'Thus says the Lord God, Because you said, Aha, over my sanctuary when it was profaned, and over the land of Israel when it was made desolate, and over the house of Judah when it went into exile, therefore I am handing you

---

[1] See the present writer 'The "Thirtieth" Year in Ezekiel 1 : 1', *V.T.* 9, 3, 1959, pp. 328 f. for the suggestion that Ezekiel was called to his work in the year 595-4.

over to the people of the East for a possession' (25 : 3-4). Referring again to the fall of Jerusalem, Moab complacently remarked, 'Judah is like all the other nations' (24 : 8). But while Ezekiel did not pretend to dispute that Judah was no exception to the rule that all nations have their day, he maintained that her fall was in accord with the will of God and that Moab herself would soon experience similar humiliation. Like the Ammonites she will be given into the hands of a people from the East, for Yahweh's words are: 'I will execute judgments upon Moab. Then they will know that I am the Lord' (25 : 11). Edom and Philistia adopted an equally vindictive attitude towards the fallen Jerusalem, but they too will be punished by Yahweh and so will be brought to acknowledge him as Lord (25 : 15-17; 35 : 1-15).

In demonstrating his sovereignty over the nations Yahweh will not, however, confine his activity to the minor states of the west. The more powerful and ambitious states of Tyre and Egypt will also be included in the impending doom; and Nebuchadrezzar will again be the instrument of humiliation. Tyre was one of these states which attempted to incite Judah to rebellion, but having heard the news of her fall she joyously exclaimed 'Aha, the gate of the peoples is broken, it has swung open to me; I shall be replenished, now that she is laid waste' (26 : 2). Having monopolised the maritime commerce of the ancient world Tyre envied the financial advantages which accrued to Jerusalem by virtue of her situation on one of the main trade routes of the Orient. She will not, however, derive much benefit from the trading facilities now thrown open to her; for the power which devastated Judah will in due time turn its attention to Tyre. She who had boasted of the perfection of her architectural beauty (27 : 3) shall become 'a city laid waste like the cities that are not inhabited' (26 : 19): she who claimed to enrich 'the kings of the earth' with her 'abundant wealth and merchandise' shall 'come to a dreadful end and shall be no more for ever' (27 : 33, 36). Yahweh has irrevocably decreed, 'Behold, I will bring upon Tyre from the north Nebuchadrezzar king of Babylon . . . with horses and chariots and with horsemen and a host of many soldiers . . . They will make a spoil of your riches and a prey of your merchandise; they will break down your walls and destroy your pleasant houses . . .' (26 : 7, 8, 12). But Yahweh's vengeance on Tyre was not solely provoked by her taunts against the stricken Jerusalem. More unpardonable was her assumption of the status of a god amongst the commercial nations of the day:

'Because your heart is proud,
and you have said, I am a god,
I sit in the seat of the gods,
in the heart of the seas,
yet you are but a man, and no god,
though you consider yourself
as wise as a god . . .
therefore, behold, I will bring strangers upon you,
the most terrible of the nations;
and they shall draw their swords
against the beauty of your wisdom
and defile your splendour' (28 : 2, 7).

Egypt's destruction will be equally severe and her humiliation no less bitter. And this is the more significant in view of the influence she exerted over Israel in the past. Ever since the Exodus Egypt had manifested an interest in Israel (cf., 1 Kgs. 9; 6; 14 : 25; 2 Kgs. 17 : 4); and Israel's association with her was in turn condemned by the prophets (Hos. 7 : 11; Is. 30 : 2; Jer. 2 : 36-37). Indeed Egypt's intervention in Palestinian affairs led to Nebuchadrezzar's final

reduction of Judah. Consequently Egypt will now suffer
for this long and unfortunate influence upon Israel:

> 'Thus says the Lord God:
> I will put an end to the wealth of Egypt
> by the hand of Nebuchadrezzar king of Babylon.
> He and his people with him,
> the most terrible of the nations,
> shall be brought in to destroy the land;
> and they shall draw their swords against Egypt,
> and fill the land with the slain' (30 : 10-11).

Again, as Tyre was condemned for assuming the status of
deity so the Pharaoh is censured for presuming to say 'My
Nile is my own; I made it' (29 : 3). The Nile was essential
to Egyptian commerce and traffic and for the irrigation of the
soil: on it depended the whole of Egyptian life, but its
waters ultimately derive from Yahweh. In accordance with
Egyptian belief in divine kingship the Pharaoh regarded
the river as his own creation, and for thus arrogating to
himself a claim that could be made by Yahweh only both he
and his land will be punished:

> 'Behold, I am against you, Pharaoh king of Egypt,
> the great dragon that lies
> in the midst of his streams . . .
> I will put hooks in your jaws . . .
> and I will draw you out of the midst of your streams . . .
> and I will cast you forth into the wilderness . . . (29 : 3-5).
> And I will dry up the Nile,
> and will sell the land into the hand of evil men;
> I will bring desolation upon the land
> and everything in it,
> by the hand of foreigners . . .' (30 : 12).

But in addition to the land being desolated and its wealth
despoiled, the idols and images for which Egypt was so
well known will also be destroyed and become objects of
disdain and contempt (30 : 13).

The restlessness and uncertainties of the age tended, moreover, to emphasise the importance of the individual national gods. Not only the great and many gods of Egypt, but Melkart of Tyre, Milcom of Ammon and Chemosh of Moab were revered by their worshippers as never before and exorbitant claims made for them. Indignant at such pretensions Ezekiel maintained that these peoples would be destroyed as in the course of historical events Yahweh's purpose is unfolded. And such destruction will be amply justified if it leads to the acknowledgment of Yahweh as a God of international sovereignty (25 : 17; 28 : 23; 30 : 19).

It is, however, in the utterances of Deutero-Isaiah that we find the most sublime expression in the Old Testament of God's sovereignty over the nations and indeed over all history and creation. Assuming his prophetic burden as the Persians were engaged on their campaigns of conquest, he was concerned to assure the exiles that Yahweh was not indifferent to the developments of the contemporary political scene. Having attacked and subdued the Medes, Cyrus was now pursuing the Lydians and it was obvious that Babylon must soon fall to his forces. It was thus with some apprehension that the Babylonians witnessed these portentous events, while the Jews were wondering what fate would befall themselves as exiles. But observing the movements and tensions of the hour, Deutero-Isaiah was convinced that in the eyes of God 'the nations' are but as 'a drop from a bucket' (40 : 15) and 'are as nothing before him' (40 : 17). Yahweh 'brings princes to nought and makes the rulers of the earth as nothing' (40 : 23), and he exercises this sovereignty because he can say,

'I made the earth
and created man upon it' (45 : 12).

In this Babylonian evironment there were many claims to the

feat of creation. The epic *Enuma Elish* had described in laudatory terms the creative activity of the god Marduk, [1] while other views of creation were doubtless expounded by the different elements of the Babylonian population. But, although the Israelites seem to have forgotten, it was Yahweh alone who brought the ordered world into being and who has long since sustained it:

> 'Have you not known? Have you not heard?
> Yahweh is the everlasting God,
> the Creator of the ends of the earth' (40 : 28).

It is again Yahweh

> 'who created the heavens . . .
> who formed the earth and made it,
> he established it;
> he did not create it a chaos,
> he formed it to be inhabited' (45 : 18).

It is he too who made the waters of the sea and who fashioned the hills and mountains (40 : 12), while the 'hand' that 'laid the foundations of the earth' (48 : 13) is that of 'Yahweh who made all things' (44 : 24).

His creation of the world and its inhabitants enables him, moreover, to direct the course of history. He took Israel from the ends of the earth (41 : 9), but in reality he called all 'the generations from the beginning' (41 : 4). Even Cyrus himself was called to his place in history by God and sustained by him in his triumphant marches (44 : 28). Not only Israel but all the nations of the day might consider this; and it is thus with some significance that Yahweh asks,

> 'Who stirred up one from the east
> whom victory meets at every step?
> He gives up nations before him,
> so that he tramples kings under foot;

---

[1] Tablets 4-6, see *A.N.E.T.*, pp. 66 f.

he makes them like dust with his sword,
like driven stubble with his bow' (41 : 2)

But although brilliantly victorious in his campaigns Cyrus is
entirely unaware of the true end he is serving. Yahweh
will give him the treasures and riches of Babylon (45 : 3), but
it is not to gratify the greed of a conqueror. It is rather
because he is forwarding the universal purpose of God and
because Israel has a special place within that purpose:

'For the sake of my servant Jacob,
and Israel my chosen,
I call you by your name, I surname you,
though you do not know me' (45 : 4).

Yahweh who initiated all history is directing it towards a
definite goal. He who has been 'declaring the end from the
beginning and from ancient times things not yet done'
(46 : 10) will now manifest his plans before the nations and
can say of Israel, 'I give men in return for you, peoples in ex-
change for your life' (43 : 4). But while Yahweh has purpose-
fully conceived and directed the events of history he was
influenced by no one. It is thus with some rhetorical effect
that the prophet asks,

'Who has directed the Spirit of Yahweh,
or as his counsellor has instructed him?
Whom did he consult for his enlightenment,
and who taught him the path of justice . . .?' (40 : 13-14).

Having indicated the self-existent nature of Yahweh,
Deutero-Isaiah now proceeds to establish that he is incomparable in his divine properties: 'To whom then will you
liken God, or what likeness compare with him?' (40 : 18).
There were a multitude of gods in Babylon, but what of
their claims to deity? The popular gods of the day were
fashioned from wood or metal, mere products of the hands
of man (41 : 6-7; 44 : 13-17); but in common with all

creation, craftsmen were themselves made by God (54 : 16). Consequently it requires but little discernment to realize that a man who falls 'down before a block of wood . . . feeds on ashes' and that he has become so spiritually and mentally degraded that he cannot say 'Is there not a lie in my right hand?' (44 : 19-20).

The idolatrous nature of the great Bel and Nebo was, however, no less apparent, and without fear or hesitation the prophet exclaims:

> 'Bel bows down, Nebo stoops,
> their idols are on beasts and cattle . . .
> They stoop, they bow down together,
> they cannot save the burden,
> but themselves go into captivity' (46 : 1-2).

Nebuchadrezzar claimed to have organised his armies by the help of his 'lord Nebo and Marduk',[1] but the prophet knows that for all the gold and silver which contributed to their manufacture, these gods of Babylon are lifeless and impotent. Unable to move from its pedestal such a god is a pathetic yet contemptible figure, and it is little wonder that 'if one cries to it, it does not answer or save him from his trouble' (46 : 7). In contrast to such helplessness Yahweh is a God of life and activity: 'He does not faint or grow weary . . . he gives power to the faint, and to him who has no might he increases strength' (40 : 28-29).

But although the artificial nature of the Babylonian gods is evident, Deutero-Isaiah still invites them to substantiate their claims to deity on the grounds of prophecy:[2]

> 'Set forth your case says Yahweh;
> Bring your proofs, says the King of Jacob.

---

[1] The Annals of his expedition to Syria, *A.N.E.T.*, p. 307a.
[2] Cf. here S. H. Blank, 'Studies in Deutero-Isaiah', *H.U.C.A.*, 15, 1940, pp. 1-6.

Let them bring them, and tell us what is to happen.
Tell us the former things what they are,
that we may consider them,
that we know their outcome;
or declare to us the things to come.
Tell us what is to come hereafter,
that we may know that you are gods;
do good, or do harm
that we may be dismayed and terrified' (41 : 21-23).

The prophet was here referring to contemporary political developments and was appealing to the Babylonian gods to interpret their significance for the course of future events. Claiming to have brought Cyrus on the stage of history and to have predicted the sequence of his victories (41 : 25) Yahweh pointedly asks,

'Who declared it from the beginning that we might know
and aforetime that we might say, He is right' (41 : 26).

Of the many gods of Babylon there was none among them who could attempt a pronouncement (41 : 26), and their failure to do so points to the inevitable verdict,

'Behold, they are all a delusion;
their works are nothing;
their molten images are empty wind' (41 : 29).

Yahweh, on the other hand, not only claims to have accurately forecast the pattern of past events, but also to be able to predict the future:

'Behold, the former things have come to pass,
and new things I now declare;
before they spring forth
I tell you of them' (42 : 9).

But Yahweh predicts the sequence of future developments only because it is he who determines the course they will assume. This is in fact the source of his infallible prescience (43 : 13). And the prophet now appeals to the Israelites

themselves in support of this contention; for they have
experienced God's grace in the past and can thus testify to
his influence in history (44 : 8). On the other hand, though
the gods of the nations had their worshippers, they had in
effect neither prophets who could declare their intentions
nor witnesses to confirm their acts. So now in an appeal
both to the nations and to Israel herself Yahweh says:

'Let all the nations gather together,
and let the peoples assemble.
Who among them can declare this
and show us the former things?
Let them bring their witnesses to justify them,
and let them hear and say, it is true.
You are my witnesses, says the Lord,
and my servant whom I have chosen,
that you may know and believe me
and understand that I am He . . .' (43 : 9 f.).

Unlike the speechless idols of the nations who have neither
prophets nor witnesses, and who in consequence can present
no credentials to deity, Yahweh can justly say, 'I declared
and saved and proclaimed' (43 : 12).

Having skilfully exposed the idolatrous nature of the
gods of the nations, Deutero-Isaiah at length represents
Yahweh as asking, 'Is there a God beside me?' (44 : 8).
For if Yahweh was active in history from the beginning
of time and if the alleged deities of the day have been shown
to have no existence, then, it follows that he is the only
God of the universe and is accordingly justified in exclai-
ming:

'I am the Lord and there is no other,
besides me there is no God' (45 : 5).

Even the Babylonians with their boastful claims for their
gods had to admit that there was a time 'When no gods

whatever had been brought into being', [1] but Yahweh could say, 'From the time it came to be I have been there' (48 : 16). He is, further, a God of the present as well as the past, and will be to all future ages:

'I am God, and also henceforth I am He (43 : 13);
I am He, I am the first and I am the last' (48 : 12).

Yahweh is the only 'Existent One', [2] and in predicating the existence of him only as God Deutero-Isaiah is the first of the Hebrew writers to give definite and unequivocal expression to a doctrine of pure monotheism. For while Jeremiah assumed that Yahweh wielded an unquestionable authority over the peoples of the day, and Ezekiel derided the gods of the western nations, they did not categorically deny existence to other gods or formally state that Yahweh alone is God.

Nor were Jeremiah and Ezekiel concerned with the formulation of the doctrine of monotheism; but Deutero-Isaiah, by virtue of the circumstances of his ministry, could not be indifferent to it. Although Ezekiel also prophesied in Babylon the immediate preoccupation of the exiles of his day was with other and more practical questions. Deutero-Isaiah, on the other hand, had to deal with a later generation of Jews who had grown up in Babylon and who were impressed as well as attracted by the imposing gods of their environment. Furthermore, the population of Babylon now included Greeks, Lydians, Egyptians and Persians, [3] and in consequence there were many and conflicting views regarding the nature of the universe and the causes underlying it. The

---

[1] *Enuma Elish*, *A.N.E.T.*, p. 61a.
[2] See here the suggestive comments of J. Morgenstern, 'Deutero-Isaiah's Terminology of the Universal God', *J.B.L.*, 69, 1943, pp. 269-280.
[3] *A.N.E.T.*, p. 308b.

Babylonians themselves were subjecting the heavenly planets
to a more methodical examination, with the resultant
development of a rudimentary scientific astrology. The
Greeks had been investigating the forces which inaugurated
and sustained the cosmic order, while Zoroaster had only
recently made astonishing claims for his god Ahura Mazda. [1]
Thus, in a city which was the centre of so many claims to
enlightenment the simple Hebrew must have wondered
how he was to conceive of his ancestral God. Such circumstances explain why Deutero-Isaiah so freely used the
methods of an apologist and why indeed he made such
exclusive claims for Yahweh. Fundamental to his purpose
was the exposure of the idolatrons nature of the gods of
Babylon, while in the face of contentions to the contrary
it was equally necessary to represent Yahweh as the Lord
of history and as the sole Creator of man and the universe.

It is, however, of interest to note here that in an article
entitled 'The Dual Origin of Hebrew Monotheism' R. H.
Pfeiffer questioned the originality of Deutero-Isaiah in
attributing the creation of the physical universe to Yahweh. [2]
Few scholars have more ably contended that we can only
speak of monotheism in the Old Testament before Deutero-
Isaiah 'by using the word in a sense other than the belief
that there is only one God, or by reading this doctrine
between the lines of our sources through inductions, deduc-
tions, and analogies of questionable force' (p. 194). But
Pfeiffer now asks a significant question: 'What elements in
the contemporary religious thought paved the way for the
monotheistic theology of Second Isaiah and made it
possible?' (*ibid*). He admits that the presentation of Yahweh

---

[1] See further *The Exilic Age*, pp. 136 ff.
[2] *J.B.L.*, 46, 1927, pp. 193-206.

as a God of history was typical of traditional Israelite religion, but maintains that, while Deutero-Isaiah would already have been acquainted with this notion, he would not have been familiar with the idea that Yahweh was also concerned with the realms of nature as this only became current in Israel through the influence of the Book of Job. Thus 'with the enthusiasm of a discoverer and with the zeal of a neophyte Second Isaiah proceeds to identify the God of Israel with the creator of the world' (p. 201). This view of the prophet is largely based on the assumption that 'Second Isaiah had neither the inclination nor the opportunity for speculation concerning the mysteries of the universe' (p. 202).

Apart, however, from the question of the priority of Job to the Second Isaiah it is evident from a reading of the prophet's work that he was not unconcerned with the creation of the universe. Indeed it is one of the main themes of his argument and one to which he returns with repeated emphasis.[1] Pfeiffer attributes the concept of Yahweh's power over nature to Edomite sources,[2] but whatever special interest the Edomites manifested in the physical world it is not at all clear how their views could have influenced the prophet; for although the thought of the age converged at Babylon there is no evidence that Edomite views of creation were represented there. Many of Deutero-Isaiah's references to the physical world appear on the other hand to have been prompted by the intellectual climate of his Babylonian environment. There is, for example, an obvious reference to the Babylonian 'Doctrine of the Name' when he represents Yahweh as saying:

---

[1] E.g., 40 : 18-19; 42 : 5, 15; 44 : 24; 45 : 18.
[2] Pfeiffer of course also thinks that a special Edomite or Seir (S) source may be discerned in the pages of Genesis; see his article 'A Non-Israelite Source in the Book of Genesis', *Z.A.W.N.F.*, 7, 1930, pp. 66-73.

'Lift up your eyes on high and see:
Who created these?
He who brings out their hosts by number,
calling them all by name . . .' (40 : 26).

Thus, while the Babylonians could ascribe the creation of
the heavenly bodies to Marduk [1] the prophet attributes their
origin to Yahweh. The notion of Yahweh as creator of the
physical world was, moreover, so essential to his thought
that he not only conceived of Yahweh as creator of the
world from the beginning of time (45 : 18), but also as
intervening in the ordered course of nature and transforming
it at will: the valleys will be filled and the mountains levelled
(40 : 4), the wilderness becomes a pool of water and the
desert will bloom with luxuriant plants (41 : 18-19). It can,
therefore, scarcely be doubted that, apart from the influence
of divine revelation, Deutero-Isaiah was himself responsible
for a concept which was so basic to his theology and so
expressive of the universal sovereignty of God.

---

[1] *Enuma Elish*, V, lines 1-20, *A.N.E.T.*, p. 67b-68a.

CHAPTER SIX

THE DIVINE JUSTICE

The conception of God's sovereignty over nature and the events of history inevitably leads to the question of the divine justice. The problem was not, however, experienced by the Israelites before the late seventh century. But, although Jeremiah himself had occasion to reflect on this problem, it was the exiles in Babylon who first seriously raised the question. In the exile too the individual became aware of a severance of the bonds which connected him with the nation, and in consequence the traditional, communal conception of religion was subjected to some review.

It was a people that Yahweh delivered out of Egypt and it was, therefore, with a people that he entered into relationship. [1] The continuance of this association depended on the observance of Yahweh's ordinances, and this was an obligation incumbent on the people as a whole. It is recorded that when Moses communicated to the Israelites the words and injunctions of God 'all the people answered and said, All the words which Yahweh has spoken we will do' (Exod. 24 : 3). Adherence to these words ensured the well-being of the group, while departure from them forfeited the protection of the deity and incurred his displeasure (cf. Exod. 18 : 23; 32 : 34). A corollary of this conception of a communal association with Yahweh was the notion that

---

[1] Cf. here S. A. Cook: 'Old Testament religion is concerned with Yahweh, Israel and Israel' s land. People and land are essentially one . . .', *The Old Testament: A Reinterpretation*, p. 119.

the offences of even a single member may affect the whole community. In partaking of the forbidden booty Achan brought sin on all Israel, and in consequence not only he, but his whole family suffered the penalty of death (Josh. 7). This instance is later quoted by certain Israelite leaders in condemning the Trans-Jordan tribes who had acted irregularly in building an altar: 'If you rebel against Yahweh today he will be angry with the whole congregation of Israel tomorrow ... Did not Achan, the son of Zerah, break faith in the matter of the devoted things, and wrath fell upon all the congregation of Israel? And he did not perish alone for his iniquity' (Josh. 22 : 18-20). The wickedness of the Benjamites similarly imperilled all the Israelite tribes, and so it was resolved to 'put them to death and put away evil from Israel' (Jud. 20 : 13). The sin of an individual likewise endangered the group or family to which he belonged. Thus Korah's rebellion against Moses led not only to the destruction of those who participated in it, but also 'their households and all the men that belonged to Korah' (Num. 16 : 32). On a well-known occasion Ahimelech, the priest of Nob, befriended David, but for this he is told by Saul, 'You shall surely die, Ahimelech, you and all your father's house' (I Sam. 22 : 16). In the event not only he and his colleagues suffer, but 'the city of the priests ... both men and women, children and sucklings' were put to the sword (I Sam. 22 : 19). Again, in the reign of David a three year famine was attributed to a former sin of Saul, and Yahweh himself is reported as saying, 'There is blood guilt upon Saul and on his house, because he put the Gibeonites to death' (2 Sam. 21 : 1). The man who rebuilds Jericho is accursed in the sight of God, but it is upon his eldest and youngest sons that the penalty falls (I Kgs. 16 : 34). Finally, thinking that her child's death must be due to her own sins, the woman of Zarephath addressed Elijah thus: 'What have you against me, O man of God? You have come to bring my sin to remembrance, and to cause the death of my son' (I Kgs. 17 : 18). It was, therefore, in accordance with the retributive principle inherent in such passages that Yahweh was conceived as 'visiting the iniquity of fathers upon children, upon the third and upon the fourth generation' (Num. 14 : 18). [1]

This is scarcely a worthy conception of Yahweh; yet as long as the Hebrews thought in terms of the nation it might be said to have some claim to credibility. For the notion that sin and immorality incline to decay, while righteousness and goodness contribute to strength and stability, is more easily demonstrable in respect of the community than the individual. The tyrannical measures of the despot and the indifferent rule of a bureaucracy lead to national degeneracy, but humane, beneficent government invites the co-operation of the individual and is conducive of a vigorous and progressive people. Thus, while the Israelites retained even a semblance of nationhood the notion that Yahweh rewarded righteousness with prosperity and iniquity with adversity was unquestionably accepted. [2] But when the nation suffered dismemberment by the Babylonian deportations the concept of racial solidarity had little significance. Alienated from his native land, the exile could no longer regard himself as a constituent member of the Israelite community in Judah. Yet, according to the tenets of traditional dogma, his plight was the consequence of the misdemeanour of Israel's

---

[1] Cf. also Exod. 20 : 5 and Dt. 5 : 9.
[2] So commenting on the problem of individual suffering Louis Finkelstein said: 'Isaiah had not asked the question, for individual prosperity or adversity were irrelevant in the social scheme as a whole', *The Pharisees*, vol. 1, 2nd edn., 1940, p. 151.

past. Hence, separated as he was from the parent body and forced to adapt himself to more individualistic conditions, he now began to reflect on the validity of this principle; and so finally we hear the complaint, 'The way of Yahweh is not just' (Ezek. 18 : 29), and the even more cynical comment, 'The fathers have eaten sour grapes and the children's teeth are set on edge' (Ezek. 18 : 2).

Some writers have recently claimed that the importance of the individual was recognised long before the time of Jeremiah and Ezekiel. According to G. E. Wright we need only consider 'the stories of the Judges, of Samuel and his mother, of David, Elijah and Elisha, and even of the Patriarchs, to realise that before the seventh century the relationship between the individual worshipper and his God was already thought to be very close'. [1] Similarly, with regard to the suggestion that Jeremiah and Ezekiel discovered the individual, H. H. Rowley comments: 'This is a gross exaggeration. It is true that these prophets stressed individual responsibility, but they were not the first to recognise the importance and worth of the individual. [2] In support of this claim Professor Rowley mentions the case of David and Bathsheba and says 'it was to David as an individual sinner that Nathan went. He did not wait until divine sanctions against the community . . . involved society in the effects of David's sin'. [3] But this does not alter the fact that the consequences of David's sin do not rest with himself alone. His whole dynasty is affected in that Yahweh says 'the sword shall never depart from your house' (2 Sam. 12 : 10), while in addition his wives will be given to his neighbour and humiliated 'before all Israel'

---

[1] *The Challenge of Israel's Faith*, 1946, pp. 96-97.
[2] *The Faith of Israel*, 1956, p. 99.
[3] *Op. cit.*, p. 101.

(vs. 11). Nor is this all; for, although David is represented as confessing his sin, Nathan further says, 'because by this deed you have utterly scorned the Lord, the child that is born to you shall die' (vs. 14). Dr. Rowley again remarks: 'When Jezebel invaded the private rights of Naboth and had him judiciously murdered, Elijah took up the cause of Naboth in the name of the Lord'. [1] But the purpose of Elijah's meeting with Ahab is to represent Yahweh as saying: 'Behold, I will bring evil upon you; I will utterly sweep you away, and will cut off from Ahab every male . . . Anyone belonging to Ahab who dies in the city the dogs shall eat' (1 Kgs. 21 : 21 f.). E. F. Sutcliffe likewise claims that 'The doctrine of individual responsibillity was not new in the sixth century', but rather, 'goes back to the beginning of Hebrew history'. [2] Some individuals, indeed, appear in a prominent capacity in the early history of Israel. But it is necessary to remember that such figures appear as leaders of the community and that it was on behalf of the community that they were called to serve. Moses is called to his office to deliver the Israelites as a people, and Yahweh's commission is, 'Come, I will send you to Pharaoh that you may bring forth my people, the sons of Israel, out of Egypt' (Exod. 3 : 10). Gideon is called 'to deliver Israel from the hand of Midian' (Jud. 6 : 14), and his immediate successors were commissioned for a similar task. Again, Saul is appointed king over Israel, because, as Yahweh says, 'he shall save my people from the hand of the Philistines' (1 Sam. 9 : 16). Such individuals were called from ordinary walks of life, and it was their election to serve the community as a whole which alone distinguished them from their fellows. Indeed, as Ludwig Koehler contends, 'in the Old Testament

---

[1] *Ibid.*
[2] *Providence and Suffering*, 1955, p. 96.

it is taken for granted that *man lives in a community*, comprehensive to a degree which we can scarcely imagine. The community of the individual with the unit to which he is by nature assigned is unquestionable'. [1] For this reason the individual had his obligations within the community and was expected to observe the laws and customs designed to preserve its continuance and identity. Hence we find that the death penalty was exacted from members of the group who departed from established practice (Exod. 21 : 21 f.); but this, rather than illustrating the principle of individual responsibility, is but indicative of the solidarity subsisting between the individual and the community to which he belongs. Even the ancient *lex talionis* which demanded 'life for life' and 'eye for eye' (Exod. 21 : 23 f.) is expressive of 'the inviolable sacredness of the ties of kinship'. [2] But even here retaliation was not strictly commensurate or individual for 'Cain is avenged sevenfold' and 'Lamech seventy-sevenfold' (Gen. 4 : 23), while the death of no less than seven of Saul's sons is required to atone for his treatment of the Gibeonites' (2 Sam. 21 : 1-6).

In maintaining that the principle of individual retribution was characteristic of early Israelite belief Professor Sutcliffe appeals to certain passages which, he thinks, illustrate his view. [3] Referring to Genesis chapters 6-7 he writes: 'Noe was saved out of the midst of the corruption universally reigning in his day' (p. 88). Noah was not, however, the only one saved from the waters of the flood. And although

---

[1] *Old Testament Theology*, Eng. trans. 1957, p. 161.

[2] R. H. Pfeiffer, *Intro. to the Old Test.*, p. 219. Pfeiffer further observes: 'The whole clan is responsible for the life of each of its members ... In the primitive conception the blood of the slain cries unto the deity from the ground' (p. 220).

[3] *Op. cit.*, pp. 88-89.

the Priestly writer states that 'Noah was a righteous man' (Gen. 6 : 9) the story is not really illustrative of individual retribution; for the members of Noah's family were also saved from the ark (Gen. 6 : 18) but there is no indication of their righteousness. If, moreover, it is objected that the family was preserved by virtue of Noah's righteousness, then, the story rather exemplifies the principle of social solidarity than that of individual retribution. The incident of Miriam's punishment for her criticism of Moses (Num. ch. 12) is similarly quoted. But, again, this is not strictly an instance of individual retribution; for although Aaron was equally critical of his inspired leader it was Miriam alone who was afflicted with leprosy (vs. 10). Appealing to Numbers 25 : 7-13 as representing another instance of individual punishment Professor Sutcliffe observes: 'Phineas received a special blessing for the zeal he manifested in the honour of God'. Yet there is little emphasis on individualism in this passage. We read that an Israelite brought a Midianite woman to his family 'while they were weeping at the door of the tent of meeting' (vs. 6). For this offence both were slain by Phineas, an act which the Priestly writer regards with considerable approval (vv. 12-13). But despite this piety of Phineas the Israelites were afflicted by a plague and we find that 'those who died . . . were twenty-four thousand' (vs. 9). The story of the withering of Jeroboam's hand (1 Kgs. 13 : 1-4) is likewise mentioned as an example of individual retribution in early Israelite history. It is commonly recognised, however, that this is but a section of 'the first extensive case of Midrash in the historical books'. [1] The words 'Behold, a son shall be born to the house of David, Josiah by name, and he shall sacrifice

---

[1] J. A. Montgomery, *Kings*, *I.C.C.*, 1951, p. 260.

upon you the priests of the high places who burn incense upon you . . .' (vs. 2) are clearly a *vaticinium post eventum*, and in condemning the heathen altars of Jeroboam and exalting the dynasty of the ideal David manifest all the characteristics of the late Judean redactor. [1]

On the basis of certain passages in Kings Professor Sutcliffe further implies that there have been instances in the period of the monarchy in which the principle that the children suffer for the sins of the fathers was in abeyance. [2] In 2 Kings 14 : 5 we read that on ascending the throne Amaziah put to death those servants who slew his father; that is, he was satisfied with the exactions of *lex talionis*. Verse 6, however, adds: 'But he did not put to death the children of the murderers, according to what is written in the book of the law of Moses, where the Lord commanded, The fathers shall not be put to death for the children, or the children be put to death for the fathers; but every man shall die for his own sin'. Sutcliffe thinks that 'it was out of deference to this law that' Amaziah 'abstained from including their children in the sentence' (p. 89). It is, however, probable that commentators like Montgomery are right in regarding this verse as the 'moralizing addition' of a late editor. [3] We also read in Deuteronomy 24 : 16: 'The fathers shall not be put to death for the children, nor shall the children be put to death for the fathers; every man shall be put to death for his own sin'. It has accordingly been suggested that the principle of individual responsibility enunciated here is in effect one of the prescriptions of the Mosaic law. [4] But

---

[1] Cf. here J. P. Hyatt, *Prophetic Religion*, p. 104, and T. K. Cheyne in W. R. Smith's *The Prophet's of Israel*, new edn., 1902, pp. xviii f.

[2] *Op. cit.*, p. 89.

[3] Montgomery, *op. cit.*, p. 439.

[4] So Sutcliffe, *op. cit.*, p. 89.

whatever the origin of the legal material in Deuteronomy 24 it is obvious that verse 16 is an intrusion in the present text and is itself dependent on the teaching of Ezekiel. There is, therefore, but little evidence for the view that the concept of individual responsibility in religion obtained in Israel before the exilic period, while the surprise which members of Ezekiel's audience manifested at his enunciation of the doctrine (Ezek. 18 : 19) shows how novel it was in his day. [1]

It was the belief that the children suffered for the guilt of the fathers which raised the issue of the justice of God for the exiles; but Jeremiah's reflections on the sad circumstances of his own life and ministry indicate that he too had pondered on the question. [2] Having proclaimed that it was Yahweh's inexorable decree that Judah must submit to the power of Babylon, Jeremiah not only incurred the resentment of his fellow men, but was subjected to the most violent treatment (11 : 19; 18 : 18). Persecuted thus by the leaders of the nation and alienated from the populace as a whole, he was forced to lead a more individualistic life than any prophet before or after his day. It was therefore with some misgiving that he contemplated certain aspects of his ministry. He had believed in the supremacy of the divine purpose over world events, but there was much in his experience which seemed incompatible with this belief.

---

[1] Cf. here W. A. Irwin, *The Old Testament: Keystone of Human Culture*, 1952, p. 210.

[2] In a chapter on 'Suffering in the Old Testament' H. W. Robinson wrote: 'Through the religious isolation of Jeremiah and in the explicit teaching of Ezekiel the individual attained more adequate religious and social recognition. This had the result of bringing the problem of suffering to the front, for it was no longer so natural to spread out some misfortune over the misdeeds of a whole group, or even its ancestors; the justice of God must vindicate itself within the course of a single life', *Suffering Human and Divine*, 1940, p. 53.

He was himself called to the office of a prophet, but the prophetic word had come to be regarded as an occasion for mockery, the people derisively saying, 'Where is the word of Yahweh? Let it come' (17 : 5). Discouraged and humiliated, he frankly confesses 'the word of Yahweh has become for me a reproach and derision all day long' (20 : 8). Isolated from the crowd and from the ordinary pleasures of man (15 : 17), he finds no pleasure in being the herald of evil tidings:

> 'I have not pressed thee to send evil,
> nor have I desired the day of disaster,
> thou knowest; that which came out of my lips
> was before thy face' (17 : 16).

Indeed at one period he considered himself as intercessor for his countrymen: 'Remember how I stood before thee to speak good for them, to turn away thy wrath from them' (18 : 20). He recalls too a time when he rejoiced in his task and in the knowledge that he was called to the service of God:

> 'Thy words were found, and I ate them,
> and thy words became to me a joy
> and the delight of my heart;
> for I am called by thy name' (15 : 16).

He was likewise confident that despite the opposition of his enemies Yahweh would vindicate his servant. For he is sure that while Yahweh is his own 'refuge in the day of evil' he is able to bring upon his critics 'the day of evil' which can 'destroy them with double destruction' (17 : 17-18).

But this fortitude of mind became less resolute before the constant criticism to which he was exposed, and he wonders if even a prophet of Yahweh should be called upon to endure so much. He could scarcely contemplate that Yahweh in his sovereignty could be indifferent to his

circumstances, and yet the presence of so much evil in a
world governed by a righteous God could not but perplex
him:

> 'Righteous art thou, O Lord, when I complain to thee;
> Yet I would plead my case before thee,
> Why does the way of the wicked prosper?
> Why do all who are treacherous thrive?' (12 : 1).

The loneliness of his life, the mounting hostility of his
enemies, the increasing humiliation to which he was
subjected, finally led him to doubt the purpose of his mission.
Toil and sorrow, frustration and defeat, characterised so
much of his ministry that he curses the day he was born and
wishes he had died at birth (20 : 14 f.). Yahweh had promised
to fortify him against the difficulties of his work (1 : 8), but
he has become so overwhelmed at the seeming futility of
his task that in desperation he cries:

> 'Why is my pain unceasing,
> my wound incurable, refusing to be healed?
> Wilt thou be to me like a deceitful brook,
> Like waters that fail?' (15 : 18).

Yet try as he may he finds to his surprise that he cannot
detach himself from the divine constraint, and after much
travail of soul is at length forced to confess,

> 'If I say, I will not mention him,
> or speak any more in his name,
> there is in my heart as it were a
> burning fire shut up in my bones,
> and I am weary with holding it in, and I cannot' (20 : 9).

Thus, however he doubts the efficacy of his mission, he
feels within him an irrepressible urge compelling him to
continue as a prophet of God. It may be difficult, even
ignominious, to face the people, but it is impossible to
withdraw from the scene and abandon his work. The

purpose of God is irrevocable, his voice irresistible, and no
man who has heard his call can ever choose otherwise.
Jeremiah cannot therefore retreat from his commitments;
a consuming fire within his soul bids him to accede to the
demands of God, and he can only submit and acknowledge,

'Thou art stronger than I and thou hast prevailed' (20 : 7).

This recognition of the futility of contending against the
will of God led the prophet to meditate on the manner in
which God reveals his purpose to man, and also to examine
his own thoughts and motives. Throughout his spiritual
tensions he was never in doubt as to Yahweh's power. Even
the wicked enjoyed their existence and material prosperity in
a realm supported by him. Certain, therefore, that Yahweh
was aware of his plight and, if he chose, could make him
triumph over his enemies, he pleads:

'O Lord, thou knowest, remember me and visit me,
and take vengeance for me on my persecutors' (15 : 15).

However perplexed he may, then, have been by the circumstances of his own ministry he could not question the
sovereignty of Yahweh. It thus occurred to him that he
may have been considering his problems from the limited
perspective of human experience and that in consequence
he was unduly concerned with his own inclinations; or it
may be that he lacked tenacity of purpose to persist in the
work to which he was called. On sober reflection he realised
that it was impossible to conceal his weaknesses and motives
from an omniscient God who 'could search the mind and try
the heart' (17 : 10), while again his own knowledge of human
nature convinced him that

'the heart is deceitful above all things,
and desperately corrupt,
who can understand it'?' (17 : 9).

Honest self-examination disclosed that he himself was no
exception to the imperfections of the human personality and
that Yahweh's dealings with him thus far but served to
reveal the extent of his shortcomings. It is, then, in all
heartfelt sincerity that he now penitently cries:

'But thou, O Lord, knowest me; thou seest me,
and triest my mind toward thee' (12 : 3).

He thus becomes remorsefully aware that under the searching
vision of God it was himself who had been found wanting.
In yielding under adversity he had proved unworthy of his
task, and it is with chastened spirit that he grasps the significance of Yahweh's words:

'If you have raced with men on foot,
and they have wearied you,
How will you compete with horses?' (12 : 5).

Jeremiah erred in judging the standards of God by those
of men; and in thus confusing his values he lost confidence
both in himself and his ministry. But he now discovers that
as well as chastening, Yahweh also forgives and is, therefore,
willing to receive him back to favour:

'If you return, I will restore you,
and you shall stand before me.
If you utter what is precious,
and not what is worthless,
you shall be as my mouth.
They shall turn to you,
but you shall not turn to them' (15 : 19).

These are the conditions of his return to the privilege of
service with God, and involve nothing less than a rededi-
cation of himself to his mission. [1] For by his querulous

---

[1] Cf. Skinner here: 'Jeremiah appears to realise that he had come near
to forfeiting his office by losing its spirit, and that he needed a renewal
of his vocation, a reinstatement in his mission, if he was to continue
to act as a prophet of Yahweh', *Prophecy and Religion*, p. 214.

attitude to his work he had impaired the dynamic of his
ministry and prejudiced his fellowship with God. But in
dedicating himself afresh to his calling he hears Yahweh
reassuringly say:

> 'I will make you to this people
> a fortified wall of bronze;
> they will fight against you,
> but they shall not prevail over you,
> for I am with you to save and deliver you . . .
> I will deliver you out of the hand of the wicked,
> and redeem you from the grasp of the ruthless' (15 : 20-21).

Assured that he was again a chosen vessel of Yahweh's
will he zealously applies himself to his task. He had once
pleaded with God on behalf of his countrymen, but he now
realised that because of their continued sin further intercession was futile. In attempting to convince them of the
course which history must now take Jeremiah became
subject to even more impassioned assault (*e.g.*, 38 : 5 f.). But
he was no longer disconcerted by the taunts of men and
regarded it but vain and unrewarding to consider their
views; for,

> 'Thus says the Lord:
> Cursed is the man who trusts in man
> and makes flesh his arm,
> whose heart turns away from the Lord.
> He is like a shrub in the desert,
> and shall not see any good come . . .' (17 : 5-6).

Henceforth his trials and persecutions were willingly borne
in the certainty that through them he attained to closer
fellowship with God. As the bonds between himself and the
nation became more tenuous he found himself drawn more
to the will and guidance of God. And 'in this individual
response to the voice of God he discovered an earnest of
that instinctive and universal sense of the divine in which

he recognised the permanent essence of religion'. [1] Through this radical change in Jeremiah's heart the question of divine justice resolved itself into a conception of God as a Being of overwhelming mercy and forgiveness. But equally significant was the discovery that he was a supremely personal God with whom individual communion was possible. Self-sacrifice in the service of God accordingly became the highest aspiration of his soul. And even though such service involved suffering it could not affect his dedication to his work. It was not for him now to choose; he only knew that in the service of God lay the purpose and fulfilment of his life. Completely surrendering himself to the divine will he could thus in effect say:

> 'Smooth let it be or rough, it will be still the best . . .
> As best to thee may seem, choose thou my good and ill'. [2]

What Jeremiah had to solve for himself Ezekiel had to solve for others. We have no direct evidence that Ezekiel benefited from the Confessions of his older contemporary, but it is significant that he was never prompted to question the justice of God. Though ministering in exile he experienced none of the frustrations of Jeremiah; nor again, although his message was largely concerned with the individual, did he hold himself aloof or detached from his fellow exiles. He was able to enjoy the company of elders in his own house (8 : 1), and was apparently accorded all the respect due to an accredited prophet of God. Never, then, discontented with his lot, or confronted with dangerous opposition, he was able to pursue without interruption the task to which he was called.

The exiles did not, however, share in this confidence. For although they could scarcely complain of their material

---

[1] Skinner, *op. cit.*, p. 219.
[2] The Hymn 'Thy way, not mine, O Lord' by H. Bonar.

circumstances, deportation to Babylon raised serious religious
issues for them. It was obvious that the Israelite nation was
dismembered and that, exiled as they were, they could have
but little association with the remnant in Judah; but,
according to the accepted principles of religious interpretation, their exile was due to the accumulated transgressions
of the nation as a whole. The suffering of individuals for
the sins of the community appeared to them as an injustice
and as a reflection on Yahweh who ordained it. [1] For
however they may resolve to live in accordance with the
divine injunctions they inevitably inherited the effects of
the sins of an earlier generation. Regarding 'the way of
Yahweh' as 'unjust' they could only complain, 'Our transgressions and our sins are upon us and we waste away
because of them; how then can we live?' (33 : 10). The
urgency and extent of the task awaiting Ezekiel is therefore
apparent. For in expressing dissatisfaction with a cardinal
tenet of traditional religion the exiles were in danger of
abandoning all faith in Yaweh. Confronted with the challenge
of presenting a conception of God adequate to the crisis the
exiles were experiencing, Ezekiel thus asks: 'What do you
mean by repeating this proverb . . . The fathers have eaten
sour grapes and the children's teeth are set on edge?' (18 : 2).
The fact that the prophet should question the validity of this
saying was in itself significant, but he is further determined
to expose its falsity. To this end he continues: 'As I live says
the Lord God, this proverb shall no more be used by you
in Israel. Behold, all souls are mine; the soul of the father
as well as the soul of the son is mine; the soul that sins shall

---

[1] Cf. Eichrodt, 'The solidarity of connexion with the whole nation
and with earlier generations is rejected as an intolerable assault upon
life, condemning it to despair'. *Man in the Old Testament*, (Studies in
Biblical Theology, no. 4) 1951, p. 57.

die' (18 : 3-4). Not content with enunciating this general principle he now illustrates his argument by applying the principle to individual cases: 'If a man is righteous and does what is lawful and right . . . withholds his hand from iniquity, executes true justice between man and man . . . he is righteous, he shall surely live says the Lord God' (18 : 5-9). He thus establishes the point that provided a man is faithful to Yahweh and observes his moral laws, he is righteous before him. But Ezekiel now considers the son of this man: 'If he begets a son who is a robber, a shedder of blood . . . shall he then live? He shall not live . . . he shall surely die; his blood shall be upon himself' (18 : 10-13). As, therefore, the righteous acts of the father ensured his righteousness in the sight of God, so the wickedness of the son incurs the divine displeasure and condemnation. Further elaborating his doctrine of divine retribution the prophet then considers the son of this wicked man: 'If this man begets a son who sees all the sins which his father has done and fears, and does not do likewise . . . withholds his hand from iniquity . . . he shall not die for his father's iniquity; he shall surely live' (18 : 14 f.). It was the notion that even a righteous man incurred his father's guilt which particularly perplexed the exiles, and in thus stating that God does not punish the sons for the sins of the fathers, Ezekiel gave expression to a proposition which was revolutionary in its theological implications. So startling did the announcement appear that the exiles instinctively exclaimed: 'Why should not the son suffer for the iniquity of the father?' (18 : 19). They had complained of the injustice of Yahweh, but so persistent are the tenets of religious belief that they could now scarcely believe otherwise. [1] And so Ezekiel was compelled to repeat:

---

[1] It will be noted that the traditional view was still believed by the

'The soul that sins shall die. The son shall not suffer for the iniquity of the father, nor the father suffer for the iniquity of the son' (18 : 20). [1] Indeed the principle of God's dealings with men may be summarily expressed thus: 'the righteousness of the righteous shall be upon himself, and the wickedness of the wicked shall be upon himself' (18 : 20). Inherent in the concept of social solidarity was the idea, that, as the evil deeds of earlier generations reflected on the lives of their descendants so their righteous deeds redounded to their credit. But according to Ezekiel there can be no transfer of individual merit: 'When a land sins against me by acting faithlessly, and I stretch out my hand against it . . . even if . . . Noah, Daniel, and Job were in it, they would deliver but their own lives by their righteousness, says the Lord God . . . they would deliver neither sons nor daughters; they alone would be delivered' (14 : 13 ff.). [2]

But the principle of the freedom and responsibility of the individual was so basic to Ezekiel's teaching that he was in danger of pursuing his doctrine of individualism to an extreme degree. In exercising his freedom a man may indeed change the whole course of his life; but Ezekiel presents this in a manner which appears to benefit the wicked rather than the righteous: 'If a wicked man turns away from all his

---

author of Lamentations 5 : 7: 'Our fathers sinned and are no more; and we bear their iniquities'.

[1] The significance of the statement that the father cannot suffer for the sins of the son may be seen in A. S. Peake's observation: 'Once he had said one generation cannot suffer for the sins of another, it was only a step further to say that one individual cannot suffer for the sins of another', *The Problem of Suffering in the Old Testament*, 1904, pp. 260-261.

[2] It is noteworthy that while in the Genesis narrative Noah's family is saved with him, here, according to Ezekiel, he would save but himself. On the question of the provenance of these three figures, however, see M. Noth, 'Noah, Daniel und Hiob in Ezechiel', *V.T.*, 1, 4, 1951, pp. 251-260.

sins which he has committed . . . and does what is lawful and right, he shall surely live; he shall not die. None of the transgressions which he has committed shall be remembered against him' (18 : 21 f.). This same freedom of choice may, on the other hand, lead to unfortunate consequences for the godly man; for as the wicked could turn from his wickedness and be saved, so the righteous may turn from his righteousness and perish: 'But when a righteous man turns away from his righteousness and commits iniquity . . . shall he live?' (18 : 24). And while this principle may in itself be justified we may detect some harshness, if not inconsistency, in the phrase, 'None of the righteous deeds which he has done shall be remembered' (18 : 24). It has thus been doubted if in proclaiming 'a doctrine of moral atomism which breaks life into a series of separate acts' Ezekiel presents a satisfactory view of God's justice. [1] Whether a man will be judged righteous or evil does not depend on the conduct of his life as a whole but on the state of his soul at the time of Judgment. As Peake has said, 'If judgment came a day sooner or later in how many cases would fate be reversed'. [2]

Yet the prophet's utterances were not based on the conclusions of syllogistic reasoning, but sprang rather from his zeal for righteousness and his impassioned hatred of evil. [3] If he thus appears to be more lenient on the sinner who repents than on the righteous man who lapses into sin, it is doubtless because he considered that the good man, by virtue of the righteousness he enjoyed, should have been

---

[1] C. H. Patterson, *The Philosophy of the Old Testament*, 1953, pp. 260-261.

[2] *Op. cit.*, p. 26.

[3] And as W. A. Irwin remarked 'Ezekiel's formulation of the doctrine of individualism in religion was still sufficiently new to provoke the excesses that usually attend novelty', *op. cit.*, p. 211.

the more able to withstand evil. In the words of a later
teacher, 'to whom much is given, of him will much be
required; and of him to whom men commit much they will
demand the more' (Luke 12 : 48). Even the righteous need
to be reminded that they cannot presume on their past
records but that to remain righteous before God demands
constant and exacting vigilance. On the other hand, the
sinner who becomes aware of his guilt derives hope from
the knowledge that he may turn from his sin and live unto
God. [1] It is, moreover, God's will that man should live
rather than die: 'Have I any pleasure in the death of the
wicked, says the Lord God, and not rather that he should
turn from his way and live'? (18 : 23). And this was a welcome truth to people who must have thought of Yahweh in
terms of a stern, indifferent being. However, then, we may
question Ezekiel's presentation of the justice of God it had
the merit of enabling the individual exile to recover his
faith at a time when he almost despaired of life itself.

But once raised the problem of theodicy was likely to
recur in one form or another, and thus it was that Deutero-
Isaiah was also concerned with the issue in his ministry
to a later generation of exiles. [2] Indeed because of his particular emphasis on the doctrine of monotheism the onus
of vindicating the divine righteousness was more incumbent
on him than his predecessors. In chapter III we have referred
to Deutero-Isaiah's use of the term 'Righteousness' in

---

[1] Cf. C. G. Montefiore: 'The descent from righteousness to sin, and
the ascent from sin to righteousness, are alike possible within the limits
of a single life. In these cases the law of retribution is modified to meet
the altered circumstances: the sinner, who was once righteous, shall
be punished; the righteous, who was once sinful, shall "live" '. *Origin
and Growth of Religion*, p. 252.

[2] The question is, of course, later the subject of the Book of Job, and
although it is also raised in Habakkuk 1 : 12 f. the passage is of uncertain
date, see, e.g., the discussion by Peake, *op. cit.*, pp. 151-171.

connection with Yahweh's activity in history and nature, and have further noted his application of the term to Israel's divine call. Israel, however, proved unworthy of the purpose of her call and did not herself act righteously (48 : 1). Hence although she may now complain that her 'right is disregarded by . . . God' (40 : 27) she has forfeited her own 'right' of fellowship with him. And if she has any doubt as to the justice of Yahweh's dealings with her she is invited to reflect on her past and consider her case before him:

'Put me in remembrance, let us argue together;
set forth your case, that you may be proved right.
Your first father sinned,
and your mediators transgressed against me' (43 : 26-27).

Thus it was that deaf to Yahweh's word, blind to his paths and indifferent to his cause, Israel became 'a people robbed and plundered . . . a prey with none to rescue, a spoil with none to say, Restore' (42 : 22). Nor is there any question of Yahweh himself being dissociated from her plight; for if it be asked 'Who gave up Jacob to the spoiler, and Israel to the robbers?' the answer is 'Was it not Yahweh against whom we have sinned?' (42 : 24). But Yahweh found no satisfaction in beholding her affliction, and yearned rather that her condition were otherwise. As Ezekiel had earlier stated, he found no pleasure in the death of even the wicked:

'O, that you had hearkened to my commandments!
Then your peace would have been like a river,
and your righteousness like the waves of the sea;
your offspring would have been like the sand . . .
their name would never be cut off
or destroyed from before me' (48 : 18-19).

Deutero-Isaiah has now reached a point in his argument at which it is desirable to intimate that the righteousness of God is but a corollary of his omnipotence. Having passionately insisted on the supremacy of God over nature and history he recognised that the circumstances which permit of evil cannot be regarded as lying outside the realms of the divine sovereignty. He was, moreover, aware that the physical universe did not in itself constitute the totality of human consciousness. Man was painfully conscious of the obscure and sinister aspects of life; but the evil, the spiritual conflicts and tensions, which contributed to such experience, could not be accorded autonomous existence. He was accordingly compelled to quote Yahweh as saying:

'I form light and create darkness,
I make weal and create woe,
I am the Lord who do all these things' (45 : 7).

This was an announcement of singular novelty; for however negligent the exiles may have regarded Yahweh, they could scarcely associate evil with him. [1] The ultimate dissociation of Yahweh from evil would be tantamount to the recognition of the existence of an independent force as powerful as, and opposed to, Yahweh himself. But in the thought of Deutero-Isaiah Yahweh was nothing if not the sole cause in the universe. As therefore he created the earth and man upon it so he 'created the ravager to destroy' (54 : 16) and lays 'waste mountains and hills' (42 : 15). Refusing, then, to make the least concession to a view of deity which was

---

[1] Cf., e.g., Zephaniah (1 : 12) who speaks of
'those who say in their hearts,
The Lord will not do good,
nor will he do ill'.
Of course in Lamentations 3 : 38 we read, 'Is it not from the mouth of the Most High that good and evil come?'; but, although N. K. Gottwald (*Studies in the Book of Lamentations*, Studies in Biblical Theology No. 14, 1954, p. 21) thinks that all the poems in this Book derive from the exilic period, Pfeiffer aptly remarked that the reflections in chapter 3 : 18-39 are 'commonplaces in the Psalter' and are probably as late as the third century B.C., *Intro. to the Old Test.*, p. 723.

suggestive of dualism he had no choice but to declare unequivocably that God was Lord alike in the psychical as well as in the physical realms of the universe. [1] This did not mean that Yahweh purposely created evil for the misfortune or hindrance of man; it implied rather that he was the ultimate source of those forces which, through natural and human agencies, develop as influences for evil and become the almost inevitable concomitants of life.

Finally, a conception of God as having exclusive association with goodness not only prompts a dualistic view of the forces behind the universe, but tends to confuse mere kindness with justice. An indulgent deity may overlook the sins and shortcomings of man, but a God who is himself the source of justice (40 : 14) must also demand righteousness from his people. Hence according to Deutero-Isaiah only those 'who know righteousness' have the privilege of converse with God (51 : 7). And while even to the righteous there may be much that is mysterious in this world, it must be remembered that to mortal man Yahweh is inscrutable and 'his understanding unsearchable' (40 : 28). It is futile for man to question his maker (45 : 9-11) or endeavour to comprehend the higher purposes of God;

> 'For my thoughts are not your thoughts,
> neither are your ways my ways, says the Lord.
> For as the heavens are higher than the earth,
> so are my ways higher than your ways
> and my thoughts than your thoughts' (55 : 8-9).

---

[1] The prophet was, moreover, doubtless aware of the current Persian notion that the world order was a tension between the beneficent deity Ahura Mazda and an Evil Spirit of equal power (*Yasna* 30 : 1-4).

CHAPTER SEVEN

REPENTANCE AND GRACE

Fundamental to prophetic theology was the notion that sin was the cause of Yahweh's estrangement from Israel. Amos speaks of a people whom Yahweh chose for himself but of whom he can now only say 'how many are your transgressions, and how great are your sins' (5 : 12). Failure to respond to the divine initiative involves, therefore, both punishment and isolation from the care and protection of God himself (3 : 2; 5 : 17). Hosea complains that, although Yahweh was gracious to the Israelites when he found them in the wilderness, they later gave their allegiance to Baal 'and became detestable like the thing they loved' (9 : 10). It was Yahweh who 'trained and strengthened their arms, yet they devise evil against' him (7 : 15). The divine indictment thus is: 'Woe to them, for they have strayed from me, destruction to them, for they have rebelled against me' (7 : 13). Israel's alienation is, indeed, so complete that she 'is like a dove silly and without sense' (7 : 11) and 'a wild ass wandering alone' (8 : 9). 'Bent on turning away from' Yahweh (11 : 7) she 'incurred guilt through Baal and died' (13 : 1). Isaiah, likewise, refers to the rebellion of the Israelites against Yahweh who nurtured and sustained them (1 : 3). Sin has intervened between them and their God and consequently 'they are utterly estranged' (1 : 4). Such is the effect of this estrangement that they have become sick in head and heart and wholly unsound of body, and have altogether perverted the true nature of their being

(1 : 5-6). The evil which Yahweh will bring upon the land is, again, attributed by Micah to the wickedness and immorality of the people (2 : 1-3). Yahweh is so grieved with Israel's waywardness that he is even provoked to controversy with her (6 : 2). So Jeremiah reminds the Judeans that 'it is evil and bitter . . . to forsake Yahweh' (2 : 19) and that it is to such conduct that they owe their doom (4 : 17). They may in turn complain of Yahweh's indifference, but his estrangement is due to their continuous rebellion against him (2 : 29). A 'people' with 'a stubborn and rebellious heart, they have turned aside and gone away' (5 : 23) and 'refuse to know' the living God (9 : 6). Ezekiel too speaks of 'the house of Israel who are all estranged from' Yahweh (14 : 5). Her preoccupation with idols has 'enraged' him against her (16 : 43), and she must now bear the shame and 'disgrace' consequent upon such alienation from him (16 : 52). Deutero-Isaiah, again, regarded sin as fraught with the most destructive effects. Israel's rejection by God was due to her disobedience and unfaithfulness to him (48 : 8). For such 'iniquities' she was 'sold' and for such 'transgressions' she was 'put away', and so forfeited her claims to the divine favour (50 : 1).

But while the prophets were unanimous in regarding sin as alienating man from fellowship with God it was not their last word on the question of divine and human relationship. For, despite the severity with which they pronounced the divine judgment on sin, it is doubtful if such pronouncements can be interpreted as the final and irreversible word of God. It has of course been suggested that the prophets regarded the breach between Yahweh and his people as irreconcilable and that, therefore, they were essentially messengers of impending doom. [1] Incorrigibly drawn to sin

[1] Cf., e.g., Karl Marti, *Religion of the Old Testament*, Eng. trans. by

the people could not, even if they desired, return to God. The view that the judgments uttered by the prophets were subject to the possibility of man's repentance is thought, moreover, to imply a contingency foreign to the nature of prophecy. Discerning, rather, the course of events with a certainty from which all contingency is absent the prophets were spokesmen of the fixed, unalterable, will of God. The purpose of their pronouncements was the expression of the divine judgment on evil, and they were not given to hypothetical predictions which in the nature of the case could only be a contradiction in terms. [1] It is questionable, however, if this view is fully interpretative of the utterances of the prophets. If it be maintained that the prophet's certainty of the issue of events was attained by immediate intuition, then, it is conceivable that his message was delivered with complete and absolute finality irrespective of any change which may occur in the hearts of his audience. In that case such words of warning as appear in the prophetic declamations are merely of a rhetorical nature and do not derive from the mouth of Yahweh who could only have decreed unconditional doom. But this would impute to prophecy the character of a rigid, unremitting legalism, while it would confine its function to that of mere prediction. If, on the other hand, we regard the announcements of the prophets as having a moral and spiritual basis, we should expect the nature of their utterances to vary with the response and conduct of their hearers, and that they themselves would

---

G. A. Bienemann, 1907, pp. 168 ff. So, although admitting an element of hope in the teaching of the prophets, Rudolf Kittel wrote: 'As long as the nation continued, the one theme of the prophetic preaching was the constant proclamation of doom on account of Israel's guilt', *The Religion of the People of Israel*, Eng. trans. by R. C. Micklem, 1925, p. 135.

[1] So, e.g., R. Smend, *Lehrbuch der alttestamentlichen Religionsgeschichte*, 2nd edn., 1899, p. 191 f.

endeavour to call the nation to repentance. As, however, it is difficult to accept the view that the prophets pronounced judgment with inexorable finality, so it seems equally unacceptable to suppose that the absolute element may be entirely excluded from their utterances. For there are passages which indicate that despite repeated warnings the Israelites persisted in their sinful ways, and so the decrees of Yahweh, pursuing an unrelieved and undeviating course, led finally to catastrophic ends. There is thus ground for assuming that both the absolute and contingent elements obtained in the prophetic utterances though, as Skinner remarked, 'we may not be able to see how the two were combined in the minds of the prophets themselves'. [1]

But while certain passages point to a tension in the minds of the prophets whether they should denounce the people or call them to repentance, it is possible to discern in their teaching a pattern in which they at first entertained the hope of a penitent Israel turning from her sins, but on her persistent refusal to heed their warnings they represented Yahweh's judgment as issuing in final and irrevocable doom. The extent to which this is true varies of course from prophet to prophet, while the fact that their oracles are not arranged chronologically in their present contexts makes the pattern difficult of discernment. The question is further complicated by the consideration that in our present prophetical compilations there are many passages relating to repentance which are clearly editorial in nature, [2] while, again, in other cases

---

[1] *Prophecy and Religion*, p. 77. So A. B. Davidson, remarked that it is 'a very delicate operation to strike the balance . . . between the moral element which introduced contingency into the prophecy, and the absolute element which lay in prediction', *Old Testament Prophecy*, 1904, p. 251.

[2] E.g., Jer. 3: 22b, 25; 18: 7 f.; 36 : 7; 42 : 2-3; Is. 25 : 9; 26 : 16 f.; 31 : 7.

we cannot with any confidence distinguish what is secondary from what is original. There is, however, much material of whose authenticity we are reasonably assured, and on the basis of which we are enabled to consider the prophetic teaching on the question of repentance and grace.

Amos' sense of justice was so outraged by the standards he observed in the Israelite society of his day that we are inclined to associate him exclusively with the proclamation of God's judgment on a corrupt nation. But the notion of repentance was also implicit in many of his utterances. For he conceived the burdens imposed on Israel as fraught with the redemptive purpose of God, although Israel herself was reluctant to recognise this: [1]

> 'I gave you cleanness of teeth in all your cities,
> and lack of bread in all your places,
> yet you did not return to me, says the Lord' (4 : 6).

It was, again, in the hope that Israel would return to him that Yahweh blighted her gardens and vineyards and afflicted her with pestilences such as she had known in Egypt (4 : 9-10). Refusing to discern his hand in these events Israel continued in her errors and Yahweh was obliged to subject her to an experience reminiscent of the horrors of Sodom and Gomorrah. It was, however, in vain: 'you did not return to me says the Lord' (4 : 11). But even in the hour of imminent peril it was still possible to repent of her sins and amend her ways; and in hopeful anticipation of this Amos confronts her with the solemn warning 'Prepare to meet your God O Israel' (4 : 12). Thus, although judgment was perilously near, repentance could yet avert its

---

[1] Cf. C. A. Simpson who speaks of Yahweh's judgment as 'the necessary prelude to redemption, for it is through judgment that men are brought to see things as he sees them', *Revelation and Response in the Old Testament*, 1947, pp. 124-125.

most dire consequences. Fully acquainted with Israel's sins and her perverted nature, Amos, nevertheless, willingly assumes the role of intercessor, and when Yahweh proposed 'a judgment by fire' his plea was,

'O Lord God, forgive, I beseech thee,
how can Israel stand?' (7 : 4).

But, alas, Israel made little effort to desist from her evil ways, and unable to exercise further forbearance Yahweh now declares,

'I will never again pass by them' (7 : 14).

For failing to respond to the call of repentance and for ignoring the voice of warning Yahweh will reckon with Israel (8 : 1), and the judgment which was so long threatened must finally issue in destruction.

The attribute of mercy was so basic to Hosea's conception of God that the concepts of repentance and grace found repeated expression in his oracles. Yahweh's original association with Israel was in itself a manifestation of his love:

'When Israel was a child I loved him,
and out of Egypt I called my son . . .
I took them up in my arms . . .
I led them with cords of compassion
with the bands of love' (11 : 1-4).

But Israel soon forgot this kindness (13 : 6), and indulging in the worship of Baal, became hopelessly estranged from Yahweh:

'A spirit of harlotry has led them astray,
and they have left their God to play the harlot' (4 : 12).

As therefore the Israelites sow, so shall they reap: 'they sow the wind, and they shall reap the whirlwind' (8 : 7). Having 'ploughed iniquity . . . reaped injustice' and 'eaten the fruit of lies' (10 : 13) they have provoked their God to anger.

He will consequently pour his wrath on them like water
(5 : 10), 'will drive them out of' his 'house' and 'will love
them no more' (9 : 15). Hosea, like Amos, had thought
that the afflictions endured by the Israelites would lead them
to abandon evil. But, despite their manifold humiliations
(7 : 9) and their oppression 'in judgment' (5 : 11),

> 'They do not return to the Lord their God,
> nor seek him, for all this' (7 : 10).

'Determined to go after vanity' (5 : 11) Israel can only
be abandoned to her infamy (4 : 18) and to consequent
moral and spiritual degeneracy. Sacrificing her sanity and
honour she has become 'a useless vessel' (8 : 8) and

> 'shall be like the morning mist
> or like the dew that goes early away' (13 : 3).

The pleasurable existence to which the nation has abandoned
itself is thus in reality without substance or foundation, and
like all such pursuits must prove dissatisfying and transient
(4 : 10). Thus it is that

> 'Ephraim is stricken,
> their root is dried up,
> they shall bear no fruit' (9 : 16).

Because 'they have dealt faithlessly with Yahweh' (5 : 7) he
is disposed to show little clemency:

> 'Shall I ransom them from the power of Sheol?
> Shall I redeem them from Death? . . .
> Compassion is hid from my eyes' (13 : 14).

Even now the Israelites prejudice the possibility of their
forgiveness; for as Yahweh considered exercising his
compassion they committed even worse evils and revealed
themselves as almost beyond redemption. Hence however
willing Yahweh may have been to forgive, he is constrained
to confess,

'I would redeem them,
but they speak lies against me' (7 : 13).

They may cry 'My God, we Israel know thee' (8 : 2) but their words are devoid of sincerity; for 'they do not cry . . . from the heart' (7 : 14). Resolved therefore to leave them to their own devices, Yahweh now says:

'I will return again to my place,
until they acknowledge their guilt and seek my face,
and in their distress they seek me, saying,
Come, let us return to the Lord . . .' (5 : 15 f.).

The root of Israel's apostasy lies in the fact that her 'heart is false' (10 : 2), and however she may profess to acknowledge Yahweh she cannot in effect establish communion with him. So defiled have her people become that their sin is now ineradicable:

'Their deeds do not permit them
to return to their God.
For the spirit of harlotry is within them,
and they know not Yahweh' (5 : 4).

But although Israel has most ungratefully rejected Yahweh's protection and wilfully ignored his demands he cannot finally abandon her. We hear of repeated threats of destruction (4 : 9; 5 : 9; 13 : 9) from which no one can save Israel, but remembering his early love for her, Yahweh is loth to cast her off. Yet he does not reach his decision lightly, and we learn of the claims of wrath and mercy which conflict within the divine mind:

'How can I give you up, O Ephraim,
How can I hand you over, O Israel,
How can I make you like Admah,
How can I treat you like Zeboim.
My heart recoils within me,
my compassion grows warm and tender.
I will not execute my fierce anger,

> I will not again destroy Ephraim;
> for I am God and not man . . .
> and I will not come to destroy' (11 : 8-9).

Man may requite ingratitude with all the vindictiveness of his nature; but Yahweh is God, and destructiveness is not of the essence of deity. Characteristic rather of his nature is the quality of profound and abiding love. Hence, although Israel's love [1] for Yahweh was but fitful and inconstant, as unstable as the 'morning cloud' and 'the dew that goes early away' (6 : 4), he is so actuated by compassion that he cannot treat her likewise. Drawn to her with a deep and compelling love he is thus willing not only to forgive her sins, but to endow her with grace:

> 'I will heal their faithlessness;
> I will love them freely,
> for my anger has turned from them.
> I will be as the dew to Israel' (14 : 4).

Hosea's emphasis on this redeeming love of God was doubtless influenced by the tragic circumstances of his own life. He had married a woman who, whatever her previous character, proved unfaithful to her marriage vows. [2] Yet such was Hosea's regard for her that he was

---

[1] The Hebrew word is חסד (*chesed*), a term difficult to render, 'for it expresses the moral bondage of love, the loving discharge of an admitted obligation, the voluntary acceptance of a responsibility', H. W. Robinson, *Two Hebrew Prophets* (ed. E. A. Payne), 1948, p. 47. It is not used at all by Amos, but is is very common in the Psalms and occours six times in the Book of Hosea; 2 : 19; 4 : 1; 6 : 4, 6; 10 : 12; 12 : 6. These passages are accepted by most scholars as original (e.g., G. Farr, 'The Concept of Grace in the book of Hosea', *Z.A.W.*, 70, 1958, pp. 101 and 103) but the authenticity of 2 : 19; 10 : 12 and 12 : 6 is questionable.

[2] On the question as to whether Gomer was unchaste before her marriage to Hosea, see H. W. Robinson, *op. cit.*, pp. 12-17; H. H. Rowley, 'The Marriage of Hosea', *B.J.R.L.*, 39, 1956-57, pp. 200-233; N. Snaith, *Mercy and Sacrifice*, pp. 26 ff.

prepared to redeem her and to welcome her return to him. But if Hosea could do this for his adulterous wife, Yahweh, whose love is infinitely greater, must be willing to redeem sinful Israel and to resume relationship with her:

'Therefore, behold, I will allure her,
and bring her into the wilderness,
and speak tenderly to her.
And there I will give her vineyards,
and make the valley of Achor a door of hope.
And there she shall answer as in the days of her youth,
as at the time when she came out of the land of Egypt' (2:1 4f.).

In thus teaching that God takes the initiative in restoring Israel to himself, Hosea conceives of the relationship between God and man as resting ultimately on the divine grace. And when he finally bids Israel to 'return to the Lord' (14 : 1) it is in the hope that God who is the source of whatever goodness and virtue she possesses (14 : 8) will himself effect her redemption.

Isaiah was primarily concerned with inspiring his country-men to a confidence in God in the hour of national crisis. Yet the notions of repentance and of the divine grace and forgiveness are also discernible in his utterances. Judah's salvation did not rest on alliances with the great powers of the day, but rather on returning to Yahweh from whom she has strayed:

'In returning and rest you shall be saved;
in quietness and in trust shall be your strength' (30 : 15).

Israel may thus remain in her sins with all their perversive effects, or return to Yahweh and share in his salvation (1 : 20). Repentance is the first step towards a spiritual apprehension of God, for it leads both to forgiveness and to the knowledge that however heinous her sins they may be expiated by atoning grace:

'Come now, let us reason together, says the Lord:
though your sins are like scarlet,
they shall be as white as snow:
though they be red like crimson,
they shall become like wool' (1 : 18).

Jeremiah himself heard the divine call to return. Repentance is accordingly an integral part of his message. The Judeans had provoked the anger of Yahweh, and to this may be traced the disquiet they were now experiencing at the contemporary political scene:

'If you say in your heart,
Why have these things come upon me?
it is for the greatness of your iniquity
that your skirts are lifted up,
and you suffer violence'. (13 : 22).

But while Jeremiah probably regarded the destruction of the state as inevitable, he hoped that by repentance its people would be saved from spiritual doom. Concerned, not with the preservation of the state, but with the relationship between Israel and her God his plea is,

'Only acknowledge your guilt,
that you rebelled against Yahweh your God' (3 : 13).

This preoccupation with the spiritual restoration of Israel proceeded from the conviction that she belonged to Yahweh by virtue of his kindness to her in the wilderness days (2 : 1 f.). Yahweh has therefore a claim on both her gratitude and loyalty, and Israel has little right to boast 'We are free, we will come no more to thee' (2 : 31). On the contrary, it is Yahweh's inalienable right to demand,

'Return, O faithless children,
for I am your master' (3 : 14).

The Judeans have, however, become 'utterly faithless' (5 : 11) and, scorning the claims of Yahweh (9 : 6), are determined to follow their 'own course like a horse plunging headlong into battle' (8 : 6). Freely participating in the idolatrous practices of their environment they pervert their moral and spiritual sensibilities:

'For my people are foolish,
they know me not;
they are stupid children,
they have no understanding.
They are skilled in doing evil,
but how to do good they know not' (4 : 22).

So dissolute have the inhabitants of Judah become that though Yahweh has 'smitten' and 'consumed them . . . they refused to take correction. The have made their faces harder than rock' (5 : 3). But although they have grievously sinned Yahweh is ready to condone their offences if they would repent:

'I have given heed and listened,
but they have not spoken aright;
no man repents of his wickedness,
saying, What have I done?' (8 : 6).

It is as natural for a sinful man to 'return' to God as for a fallen man to 'rise again' (8 : 4), but this is now beyond Israel's power: 'The sin of Judah is written with a pen of iron; with a point of diamond it is engraved on the tablet of their heart' (17 : 1). Thus, so obstinately has she persisted in her waywardness that sin has become engraved in her soul and become the very essence of her nature:

'Can the Ethiopian change his skin
or the leopard his spots?
Then also you can do good
who are accustomed to do evil' (13 : 23).

Judah may profess her innocence in the hope of escaping Yahweh's wrath (2 : 35), but as there is no indication of a change of heart she is fully deserving of punishment:

> 'Shall I not punish them for
> these things? says the Lord;
> and shall I not avenge myself
> on a nation such as this?' (9 : 9).

Yet Yahweh is reluctant to execute vengeance on her and is even now prepared to withhold his hand. It is however to little purpose, for

> 'When I would gather them, says the Lord,
> there are no grapes on the vine,
> nor figs on the fig tree;
> even the leaves are withered,
> and what I gave them has passed away from them' (8 : 13).

So heedless has Israel been of his warnings and so utterly unresponsive to his call that at last Yahweh exclaims 'How can I pardon you?' (5 : 7); and in deference to the demands of justice he can only say:

> 'I have spoken, I have purposed;
> I have not relented nor will I turn back' (4 : 28).

Jeremiah himself had been reminded that penitence was a necessary preliminary to restoration to fellowship with God (15 : 19); but such is the apathy of his countrymen that they 'are too weary to repent' (9 : 5). Indeed, they now openly confess their inability to return to God and unashamedly say, 'That is in vain, we will follow our own plans, and will everyone act according to the stubbornness of his evil heart' (18 : 12).

Israel is thus too helplessly emburdened by sin ever to amend her ways, but such is Yahweh's regard for her that he cannot finally abandon her. There was a time when she was faithful and devoted to him (2 : 2), and it is with approval that he reflects on this phase of their relationship. Essentially a God of mercy and forgiveness he would find little satisfaction in irrevocably committing Israel to spiritual doom. Promising therefore to deal leniently with her he pleads,

'Return, faithless Israel,
I will not look on you in anger,
for I am merciful . . .
I will not be angry for ever' (3 : 12).

But even in his mercy Yahweh cannot overlook the sin of his people; and if they are too depraved to return to him he must, then, take the initiative of redeeming grace and transform their rebellious hearts. [1] That was Jeremiah's conception of the new and closer relationship which would henceforth subsist between Yahweh and his people, and which in the present text of his prophecies is defined thus: 'Behold, the days are coming says the Lord, when I will make a new covenant with the house of Israel and the house of Judah . . . I will put my law within them, and I will write it upon their hearts; and I will be their God, and they shall be my people. And no longer shall each man teach his neighbour and each his brother, saying, Know the Lord, for they shall know me, from the least of them to the greatest, says the Lord; for I will forgive their iniquity, and I will remember their sin no more' (31 : 31-34). Jeremiah's authorship of these words has, of course, long been questioned, [2] and it is indeed probable that the passage is at least in

---

[1] This is probably the point of the reference to the potter and his clay in 18 : 1-6. As the potter may reshape the clay of a faulty vessel into a good vessel so God by his sovereign grace may transform sinful man: 'O house of Israel, can I not do with you as this potter has done? says the Lord. Behold, like the clay in the potter's hand, so are you in my hand' (vs. 6). The interpretation offered by the present text (vv. 7-10) is clearly Deuteronomic in form and it is doubtful if it correctly represents the teaching of Jeremiah. For, the view that Yahweh's forgiveness is conditional on a nation's turning from evil is not analogous to the potter's handling of his impassive clay.

[2] So, e.g., B. Duhm *Israels Propheten*, 2nd edn., 1922, pp. 456 f.

editorial form. Our concern, however, is not with the question whether the prophet thought in terms of law or covenant, but rather with the extent the substance of the passage might express his ideal of religion. It is clear that the relationship between God and man here envisaged rests on the divine forgiveness of sin and on the subsequent cleansing of the human heart. And this is certainly in accordance with what we know of Jeremiah's theology of grace and redemption. Having himself experienced the deceitfulness of the heart (17 : 9), he knew that a cleansed heart was a necessary prerequisite to true fellowship with God. His own temporary estrangement had, again, assured him that only God could 'heal' the broken bonds and effect a spiritual reconciliation (17 : 14). Recalling, further, the intensely personal nature of his own approach to God, he emphasises the significance of the individual awareness of the divine presence. His knowledge of the sinful nature of humanity convinced him, moreover, that without the atoning grace of God, man must inevitably meet with spiritual destruction. The material of chapter 31 : 31-34 but expresses, then, in summary form what Jeremiah himself had earlier conceived and experienced. True religion must spring from the innermost soul of man, but only the implanting of the divine law, by God himself, within the heart could displace the sin so indelibly engraved. Mercy and forgiveness were essential properties of the God of the prophet's experience, and it is thus in full conformity with his theology that Yahweh here says, 'I will forgive their iniquity and I will remember their sin no more'.

The conception of Yahweh as a gracious and forgiving Being is, again, an element in Ezekiel's theology. It was indeed a necessary consequence of his particularly unfavourable opinion of Israel's religious history. For, while

earlier prophets credited Israel with some degree of faithfulness to Yahweh during the wilderness period, Ezekiel
represents her as being rebellious and ungrateful from the
beginning. Delineating her history in the most vivid terms
he intimates that in view of her origin but little could be
expected from her: 'Your origin and your birth are of the
land of the Canaanites; your father was an Amorite, and
your mother a Hittite' (16 : 3). It was wholly through
Yahweh's compassion that she was rescued from the wayside
at birth and through his continuing generosity that she
developed to maturity (16 : 6 f.). But, inheriting the sensuous
tendencies of her Canaanite ancestry, she indulged in the
most gross and degrading practices (16 : 15 f.). Thus even
as early as the days of her bondage she 'played the harlot
with the Egyptians' (16 : 26) and later defiled herself with
the idolatry of the Philistines and Assyrians (16 : 27-28).
'Like mother, like daughter' (16 : 44), but of all the daughters
of Canaanite stock Judah was the most profane; for in the
intensity and range of her sin she surpassed Samaria, her
elder sister, and even Sodom, her younger sister. Indeed
in comparison with Judah these 'sisters appear righteous'
(16 : 50-52). Samaria and Sodom were most certainly
abominable in the sight of Yahweh, but because of the
vicissitudes of history they did not enjoy his care and
protection. Judah, on the other hand, had the constant
advantage of Yahweh's counsel, but, irresistibly drawn to
evil, she utterly failed in his purpose for her and so became
completely abject and worthless.

Ezekiel now emphasises this point by adopting the
metaphor of the wild vine of the forest: 'How does the wood
of the vine surpass any wood, the vine branch which is
among the trees of the forest? Is wood taken from it to make
anything? Do men take a peg from it to hang any vessel

on? Lo, it is given the fire for fuel; when the fire has consumed both ends of it, and the middle of it is charred, is it
useful for anything? Behold, when it was whole it was
used for nothing; how much less, when the fire has consumed
it and it is charred, can it ever be used for anything! Therefore
thus says the Lord God: Like the wood of the vine among
the trees of the forest, which I have given to the fire for fuel,
so will I give up the inhabitants of Jerusalem' (15 : 2-6).
A dead vine is the most worthless of trees because its wood
can be put to no practical use. The only virtue of the vine
resides in the fact that, as Jotham had earlier observed, it
is the source of the 'wine which cheers gods and men'
(Jud. 9 : 13). If it therefore failed to produce grapes it failed
in the one purpose of its creation. Like the fig tree of a
later time which produced no fruit (Mat. 21 : 19) it was
doomed to destruction. But if the wood of the vine is only
fit for fuel, a charred, burnt vine is even more useless still.
And this is the state of uselessness to which Israel is now
reduced. As, then, Ezekiel referred to her spiritual degeneracy
in terms of the withered vine, so he depicts her punishments
by the apt metaphor of the forging of a sword:

'Thus says the Lord, say,
A sword, a sword is sharpened
and also polished, sharpened for slaughter,
polished to flash like lightning' (21 : 8).

A sword is sharpened and polished 'to be given into the
hand of the slayer', and it is for the purpose of destruction
that it will now be used against Israel (21 : 11-12).

But as Yahweh was about to destroy Israel the consideration that her destruction would unfavourably reflect on
himself led him to repent of his purpose: 'I withheld my
hand, and acted for the sake of my name, that it should not
be profaned in the sight of the nations' (20 : 22). This

statement of Ezekiel is expressive of his concern to preserve the honour and dignity of the holy, transcendent God. The divine purpose must not appear to be frustrated in the eyes of the heathen, and Israel's doom is accordingly averted. In referring to the honour of Yahweh's name (36 : 21, 22, 24) he is not, however, consciously representing Yahweh as a vain, egoistic being. For, according to Semitic thought the 'name' is indicative of the character and person to whom it is applied. 'To know the name of a man is the same as to know his essence'. [1] Yahweh's appeal to his name is therefore an appeal to his nature. [2] It is consequently in deference to the law of his being that his actions and dispositions are motivated. His decision to withhold his hand from Israel is an expression not only of his mercy, but of his hope that she will yet realise his purpose for her. Indeed, Israel herself will come to know and appreciate what that purpose is: 'And you shall know that I am the Lord, when I deal with you for my name's sake' (20 : 44). Yahweh alone possesses the attributes of deity and, therefore, it is only right that his sovereignty and holiness should be acknowledged by the heathen nations.

The implication that God is forgiving only because he is powerful is likewise evident in Ezekiel's interpretation of his vision in the Valley of Dry Bones. It was incredible to man that dry, dismembered bones could again become the vehicle of life. Yahweh could, however, say: 'Behold, I will cause breath to enter you, and you shall live. And I will

---

[1] J. Pedersen, *Israel, I-II*, p. 245. See also George Contenau, *Everyday Life in Babylonia and Assyria*, p. 160, for the Babylonian conception of 'name'. Elsewhere in the Old Testament Yahweh is similarly conceived as acting through his name. So, for example, Psalm 20 : 1:
'The Lord answer you in the day of trouble
the name of the God of Jacob protect you'.
[2] Cf. here too H. W. Robinson, *Two Hebrew Prophets*, p. 97.

lay sinews upon you, and will cause flesh to come upon you, and cover you with skin, and put breath in you, and you shall live; and you shall know that I am the Lord' (37 : 5-6). But although the bones had assumed their normal place in the structure of the human body and were covered with sinews and flesh, there was yet no life in them. Yet Yahweh could also supply this vitalising principle of life: 'Come from the four winds, O breath, and breathe upon these slain, that they may live . . . and the breath came into them and they lived, and stood upon their feet' (37 : 9-10). From the realism with which this vision demonstrated the divine power, Ezekiel was able to declare that Yahweh could likewise restore Israel to her own land: 'I will bring you home into the land of Israel . . . and I will put my spirit within you, and you shall live . . . then you shall know that I, the Lord, have spoken and . . . done it' (37 : 12 f.).

In thus restoring Israel Yahweh will vindicate his power and his holiness in the eyes of all the nations (36 : 22-23). But although Israel's restoration is assured she is not yet purged of her sin and purified in spirit, and still awaits the direct intervention of Yahweh's cleansing action: 'I will sprinkle water upon you, and you shall be clean from all your uncleanness . . . A new heart I will give you, and a new spirit I will put within you; and I will take out of your flesh the heart of stone and give you a heart of flesh' (36 : 25-26). Ezekiel had earlier called man to repentance, commanding him to 'cast away' his 'transgressions' and to get 'a new heart and a new spirit' (18 : 31). Now he realised that man is helpless to do this for himself and that conversion is impossible without the prevenient grace of God. Israel was by nature prone to sin, and with her unrepentant heart of stone had no power to do good works, 'pleasant and acceptable to God'. But displacing this heart of stone by one

of flesh, God effects a radical change within her. She is
therefore conscious not only of a changed heart but, more
significant still, is aware of a loathing revulsion towards sin
itself: 'Then you will remember your evil ways, and your
deeds that were not good; and you will loathe yourselves
for your iniquities and your abominable deeds' (36 : 31).
This acknowledgment that sin can only be eradicated through
the unmerited favour of God is thus characteristic of the
truly penitent and regenerate soul; and it is also an indication
that the nature of sin can ultimately be comprehended
only in the context of divine salvation. In attributing
Israel's spiritual regeneration to the atoning activity of God
Ezekiel, accordingly, makes a notable contribution to the
theology of grace and forgiveness.

Deutero-Isaiah's comprehensive theology of salvation
necessarily presupposed the divine initiative of pardon and
grace. Yahweh's election of Israel in the first instance was
a clear expression of his grace (43 : 21; 44 : 21, 24), but
alas the alienating effect of sin had long been manifest.
Obstinate in her waywardness and intent in her idolatry
(48 : 1 f.), she had been unresponsive through the centuries
to the guiding hand of God:

> 'You have never heard, you have never known,
> from of old your ear has not been opened' (48 : 8).

But Yahweh has no pleasure in profaning his 'heritage'
(47 : 6) and complains that if Israel had hearkened to his
commandments she would neither be disinherited nor
destroyed before him (48 : 17). The divine purpose cannot,
however, be thwarted, and hence, despite Israel's faithless-
ness, Yahweh's honour and name must be vindicated:

> 'For my name's sake I defer my anger,
> for the sake of my praise I restrain it for you,
> that I may not cut you off.

Behold, I have refined you, but not like silver;
I have tried you in the furnace of affliction.
For my own sake, for my own sake, I do it,
For how should my name be profaned?
My glory I will not give to another' (48 : 9-11).

But although Yahweh is here represented as acting for the sake of his honour, his relationship with Israel prompts him to take a compassionate view of her apostasy. Elected as 'witnesses' to his redemptive purpose (43 : 10) she is 'honoured' and 'precious' in his sight. It is thus in accordance with his steadfast love (*chesed*) for her that he now confesses:

'For a brief moment I forsook you,
but with great compassion I will gather you,
In overflowing wrath for a moment I hid my face from you,
but with everlasting love I will have compassion on you,
says the Lord, your Redeemer' (54 : 7-8).

Such is the intensity and faithfulness of the divine love that it surpasses that of a woman for her child: 'Even these may forget, yet I will not forget you' (49 : 15). And as Yahweh's love exceeds that of human love, so his strength and protection surpasses that of frail, mortal man:

'I, I am he that comforts you;
who are you that you are afraid of man who dies,
of the son of man who is made like grass,
and have forgotten the Lord, your Maker' (51 : 12).

The young and vigorous may grow faint and weary 'but they who wait for Yahweh shall renew their strength' (40 : 30-31). Merciful and forgiving by nature (55 : 7), he displays a ready 'compassion' towards the 'afflicted' (49 : 13), and it is thus in accord with his character that he assures Israel:

'Fear not, for I am with you,
be not dismayed, for I am your God;

I will strengthen you, I will help you,
I will uphold you with my victorious right hand' (41 : 10).

As, then, Yahweh's protection of Israel ultimately derives
from his power, so her forgiveness springs from his grace:

'You will not be forgotten by me,
I have swept away your transgressions like a cloud,
and your sins like mist;
return to me, for I have redeemed you' (44 : 21-22).

Having redeemed Israel by his grace Yahweh is determined
to manifest his purpose anew for her. As her redeemer he
'will send to Babylon' and effect her deliverance (43 : 14);
and although this may seem unlikely to the exiles nothing
can now impede the divine purpose:

'Can the prey be taken from the mighty,
or the captives of a tyrant be rescued?
Surely, thus says the Lord:
Even the captives of the mighty shall be taken,
and the prey of the tyrant be rescued,
for I will contend with those who contend with you,
and I will save your children . . .
Then all flesh shall know
that I am the Lord your Saviour,
and your Redeemer, the Mighty One of Jacob' (49 : 24-26).

Yahweh's purpose will thus be definitely achieved, and when
Israel will finally depart from Babylon it will be to the
exultant cry 'Yahweh has redeemed his servant Jacob'
(48 : 20). Through the redeeming grace of God Israel
will, further, attain to spiritual salvation. Those who worship
idols and images are insensate and confused,

'but Israel is saved by the Lord
with everlasting salvation' (45 : 17).

Israel's salvation was preceded by her redemption and

the consequent regeneration of her spirit, but Deutero-
Isaiah conceives of the divine salvation being offered freely
to the heathen nations as well and now represents Yahweh
as saying:

> 'My deliverance draws near speedily,
> my salvation has gone forth,
> and my arms will rule the peoples;
> the coastlands wait for me
> and for my arm they hope . . .
> the heavens will vanish like smoke,
> the earth will wear out like a garment,
> and they who dwell in it will die like gnats;
> but my salvation will be for ever,
> and my deliverance will never be ended' (51 : 5-6).

Availing themselves of this salvation the nations of the
world will acknowledge his sovereignty (52 : 10) and every
tongue will acclaim his name (45 : 23).

Such passages from the prophetical literature indicate,
then, that the prophets did not regard the divine judgment
on sinful Israel as absolute and irrevocable. More than once
we find instances in which the people are called to repentance
and, consequently, intimations that judgment may yet be
averted. Nor can it be objected that this interpretation of
the prophetic utterances imposes a limitation on God's
omniscience or that his actions are unduly contingent on
human behaviour. For the divine disposition towards man
is not governed by cold, impersonal logic, but is rather
motivated by personal and forgiving love. The prophets
represented God as being so concerned with human sin
as to experience himself the conflicts of wrath and compassion. And although Israel herself suffered from her long and
obstinate continuance in sin yet Yahweh's love is ultimately
determinative and decisive. It is in mercy rather than justice
that he calls man to repentance, and it is again through

love that he readily pardons and forgives. Overwhelmed by the toils of sin and vice man is helpless to return to God, but freely exercising his grace God effects his redemption and restores him to fellowship with himself.

CHAPTER EIGHT

FULFILMENT IN SERVICE

The great prophets were convinced that only through a life of dedicated service could they fulfil the functions of their office. Summoned by God himself their call was the instrument and seal of their dedication. For when Yahweh hath spoken 'who can but prophesy' (Amos 3 : 8), when he puts 'forth his hand' and imparts the inspired word (Jer. 1 : 9) who can forbear. [1] Thus, when Amos was called to leave his native Tekoa to prophesy in the northern kingdom he could not refuse. At the royal sanctuary at Bethel he did not hesitate to denounce even the king himself. Charged with conspiracy, he was turned away by Amaziah the priest and warned not to present himself in Bethel again (7 : 10 f.). But undeterred by such treatment, he remained in the land demanding justice for the poor and condemning the vices and immorality of the rich. Similarly, however we interpret the circumstances of Hosea's marriage with Gomer it is clear that the unhappiness of his domestic life was symbolic of the sorrows and disappointments he experienced as a prophet. For he could scarcely condemn kings and almost every section of society (4 : 1-9; 5: 1 f.) without incurring enmity and opposition. So Micah's indictment of the nation

---

[1] So it will be observed that while the secondary character of Isaiah ch. 6 is obvious, the writer nevertheless accurately reflects the nature of the prophetic call when he represents his subject as being completely obedient to the divine will.

as a whole (6 : 9 ff) could hardly be passively accepted and must have given affront to many of its leading citizens.

But perhaps more than any of these prophets Jeremiah realised what faithfulness in the service of God involves. His call to the prophetic office alienated him from his family and brought him into immediate conflict with the ruling classes. Disapproving of the sacrificial approach to God he offended the priests and other interested officials of the temple. His attack on institutional religion gave offence on a national scale, while his prediction of the fall of Jerusalem and the destruction of the temple itself was received with bitter resentment. Subjected to the most outrageous abuse (37 : 15 f.) it is little wonder that he should regard himself a lonely, frustrated man and that, thinking he was forsaken even by God, he should contemplate abandoning his mission. Struggling with such feelings he pours out his soul in the most poignant and plaintive language. Yet through this anguish he experiences the reality of God's forgiveness, and recognising at last that he can find fulfilment only in fellowship with him, he dedicates himself afresh to his service. Nor was Ezekiel any exception to the great prophets who spent and fulfilled themselves in the service of God. Although we have no reason to think that he suffered the anguish of soul characteristic of Jeremiah, his ministry was exercised amongst a people who raised the difficult question of the justice of God and was, therefore, necessarily exacting and exhausting in its nature.

It is, however, in the pages of Deutero-Isaiah that we find the highest ideal of service in the prophetical literature, or, indeed, in the whole Old Testament. Undertaken in unquestioning obedience to the divine will, it even involved suffering on behalf of mankind itself. This ideal is presented in four passages, known since Duhm as the Servant Songs, [1] the first of which reads thus:

> 'Behold my servant, whom I uphold,
> my chosen, in whom my soul delights;
> I have put my spirit upon him,
> he will bring forth justice to the nations.
> He will not cry or lift up his voice,
> or make it heard in the street;
> a bruised reed he will not break,
> and a dimly burning wick he will not quench;
> he will faithfully bring forth justice.
> He will not fail or be discouraged
> till he has established justice in the earth;
> and the coastlands wait for his law' (42 : 1-4).

The Servant is here introduced by Yahweh himself. Choosing him for service he forthwith supports him; and as his mission is that of conveying the principles of true religion to the Gentile world he is endowed with Yahweh's own spirit. Hence although the Servant is called to a gigantic task it is discharged in a quiet, unassuming manner; not by the clamorous raising of his voice in public places but by the transforming influences of the spirit. The progress of his work will necessarily be slow but he will faithfully continue till his words reach the farthest coast where people eagerly await enlightenment.

This universal character of his mission is further emphasised in the second Song in which the Servant himself says:

> 'Listen to me, O coastlands,
> and hearken, you peoples from afar,
> The Lord called me from the womb,
> from the body of my mother he named my name.
> He made my mouth like a sharp sword,
> in the shadow of his hand he hid me . . .

---

[1] In his *Die Theologie der Propheten*, 1875. So in his commentary *Das Buch Jesaia*, 4th edn., 1922, pp. 311 f., cited hereafter.

And he said to me, You are my servant,
Israel, in whom I will be glorified.
But I said, I have laboured in vain,
I have spent my strength for nothing and vanity;
yet surely my right is with the Lord,
and my recompense with my God.
And now the Lord says . . .
It is too light a thing that you should be my servant
to raise up the tribes of Jacob
and to restore the preserved of Israel;
I will give you as a light to the nations,
that my salvation may reach
to the end of the earth' (49 : 1-6).

Addressing the coastlands and distant nations the Servant avers that he was destined for his office from birth. He is conscious, moreover, not only of his call and preparation but of the high destiny of his mission; for he is the instrument by which even Yahweh himself will be glorified. Yet as he now contemplated the magnitude of his task he entertains some misgivings as to his own effectiveness. But he immediately recovers his self-confidence and reassures himself that he will yet be vindicated by Yahweh. And now he dwells once more on the nature of his mission. If for a moment he conceived of his work as concerned with Israel only, he is forcibly reminded to the contrary. The restoration of Israel to God is indeed part of his obligation, but his mission actually includes the mediation of divine salvation to the heathen world.

The next Servant Song appears in 50 : 4-9. It is true that the word 'servant' does not occur in the passage, but the material as a whole exhibits such affinity of thought with the other Songs that it can only be regarded as belonging to their cycle. Indeed it provides a necessary connection between the first two Songs and the fourth; for while it affirms and develops certain themes of the earlier poems it introduces the element of suffering which is so prominent a feature of the last. As in the previous passage the Servant is here also the Speaker, and of his experiences and convictions he says:

'The Lord God has given me
the tongue of those who are taught,
that I may know how to sustain
with a word him that is weary.
Morning by morning he wakens . . .
my ear to hear as those who are taught . . .
I hid not my face from shame and spitting.
For the Lord God helps me;
therefore I have not been confounded;
therefore I have set my face like a flint,
and I know that I shall not be put to shame;
he who vindicates me is near.
Who will contend with me? Let us stand up together.
Who is my adversary? Let him come near to me.
Behold, the Lord God helps me;
who will declare me guilty? . . .'

Benefiting from the close relationship which exists between God and himself he is in turn able to offer an effective word of consolation to the weary and depressed. But this relationship needs continual strengthening and renewal; for it is both the source of his message and the explanation of his remarkable forbearance. Immune from the effects of scorn and insults he is thus enabled to endure the persecutions which have now become inseparable from his mission. But he has also his moments of anticipated triumph; he even challenges his adversaries to a contest and his critics to declare his guilt. Convinced of his innocence he is confident of success, for his advocate is none other than God himself.

The fourth Song is of considerable length, extending from chapter 52 : 13 to the end of chapter 53. The text is

unfortunately obscure and uncertain in places, having
suffered not only in transmission but also, apparently, from
the interpretative hand of the editor. The purport of the
author is, however, clear and the passage itself may be
conveniently considered in three sections. Chapter 52 : 13-15
comprises the first section and may be taken as providing
an introduction to the Song as a whole. Yahweh is the
Speaker and makes a brief announcement concerning the
future triumph of his Servant. This is a destiny which is in
sharp contrast with the humiliation of the present, and will
be the occasion of surprise amongst kings and nations:

> 'His appearance was so marred beyond human semblance,
> and his form beyond that of the sons of men,
> so shall he startle many nations;
> kings shall shut their mouths because of him;
> for that which has not been told them they shall see'
>   (52 : 14-15).

The second part may be recognised in the material of
53 : 1-11a. It is uncertain whether the Speakers here are the
heathen nations or the Israelites, but they are obviously
contemporaries of the Servant and hence eyewitnesses of
his history and circumstances. Like the kings in the preceding
section, they too regarded the Servant as unprepossessing
and insignificant in appearance:

> 'he had no form or comeliness that we should look at him
> and no beauty that we should desire him' (53 : 2).

Unattractive at birth, he contracted in life a loathsome,
disfiguring disease. Stricken and afflicted, he was an object
from which men in disgust diverted their gaze. But although
smitten to the point of revulsion and succumbing to the
pains of death, his onlookers now realised that it was at the
will of Yahweh he suffered and that it was the penalty of
their own transgressions he was bearing:

'All we like sheep have gone astray;
we have turned every one to his own way;
and the Lord has laid on him
the iniquity of us all' (53 : 6).

The third component of the Song consists of 53 : 11b-12, and Yahweh is again the Speaker. The theme is that of the atoning work and ultimate exaltation of the Servant. Through his close fellowship with God and his 'knowledge' of the divine purpose he is able to effect the salvation of others. But as in this mediatorial capacity he endured unmerited sufferings, so he shall now attain to an influence comparable to that of the great rulers of the day:

"By his knowledge shall the righteous one, my servant,
make many to be accounted righteous . . .
Therefore 1 will divide him a portion with the great,
and he shall divide the spoil with the strong;
because he poured out his soul to death . . .' (53 : 11-12).

Our consideration of the Servant passages thus far reveals that he was the chosen vessel by which God's purpose would be established in the world. In the first two Songs he actively pursues his mission, and although the third Song represents him experiencing some humiliation, he nevertheless continues his work in the confident hope of ultimate success. In the fourth Song, however, we meet with a different figure. Instead of the enthusiastic, hopeful Servant of God we have a despised and afflicted man of sorrows who eventually meets with death. While, therefore, in the preceding Songs the Servant fulfils an active role, his mission is fulfilled here by suffering which was to prove the most effective feature of his work, and which will later claim our attention. In the meantime we pause to ask, Who was this Servant who was capable of enduring and accomplishing so much?

The question of the identity of the Servant of Yahweh
has exercised the minds of men since, with reference to
Isaiah 53 : 7-8, the Ethiopian eunuch inquired if the prophet
were speaking of himself or of some other person (Acts
8 : 32 f.). Throughout the centuries it has remained the
most difficult problem of Old Testament exegesis and has
in consequence been the subject of keen debate and of a
voluminous literature.[1] There are, of course, passages
outside the Songs in which the term 'servant' clearly applies
to the nation Israel. Thus in 41 : 8 we read: 'But you,
Israel my servant . . . whom I took from the ends of the
earth . . . saying to you, you are my servant'. Likewise in
43 : 10 the Israelites are both 'witnesses' to Yahweh's acts
in history and the 'servant' whom he has 'chosen'. So
again, 41 : 8, 45 : 4 and 48 : 20 are instances in which
Israel is similarly designated. The 'servant' of these passages
is, however, a rather different figure from that delineated
in the Songs.[2] Israel is indeed called by Yahweh but has
little trust in him (40 : 27; 42 : 24 f.; 43 : 27-28). If, on the
other hand, the Servant of the poems experienced a moment
of hesitation it was only because he was dissatisfied with
his own service and immediately affirmed his trust in God
(49 : 4). The Songs repeatedly state that the Servant is
free from sin (50 : 5; 53 : 4, 6-12) but Israel has been
obstinate and rebellious from birth (43 : 23-24; 48 : 4, 8).
The Israelites are indifferent 'witnesses' to Yahweh (44 : 8),
whereas the Songs represent the Servant as faithful and
obedient (42 : 4; 50 : 4-5). Again, while the suffering of the
Servant is on behalf of others (53 : 4-6, 11, 12), Israel's
sufferings are but the consequences of her own sins

---

[1] See the survey of C. R. North, *The Suffering Servant in Deutero-Isaiah*,
2nd edn., 1956 pp. 1-116.

[2] Cf., e.g., Johann Fischer *Das Buch Isaias*, 2, 1939, pp. 10 f.

(42 : 22 f.; 47 : 6; 50 : 1). The Servant, moreover, suffers patiently and voluntarily but Israel's sufferings will yet be avenged (41 : 11 f.; 47 : 1 f.). Further, Israel proved inadequate to the purpose of her call (43 : 21-22), while the Servant was not only entrusted with the task of mediating true religion to the Gentile world (42 :4), but was actually charged with a mission to Israel herself (49 : 5-6). Indeed, so different is the character of the Servant—Israel from the Servant of the Songs that some scholars have regarded the Songs as the composition of a writer other than Deutero-Isaiah. [1] Pronounced, however, as this difference is, there are no really strong grounds for assuming a difference of authorship. [2] Even the fourth Song with its many peculiarities of vocabulary and thought may with some confidence be assigned to the prophet. [3]

But the probability that the Songs are from Deutero-Isaiah does not in itself materially assist us in identifying the Servant. In support of his own collective theory Wheeler Robinson could write: 'if we could assert with confidence identity of authorship, then we should have a very powerful argument for maintaining that the picture of the Servant in the Songs is really a picture of Israel, for there is no doubt that in the other poems the title 'Servant' is given to Israel as a people'. [4] But assuming that the Songs are from Deutero-Isaiah he need not necessarily have had Israel in mind when

---

[1] So Duhm, op. cit., pp. 311 ff.; M. Schian, *Die Ebed-Yahweh-Lieder in Jes.* 40-66, 1895, pp. 13 f.; R. H. Kennett, *The Servant of the Lord*, 1911, e.g., pp. 121 f.

[2] Cf. J. Muilenburg, *The Interpreter's Bible*, 5, pp. 406 f.

[3] C. R. North, *op. cit.*, pp. 169-177.

[4] *The Cross in the Old Testament*, 1955, p. 68. On another page (69), however, he remarked: 'Apart from this assumption, all we are warranted in saying ... is that the previous usage of the term leaves it an open question whether 'Servant' denotes an individual or a group'.

he sketched his ideal of service, although it is such an assumption which underlies the age-long identification of the Servant with Israel. The appearance of the words 'Jacob' and 'Israel' in the Greek version of 42 : 1 and the interpolation of the word 'Israel' in the Hebrew text of 49 : 3 testify to the antiquity of this view. It was likewise that accepted by the Rabbinical exegetes of medieval times; [1] while in varying ways it has found support in modern scholarship. Wheeler Robinson himself based the identity of the Servant with the Israelite nation on the hypothesis that the prophet was thinking in terms of corporate personality. [2] This ancient mode of thought sees little distinction between the community and the individual and so, argues Robinson, provides an explanation of both the individual traits of the Songs and the distinction which appears to exist between the work of the Servant and the attitude and characteristics of the nation. We must 'remember that we are reading a Semitic and Oriental book', written by a people who did not think in abstract terms, and who in order 'to utter a general truth at all . . . had to use the particular image' (p. 71). In support of this argument Robinson appeals to those Psalms in which it is difficult to discern whether the speaker is the community or individual, and remarks 'The true answer would seem to be that it is both, or rather that there is a consciousness of both as so united in the speaker that he can emphasise now one side, now the other, without needing to draw a definite line' (p. 78). Such considerations, then, bring us 'to a point of view from which it is conceivable that the prophet's mind held together what we can only regard as distinct' (p. 78). Otto Eissfeldt also approached the question from the standpoint of corporate personality, and came to much

---

[1] See North, *op. cit.*, p. 18.
[2] *Op. cit.*, pp. 76 ff.

the same conclusions as Robinson.[1] Conceiving of the group
as superior to the individual he thinks that 'the real entity
is the community'. We may, however, have a 'corporate
individual' distinguishable from members of the social group.
It is this corporate individual which constitutes the 'ideal
entity', and it is in terms of such an entity that the Servant
is to be regarded. In conformity with Jewish exposition as
a whole S. H. Blank contended that the Servant could only
be the nation Israel. The concept of the Servant is, indeed,
complementary to the argument from prophecy as developed
by Deutero-Isaiah, and Israel is accordingly personified in
the Songs as a prophet.[2] Proceeding from the assumption
that the Songs are the work of the Second Isaiah, Muilenburg similarly claims that the Servant represents the Israelite
people. The mission and destiny of Israel entailed service,
and in his presentation of the Servant the prophet was only
emphasising what was but a central motif in Israelite faith.
'No single person is sufficient to bear the burden of what is
disclosed in the Songs. For the reality that lies within and
behind the songs is infinitely greater than any person could
exemplify'. 'On the other hand', continues Muilenburg,
'what cannot apply to an individual may apply to a community such as Second Isaiah conceives Israel to be'.[3] The
conclusion to which the evidence, then, points is that 'Israel,
and Israel alone, is able to bear all that is said about the
servant of the Lord' (p. 411).

But while such arguments are advanced by these and
other scholars on behalf of the national view, there are

---

[1] 'The Ebed-Jahwe in Isaiah XL-LV in the Light of the Israelite
Conceptions of the Community and the Individual, the Ideal and the
Real', *E.T.*, 44, 1933, pp. 261-268.
[2] *H.U.C.A.*, 15, 1940, p. 20.
[3] *Loc. cit.*, p. 409.

certain difficulties which beset any collective interpretation
of the Servant Songs. It can scarcely be Israel who was
'afflicted' and 'wounded' for the 'transgressions' of others
(53 : 4-5), for the prophet more than once tells us that
her afflictions were but the penalty for her own sins (40 : 2;
42 : 24-25; 43: 27-28; 51 : 17). Even the Gentiles too
suffer the consequences of their guilt, being duly punished
by Yahweh:

> 'Behold, I have taken from your hand the cup of staggering;
> the bowl of my wrath you shall drink no more;
> and I will put it into the hand of your tormentors' (51 : 22-23).

Thus it is that the victories of Cyrus are regarded not merely
as a judgment upon Babylon but upon the Gentiles nations
at large (45 : 6, 20). It is, again, difficult to conceive of
Israel bearing the effects of sin not her own when in fact she
herself is ransomed by other nations: Egypt, Ethiopia and
Seba are exchanged for her; 'men' and 'peoples' are given
'in return' for her (43 : 3-4). Nor can it be justly said of
Israel that she 'was oppressed and . . . afflicted yet . . . opened
not' her 'mouth' (53 : 7); for she is not elsewhere represented as silently and humbly accepting her lot. Earlier
questioning the justice of God (Ezek. 18 : 25), she now in
Deutero-Isaiah's day complained 'My way is hid from
Yahweh, and my right is disregarded by my God' (40 : 27).
Thus with regard to chapter 53 : 7 Wheeler Robinson
deemed it expedient to remark: 'Here, obviously, the
attributes of the few are ascribed to the nation as a whole
in its corporate personality'. [1] Such words are suggestive
of the theory that the Servant represents the ideal as distinct
from the actual Israel, a view rejected by Robinson himself, [2]

---

[2] *Op. cit.*, p. 83.
[1] *Op. cit.*, p. 79.

but which has the sympathetic support of not a few scholars.
It is, for example, on the presuppositions of this view that
Skinner could say, 'the Servant-ideal is one that embraces
all that is of religious significance in the life of Israel'. [1] And
whatever its inadequacies it is at any rate free from many
of the embarrassments of the national interpretation of the
Servant. [2]

The suggestion that the Servant concept is representative
of the order of the prophets is, again, not lightly made.
For however the functions of the Servant surpass that of
the prophets the portrait of his sufferings is reminiscent of
the prophetic experiences. The persecutions of Jeremiah,
his patience and submissiveness to the will of God, come
readily to mind; and it is not therefore surprising that
some scholars have associated the Servant with him. [3] Indeed,
the equation of the Servant with a particular person seemed
a natural inference from the individualistic traits in the
Songs themselves, and thus historical figures ranging from
Moses to Cyrus have been proposed. [4] Duhm regarded the
collective interpretation as entirely inadequate and main-

---

[1] *Isaiah XL-LXVI*, 1917, p. 270.

[2] It may be observed that A. Condamin regarded the Servant of
chs. 40-48 as the historical Israelite nation and that of chs. 49-55 as the
ideal Israel. Maintaining that the Servant is always identified with
Israel in the first section, he thought that the anonymous figure of the
last section could only be the Messiah. In order to achieve this precise
distinction, however, he transferred the material of 42 : 1-9 to a point
after 49 : 1-7, e.g., 'Le Serviteur de Jahvé', *R.B.*, nouv. sér., 5, 1908,
pp. 162-181. In this view Condamin was to a large extent followed by
A. Van Hoonacker, so, e.g., 'The Servant of the Lord in Isa. XL ff.'
Expositor, 8th series, 1916, pp. 183-210.

[3] E.g., F. A. Farley 'Jeremiah and "The Suffering Servant of Jehovah"
in Deutero-Isaiah', *E.T.*, 38, 1926-27, pp. 521-524; so S. H. Blank
though that 'Jeremiah in particular hovered before' the author's 'eyes
as he limned in the figure of the Ebed', *loc. cit.*, p. 27.

[4] See here North, *op. cit.*, pp. 192 ff.

tained that the Songs are intelligible at all only if we take
them as referring to a single individual. Denying the Songs
to Deutero-Isaiah on the grounds of style and content, he
placed their composition in the early fifth century and
thought that the Servant was a teacher of the Law who was
influenced by the prophets. [1] The affliction (*Krankheit*)
mentioned in chapter 53 must apply to leprosy with which
the Servant was aflicted and from which he eventually died. [2]
Like Duhm, Bertholet also held that the Songs were from
a later hand than Deutero-Isaiah. Pertaining to an individual
who was a representative of the order of the teachers of the
Law they were composed between the exile and the publi-
cation of the Priestly Code in 444 B.C. The material of
chapter 53 : 1-11a is, however, later still and probably
refers to the sufferings of Eleazar the scribe who perished
in the persecutions of Antiochus Epiphanes as narrated
in 2 Maccabees 6 : 18-31. [3]

The view has also been advocated that the Songs are
the autobiographical record of the Second Isaiah and that
therefore the Servant is none other that the prophet himself.
Propounded first by Mowinckel, [4] it found ready acceptance
among other scholars. [5] But, recognising the difficulties

---

[1] *Op. cit.*, pp. 311, 393 f.

[2] *Op. cit.*, p. 397.

[3] A. Bertholet, *Zu Jesaja* 53, 1899, pp. 22 f. So R. H. Kennett maintained that all the Songs derived from the Maccabean age and referred
to the persecutions of the Hasidim by Antiochus, *The Servant of the
Lord*, 1911, e.g., pp. 10 ff., 92 ff.

[4] *Der Knecht Jahwäs*, 1921, e.g., pp. 9 ff. Paul Volz similarly interpreted the first three Songs, but he regarded the last as being as late as
the fourth or third century B.C., 'Jesaja 53' in *Budde Festschrift*, *Z.A.W.*,
34, 1912, pp. 180-190.

[5] E.g., Emil Balla, 'Das Problem des Leides in der israelitischen-
jüdischen Religion' in *Eucharisterion* (ed. H. Schmidt), 1923, pp. 214-261,
and Max Haller, 'Die Kyros-Lieder Deuterojesajas', *ibid.*, pp. 261-277.

inherent in the implication that the prophet described the manner of his own death, Mowinckel decided to modify his thesis. He, thus, subsequently expressed the view that the prophet did not compile his own oracles, but rather that they were were compiled by his disciples who were guided by the 'catchword' principle of compilation. Failing to discern any close 'catchword' connection between the Songs and the rest of the prophecy, Mowinckel now maintained that they were not from Deutero-Isaiah, but were in fact interpolations by members of the Trito-Isaiah circle. [1] In a more recent reference to the subject this scholar suggests that the historical Servant was a member of such a circle. [2] The poems in the first person may, therefore, be the Servant's own sayings, while those in the third person may be the work of a poet-author; or, again, it may be that in all four Songs we have 'the tradition, interpretation, and faith of the circle' (p. 251).

The autobiographical theory was, however, regarded as being so satisfactory that, despite Mowinckel's modification of his original view, Joachim Begrich argued afresh that the Second Isaiah was both the author of the Songs and the Servant of Yahweh. [3] Similarly, in a chapter dealing with recent criticism of the Second Isaiah, Sidney Smith favoured the autobiographical interpretation. But he suggested that the servant passages which seem to refer to an individual need not necessarily pertain to one and the same person. Thus, while the prophet himself is to be identified with the Servant in 49 : 1-6 and   50 : 4-10 and   probably in

---

[1] 'Die Komposition des deuterojesajanischen Buches', *Z.A.W.*, N.F., 8, 1931, pp. 242 ff.

[2] *He That Cometh*, pp. 246 ff.

[3] 'Studien zu Deuterojesaja', *Z.W.A.N.T.*, 4, 25, 1938, pp. 131 f.

52 : 13-53: 12, it is the conqueror Cyrus who is the subject of 42 : 1-4. [1]

The foregoing paragraphs indicate, then, the problematical nature of the identity of the Servant of the Lord. Defying attempts to identify him with the nation or an individual he is still 'an unsolved enigma'. [2] Hence, despite a century of close and critical research, the position is scarcely different today from that implied by the fourteenth century Rabbi who remarked: 'I have never in my life seen or heard of the exposition of a clear or fluent commentator in which my own judgment or that of others who have pondered on the same subject might completely acquiesce'. [3]

But while there is little unanimity regarding the identity of the Servant there can be no doubt as to the moral and religious significance of his mission. And of especial importance is the vicarious nature of the suffering he endured. The problem of suffering had been experienced by most ancient peoples [4] and not least by the Israelites themselves. Ezekiel had informed the first generation of exiles that, contrary to popular belief, the sons did not suffer for the sins of the fathers, and insisted that the individual was responsible only for his own sins. But there is much suffering and affliction which can scarcely be explained in terms of personal sin. The effects of evil seem more often to fall on the righteous than on the guilty, while those who are most conscientious in their observance of the divine law are most conscious of the burdens and sorrows of life. Experiences and reflections of this nature combined to create

---

[1] *Isaiah Chapters XL-LV* (Schweich Lectures 1940), 1944, pp. 19-20.

[2] Wheeler Robinson, *op. cit.* p. 65.

[3] S. R. Driver and A. Neubauer, *The Fifty-third Chapter of Isaiah according to the Jewish Interpreters,* vol. 2, 1877, p. 138.

[4] *A.N.E.T.*, pp. 405 ff.; 438 f.

the problem of the innocent sufferer for the exiles, and may partly explain why some of them sat and wept by the waters of Babylon (Ps. 137 : 1 f.). It would, accordingly, seem that it was to meet such a problem that Deutero-Isaiah conceived of the theme of the Servant Songs: and it will be observed that they are so constructed as to lead naturally to the thought of vicarious suffering. In the first Song the Servant is called by Yahweh and supported by him in his exposition of divine justice. He will be subjected to trials and humiliation, but, confident in the power of God, 'he will not fail or be discouraged' (42 : 4). In the second Song the Servant affirms the divine purpose of his call. It is thus with some vigour that he pursues his task, even though he experiences a brief moment of disquiet. But that his mission involves suffering is clearly indicated in the third Song (50 : 5 f.). Yet, although exposed to the violence of assault and to the indignities of facial disfigurement, he unrelentingly pursues his course. The point of his suffering is, however, as yet concealed from his persecutors. Even in the fourth Song popular opinion interprets his humiliation as a penalty for his own sin and regarded him as 'smitten by God and afflicted' (53 : 4). But those who were most contemptuous of his afflictions and most scornful of his appearance now suddenly realise that the Servant was suffering for sins not his own. Rather, his passion was borne entirely for the benefit of themselves, and they are accordingly moved to confess:

'he was wounded for our transgressions,
he was bruised for our iniquities;
upon him was the chastisement that made us whole,
and with his stripes we are healed' (53 : 5).

The thought that the Servant had borne their griefs and carried their sorrows was thus scarcely less than the recognition of a new factor in human experience. For the principle of vicarious suffering sheds some light on the universal fact of pain and suffering. Through it men may be led to an acceptance of their lot in life when other considerations fail. A man who has suffered for his own wrongs and expiated his own guilt may not necessarily be a changed character. He may, on the contrary, arrogantly boast that he has served his sentence, and in consequence he may become more embittered and cynical. But the thought that another might bear the burden of his guilt awakens him to worthier feelings: not only is he urged to acknowledge his transgressions but he is moved to a deep sense of shame and contrition. The knowledge that others could sacrifice their happiness and even their life for him, compels him to recognise in vicarious suffering one of the most effective instruments of humanity. When, moreover, it is realised that this suffering is not only vicarious but voluntary, then, it must be admitted that human nature has attained to its highest and noblest, and we have reached a point where we can only in admiration exclaim 'Greater love has no man than this, that a man lay down his life for his friends' (John 15 : 13).

But this sacrifice is even yet more effective when he who has given his life is himself sinless. Such was the nature of the Servant's sacrifice: he surrendered his life

> 'although he had done no violence
> and there was no deceit in his mouth' (53 : 9).

Having done no wrong he had no sin to expiate, no fears of retribution. His suffering was, again, borne in silence. There were many men of God who suffered, but none without complaint or misgiving. Jeremiah was the most steadfast and long-suffering of prophets, but he came to a stage in his mission when in desperation he asked 'Why is

my pain unceasing, my wound incurable . . . ?' (15 : 18).
The writer of Psalm 73 was, similarly, a man of exemplary
character, devoutly acknowledging the goodness of God.
Yet he became so perplexed by the prosperity of the wicked
that he impulsively remarked:

> 'All in vain have I kept my heart clean
> and washed my hands in innocence.
> For all the day long I have been stricken,
> and chastened every morning' (vv. 13-14).

Of all the Old Testament figures the Servant alone accepts
his lot with complete and unquestioning resignation. Had he
been dragged struggling and reluctant to his doom he
would have been a mere victim who would have earned our
compassion but would not have excited our wonder or admiration. Instead he submitted himself willingly and with a
sense of divine destiny. But this was due to his close relationship with God and because he had a secret entrusted to him
alone:

> 'The Lord God has opened my ear
> and I was not rebellious,
> I turned not backward' (50 : 5).

Relentlessly and faithfully he went forward to his mission
fully accepting that 'it was the will of Yahweh to bruise
him' and to 'put him to grief' (53 : 10). In thus acquiescing
in the divine will it was scarcely punishment that he was
enduring. Rather 'it was a Service he was performing, a
service laid on him by God, a service for man's redemption'. [1]

---

[1] G. A. Smith, *The Book of Isaiah*, vol. 2, p. 360. Smith was even
prepared to identify the passion of the Servant with that of God. He
could thus write: 'It was not only the human Servant who served the
nation by suffering, for God Himself had come down to *carry* His
distressed and accursed people, and *to load Himself with them* . . . Like
the Servant too, God *was afflicted in all their affliction*; and His love
towards them was expended in passion and agony for their sins. Vicarious suffering was not only human, it was Divine', p. 358.

In bearing the effects of the transgressions of man he assisted him to a restored relationship with God. Therein lies the explanation of the Servant's humiliation and the supreme purpose of his mission:

'He poured out his soul to death,
and was numbered with the transgressors;
yet he bore the sin of many,
and made intercession for the transgressors' (53 : 12).

Taking suffering and sin upon himself the Servant transmuted them into an exhibition of love. Thus his death was not a sacrifice in a penal and forensic sense, but a manifestation of what love itself was capable of achieving. Nor were the effects of this love a merely temporary force; for in contemplation of it man is inevitably reminded of his own sins and, therefore, of the need for atonement.

But as befitting one who has dedicated himself to the service of God, the Servant will be rewarded in the knowledge that his work is effective: 'He shall see the travail of his soul and be satisfied' (53 : 11). Nor is this all. In ennobling man he is himself elevated by God and accorded a place of incomparable glory:

'Behold, my servant shall prosper,
he shall be exalted and lifted up,
and shall be very high' (52 : 13).

In bearing the guilt of others, and in effecting their restoration to God, the Servant might be said to fulfil his mission. But he attained to an even greater fulfilment in his ultimate triumphant exaltation to a closer and more creative fellowship with God.

The Servant Songs, then, present a unique interpretation of suffering and a remarkable ideal of service. Nor is it likely that this delineation of the suffering of the Servant is a mere rhetorical utterance designed to meet the needs of

the exilic community but seems, to some extent, to reflect the
prophet's own experience of life. For although we have no
reason to assume that he was subjected to physical violence he
could still have 'suffered a martyrdom of soul'. [1] His fellow
Israelites amongst whom he laboured were by no means
exemplary in their devotion to Yahweh. Even in passages
where they are designated 'servant' they are 'blind' and
unresponsive (4 : 19-20), and they are more than once
rebuked for their sins and disobedience (46 : 12; 48 : 4 f.).
Despite the vital, optimistic nature of his message as a
whole the prophet was, therefore, acutely aware of the
hindrances to his mission. Cyrus too, whose conquests he
regarded as divinely ordained (41 : 2-3), and whom he
addressed as the 'anointed' of God (45 : 1), scarcely vindicated the hopes he entertained for him. For while it was
conceivable that the Persian conqueror might ultimately
recognise the universal claims of Yahweh, he professed
instead his allegiance to Bel-Marduk. [2] It may thus be that
the Songs were composed somewhat late in the prophet's
career when, realistically assessing the success of his ministry,
he became convinced that the apostle of true religion
inevitably incurs opposition and disappointment. The
synthesis of such thoughts and their presentation in writing
proved, apparently, no easy undertaking. Like the poet of a
later age it may be that he felt 'what' he could'ne'er express
yet' could 'not all conceal'. [3] This may account for the
obscurities which so often characterise the Songs. It is,
moreover, probable that the portrait of the Servant is com-

---

[1] C. R. North, *op. cit.*, p. 217.

[2] So in the Cyrus-Cylinder he says of Marduk 'I was daily endeavouring to worship him', *A.N.E.T.*, p. 316a. Cf. here also J. Hempel,
'Vom irrenden Glauben', *Z.S.T.*, 7, 1929, pp. 631 ff.

[3] Byron, *Childe Harold*.

posed of both collective and individual features, while the actual description of the sufferings of the Servant may even be influenced by the ceremonial which enacted the humiliation of the King in the Babylonian New Year Festival.[1] But, whatever the source of the portrait which the prophet delineates, we may doubt if his ideal was fulfilled in his own day. Nor is it likely that he himself regarded the figure of the last two Songs as having already come. For part of his mission is in the future: men are still in need of redemption, 'and he shall bear their iniquities' (53 : 11). It is at any rate certain that the ideal presented in the Songs was only realised once in history, and that was considerably later than Deutero-Isaiah.

Some five centuries after the prophet, Jesus of Nazareth appeared on the scene and fulfilled the ideals and experienced the sufferings prefigured in the Songs. He who is but a dim, elusive figure in the prophecy assumes definite form in the person of Jesus: he whom we could but regard as a mere ideal now appears as an historical reality. In the life and atoning work of Jesus we have the mission of the Servant portrayed in the Songs brought to fulfilment and consummation. Yet we can only regard as remarkable the extent to which the portrait of the Servant foreshadows the mission and experience of Jesus. Like the Servant, he 'came not to be served but to serve, and to give his life a ransom for many'

---

[1] The cultic aspects of the portraiture of the Servant have of course been pointed out by such scholars as Heinrich Zimmern (*Die Keilinschriften und das Alte Testament*, ed. E. Schraeder, 3, Aufl., 1903, pp. 384 ff.) and L. Dürr (*Ursprung und Aufbei der israel-jüd. Heilandserwartung*, 1925, pp. 134 ff.). More recently it has been emphasised by Scandinavian writers. See, e.g., Helmer Ringgren, *The Messiah in the Old Testament*, 1956, pp. 39-53 and the literature cited there. It is unlikely, however, that Deutero-Isaiah was indebted to Kingship ideology beyond that of mere verbal suggestiveness.

(Mark 10 : 45). But like the Servant, too, Jesus was rewarded for his service, for 'God has highly exalted him and bestowed on him the name which is above every name' (Phil. 2 : 9).

The fact that the Servant Songs were fulfilled in Jesus invests them with a singular and prophetic significance. Moved by the unsolved mystery of pain and sorrow, their author conceived of the notion of vicarious suffering. Regarding such suffering as fraught with ennobling and redemptive power he represents it as the ideal of human service. Silently and willingly borne, it may involve even the sacrifice of life itself. But as this is also life surrendered to the will of God it finds and fulfils itself anew in that higher service. It is life as exemplified in him who said, 'Whoever would save his life will lose it, and whoever loses his life for my sake, he will save it' (Luke 9 : 24).

APPENDIX

PRE-EXILIC PROPHECY AND ESCHATOLOGY

It is commonly thought that eschatology was a feature of Israelite religion from the earliest times and that, consequently, it constituted a definite element in the teaching of the pre-exilic prophets. [1] This view has long been maintained by such scholars as R. H. Charles [2] and A. B. Davidson, [3] but it was mainly through the work of Gressmann and Sellin that it tended to become an accepted principle of Old Testament exegesis. In *Der Ursprung der israelitisch-jüdischen Eschatologie* (1905) Gressmann argued that the concept of a world catastrophe and eschatology obtained amongst the ancient Semites as a whole but that its origins are ultimately to be traced to Babylonia. [4] This theory rests on the assumption that the Babylonians believed in the sun's millennial encirclement of the earth and that each cycle was regarded as a period of weal or woe. [5] Gressmann thought that such ideas were mediated by the Canaanites to the Israelites, and hence became the basis of the 'disaster' and 'restoration' elements of a prophetic eschatology. But, apart from the question of Babylonian influence on Israelite religion in this

---

[1] See J. M. Powis Smith, *The Prophets and Their Times*, revised edn. by W. A. Irwin, 1940, pp. 66 ff.; T. H. Robinson, *Prophecy and the Prophets*, 2nd edn. 1953, pp. 197 f.; Jaroslav Černý, *The Day of Yahweh and Some Relevant Problems*, 1948, p. 100; S. B. Frost, *Old Testament Apocalyptic*, 1952, pp. 43-56; G. E. Wright, *Interpreter's Bible*, 1, 1952, pp. 371 f.

[2] *Eschatology, Hebrew, Jewish and Christian*, 1899, pp. 81 ff.

[3] *Old Testament Prophecy*, 1904, pp. 72, 310.

[4] *Op. cit.*, pp. 142-158.

[5] pp. 167 f.

respect, there is no tangible evidence that eschatology was a characteristic of Babylonian belief. Gressmann has indeed been supported in his theory of a Babylonian eschatology by Jeremias [1] and others, but the Babylonian texts as examined by Zimmern, Von Gall and Mowinckel yield no such evidence. [2] The most we find in these texts is the expression of the hope that the reign of a king would be blessed by material and social prosperity and that he himself would avoid evil. It is thus recorded that at the coronation of a king the priest said: ' . . . Before Assur, thy god, may thy priesthood and the priesthood of thy sons find favour. With thy straight sceptre make thy land wide. May Assur grant thee satisfaction, justice and peace'. [3] We, likewise, read of Sargon himself asking Ea, his god for 'the waters of plenty in abundance . . . quick understanding and' prosperity in 'his work', [4] while it is reported of Ashurbanipal II that on ascending the throne 'Adad (the rain god) sent his rains . . . heavy crops and a rich yield made the fields constantly abound . . . there was fulness to overflowing . . . there was abundant plenty'. [5] But as Mowinckel commented, 'When *we* apply to this term "Paradisal" fertility, the metaphorical expression is *ours* and does not reflect the ancients' own ideas. There is no "paradise myth" behind these hyperbolical expressions of oriental imagination. The Babylonians had no conception of a primeval paradise, now lost,

---

[1] A. Jeremias, *Handbuch der altorientalischen Geisteskultur*, 2nd edn. 1929, pp. 205 ff.; cf. also W. Staerk, *Die Erlösererwartung in den östlichen Religionen*, 1938, pp. 167 ff.

[2] See S. Mowinckel, *He That Cometh*, p. 127, n. 3 and the literature cited there.

[3] Henri Frankfort, *Kingship and the Gods*, 1948, p. 247.

[4] Frankfort, *op. cit.*, p. 310.

[5] Mowinckel, *op. cit.*, p. 46.

which the new king restored when he inaugurated a new epoch'. [1]

But the king was also liable to encounter evil, and in the presence of disquieting portents he prays thus: 'In the evil eclipse of the moon . . . in the evil of the powers, of the signs, evil and not good, which are in my palace and my country, I fear, I tremble, and I am cast down in fear . . . let me live, let me be perfect . . .'. [2] There was, however, a recognised ritual, which, if performed by the king, could counteract the effects of such portents. Even in the case of a predicted earthquake a priest informs the king: 'Your gods will cause it to pass away. Ea made (the earthquake), Ea will release (us from it). (For) whoever made the earthquake has also provided the lustral incantation against it. In the time of the fathers (and) grandfathers of the king, there was no earthquake . . . That (same) god will give wisdom to the king saying, Let him spread out his hands (in prayer) to god. Let him perform the proper lustral incantations; it will surely pass away'. [3] While, then, there are many such texts relating to the good and evil fortune which a king and his people may experience, there is no indication that periods of weal and woe were thought to occur in alternate and regular cycles.

It is therefore not surprising that while Sellin contended for an Israelite eschatology he should reject Gressmann's theory of Babylonian influence. Yet it is doubtful if Sellin's own view of a native Israelite eschatology dating from Moses can be sustained. [4] The word 'eschatology' is, however

---

[1] Ibid.

[2] Frankfort, op. cit., p. 248.

[3] Frankfort, op. cit., p. 260.

[4] Der alttestamentliche Prophetismus, 1912. See also his Introduction to the Old Testament, Eng. trans. 1923, p. 170, where he speaks of 'the traditional eschatology of salvation'.

loosely used by many writers, and it is therefore necessary that we should have a clear conception of the connotation of the term. It literally means 'a theory of the last things' [1] and hence any correct use of the term must pertain to such phenomena as the ending of the natural world order and the inauguration of another of an essentially different kind. Mowinckel, again, rightly observes that a distinction must be made between a 'future hope' and 'eschatology' and maintains that 'a future hope which is national, as the Jewish hope undoubtedly was, need not be eschatological'. [2] He further holds that the eschatological 'drama has a universal cosmic character' wherein 'the universe itself, heaven and earth, is thrown into the melting pot', and that this action is brought about by supernatural powers. [3] If, therefore, we conceive of eschatology as applying to the catastrophic ending of the physical order of the world and the beginning of a new and spiritual order in which the divine will is completely observed, then, we can scarcely hold that eschatology was a tenet of Israelite religion in Mosaic times.

Like Sellin, S. B. Frost regards eschatology as indigenous to Israel, [4] and speaks of the popular expectation of the Day of Yahweh in the time of Amos in terms of a 'futuristic eschatology'. [5] It seems clear, indeed, that Amos did not originate the expression 'Day of Yahweh' but that it was an element of the popular vocabulary of the period. Yet there is no evidence that it was used in an eschatological sense by the people of the day, much less by the prophet himself. [6]

---

[1] See R. S. Cripps, *The Book of Amos*, 2nd edn. 1955, p. 55.
[2] Op. cit., p. 125.
[3] Page 126.
[4] *V.T.*, 2, 1, 1952, p. 75.
[5] *Old Testament Apocalyptic*, p. 43.
[6] Cf. here G. Von Rad who in a discussion of 'The Origin of the

The term 'day' is not used exclusively in the Old Testament
with Yahweh, but has also a number of other associations.
As R. H. Kennett wrote, it 'merely denotes a time which is
memorable in connexion with someone or something'. [1]
Thus we find such expressions as 'the day of Midian' (Is.
9 : 4), 'the day of Jezreel' (Hos. 1 : 11) and 'the day of
Jerusalem' (Ps. 137 : 7), all of which refer to significant and
memorable events in the life of Israel. The Day of Yahweh
is likewise to be connected with such an occasion. That it
may apply to a day in which Yahweh showed himself mighty
in battle on Israel's behalf is seen from Ezekiel's reference
to her failure to 'stand in battle in the day of Yahweh'
(13 : 5). This meaning is also discernible in Zechariah
chapter 14 where we read: 'Behold, a day of the Lord is
coming, when . . . the Lord will go forth and fight against
those nations as when he fights on a day of battle' (vv. 1-3).
But while most scholars connect the 'Day of Yahweh' with
Yahweh's victory for Israel in the day of battle [2] others
conceive of it differently. Gressmann, as we have noted,
connects its origin with an eschatology of weal and woe
which, he claims, was common to the ancient Semitic world.
Mowinckel, on the other hand, argues that the Day of
Yahweh 'originally means the day of Yahweh's manifestation
in the festal cult at the New Year Festival'. [3] Hölscher had
earlier advocated a cultic origin for the Day of Yahweh

Concept of the Day of Yahweh' (*J.S.S.*, 4, 1959, pp. 97-108) contended
that it 'was by no means originally eschatological' (p. 106).

[1] *The Church of Israel*, 1933, p. 177.

[2] See, e.g., H. W. Robinson, *Inspiration and Revelation in the Old
Testament*, p. 138. Cf. also J. M. Powis Smith, *American Journal of
Theology*, 5, 3, 1901, pp. 505-533. Von Rad likewise connects the phrase
with the tradition 'of the holy wars of Yahweh in the ancient history
of Israel', *loc. cit.*, p. 108.

[3] *Op. cit.*, p. 132.

in Amos 5 : 18 [1], and Mowinckel similarly interprets this
passage. Regarding the material of verses 18b-19 as an
explanatory addition, he points to the close connexion
between the Day of Yahweh and the cult as is evidenced by
verses 20-23 which are in fact a denunciation of the cult. [2]
The genuine utterance of Amos therefore was:

> Woe to you who desire the day of Yahweh!
> Why would you have the day of Yahweh?
> Is not the day of Yahweh darkness, and not light,
> and gloom with no brightness in it?

On the assumption that the Israelites experienced the coming
of Yahweh on the occasion of the New Year Festival, when
the divine presence assured them of victory over their
enemies and good fortune in life, Mowinckel thinks that
whenever they encountered trouble they longed for the
day when Yahweh would again manifest himself to them.
'In so far then', he says, as the Day of Yahweh 'might denote
any appearance of Yahweh to save and bless, we may speak
of the beginning of the separation of the idea from the cultic
festival'. [3] Mowinckel's emphasis on the fact that the Day
of Yahweh appears in Amos 5 in a cultic context is certainly
worthy of attention, but his interpretation of the passage
as a whole presupposes the existence of a New Year Festival
in ancient Israel. This is, however, a supposition not shared
by all scholars, and the festival is not mentioned with the
three main feasts of the Hebrew calendar in Exodus
23 : 14-17 although Mowinckel associates the feast of Harvest
with the New Year Festival. [4] Yet Mowinckel finds consi-

---

[1] *Die Ursprünge der jüdischen Eschatologie*, 1925, pp. 12 f.
[2] *Op. cit.*, p. 132 and n. 4.
[3] Pp. 132-133.
[4] p. 98. Cf. also Zech. 14 : 16-17, where we read that the giving of
rain is dependent on the annual attendance at the Feast of Tabernacles
in Jerusalem.

derable support for his theory of an Israelite New Year Festival in the many Psalms which refer to the enthroning of Yahweh. [1] It is, moreover, established beyond doubt that there was a New Year Festival in Babylon [2] and a similar festival in ancient Ras Shamra, [3] while the reference to 'the day of appointed festival and . . . the day of the feast of Yahweh' in Hosea 9 : 5 suggests that an important festival was also observed in ancient Israel.

But whatever the origin of the term 'Day of Yahweh' there is no evidence that it was used in pre-exilic times in an eschatological sense. Its occurrence in Amos 5 : 18 has of course often been cited as proof that it was used in this sense before the time of the great prophets. [4] It is moreover interesting that Mowinckel himself at one time adhered to this view and in his *Psalmenstudien* II he expressed the opinion that eschatology was an early development in Israelite thought (pp. 318 f.). In his *Han som Kommer*, however, which appeared in 1951, he retracts this view as being erroneous and says there is in Amos 5 : 18 'no reference to an eschatological day of Yahweh at some indefinite point in the future'. [5] The expression rather refers to contemporary cultic practice and to the emotional experience arising from it. Further, although Amos uses the term he does so in an ironical sense; for, far from Yahweh appearing to

---

[1] *Psalmenstudien* II. *Das Thronbesteigungsfest Jahwäs und der Ursprung der Eschatologie*, 1922. Cf., e.g., Psalms 24 : 7-10; 47 : 1-8; 48 : 2; 95 : 3.

[2] See H. Frankfort, *op. cit.*, pp. 313 ff.

[3] See John Gray, 'Canaanite Kingship in Theory and Practice', *V.T.*, 2, 3, 1952, pp. 193-220; Ivan Engnell, *Studies in Divine Kingship in the Ancient Near East*, 1945, pp. 149-173.

[4] E.g., R. B. Y. Scott, *The Relevance of the Prophets*, 1944, p. 128; C. R. North, *The Old Testament Interpretation of History*, 1946, p. 126. So in this context H. E. W. Fosbroke refers to "the final coming of God in power', *Interpreter's Bible*, 6, 1956. p. 817.

[5] As translated in *He That Cometh*, p. 131.

deliver his people in distress, his presence will rather mean the discomfiture and punishment of the sinful and arrogant.

But if we fail to discern any eschatological content in the Day of Yahweh as used by Amos we may wonder if there is anything else in his work which might be regarded as such. The picture of Yahweh visiting and punishing his people is, indeed, a prominent feature of his prophecy, but, as we shall see, such visitations are effected in the temporal order by human and natural agencies and therefore can scarcely be termed eschatological.

Foremost amongst the means of punishment conceived by Amos is the destruction of the nation by an invading army. Israel is censured because she does 'not know how to do right' and for the 'violence and robbery' which she commits; 'therefore thus says the Lord God:

'an adversary shall surround the land,
and bring down your defences from you,
and your strongholds shall be plundered' (3 : 11).

There will be little point in opposing this enemy, for such is the terror he inspires that

'flight shall perish from the swift
and the strong shall not retain his strength,
nor shall the mighty save his life;
he who handles the bow shall not stand . . .
nor shall he who rides the horse save his life' (2 : 14 f).

In 6 : 14 we likewise read:

'For behold, I will raise up against you a nation,
O house of Israel, says the Lord . . .
and they shall oppress you from the entrance
of Hamath to the Brook of the Arabah'.

The Israelites will, however, not only be invaded, but will also suffer the humiliation of deportation. We thus hear of Israel going 'into exile away from its land' (7 : 17) and also of the people going 'into captivity before their enemies' (9 : 4). The enemy is not actually mentioned by name,[1] but when Amos speaks of Israel going 'into exile beyond Damascus' (5 : 17) it must have been clear to his contemporaries that Assyria was in his mind. The reference to the 'entrance of Hamath' could, again, only indicate that the foe would come from the direction of Assyria.

It might of course be objected that when Amos was preaching, Assyria could scarcely be regarded as constituting a threat to Israel. Amos is generally thought of as being active in or around the decade 760-750 B.C. [2] But this dating largely rests on chapter 7 : 10 which states that the prophet visited Bethel during the reign of Jeroboam II, and according to the generally accepted chronology this king died as early as 746. [3] There is, however, no decisive evidence for such a date. We can at most claim to be suggestive in the difficult field of Old Testament chronology but we may make a computation on the basis of the definite date of Jehu's tribute to Shalmaneser III in the year 841 as attested by Assyrian records. [4] On the assumption that Jehu made this tribute at the beginning of his twenty-eight year reign,[5] then, according to the figures of Second Kings, the number of years which elapsed between his accession and the death

---

[1] In 3 : 9 the R.S.V., following the LXX, reads 'Proclaim to the strongholds of Assyria'. The M.T., however, reads 'Ashdod'.

[2] So, e.g., W. F. Albright (*The Biblical Period*, 1950, p. 39) places his call in about 752, while, thinking that 8 : 9 alludes to a solar eclipse which according to Assyrian records occurred in 763, B. D. Eerdmans places it as early as that date, *The Religion of Israel*, 1947, pp. 146, 149.

[3] So, e.g., Albright, *ibid*.

[4] See D. J. Wiseman, *Documents from Old Testament Times*, 1958, pp. 46-49.

[5] See M. Noth, *The History of Israel*, Eng. trans. 1958, p. 246; E. R. Thiele, *The Mysterious Numbers of the Hebrew Kingdoms*, 1951, p. 53.

of Jeroboam II was 102.[1] On this calculation Jeroboam died in the year 739.

We further read in the superscription to the Book that Amos was called to his office within the reign of 'Uzziah king of Judah ... two years before the earthquake'. The Begrich Chronology places Uzziah's death in 747 [2] although Albright brings it as late as 742. [3] But if we identify Uzziah, or Azariah as he is also called (2 Kgs. 15), with *Azriau of Yaudi* who was active in North Syria during the western campaigns of Tiglath-Pileser III, then he must have been alive as late as 739. [4] It is again conceivable that the earthquake referred to in the superscription may be that mentioned by Josephus in his account of Uzziah's reign. According to this account an earthquake occurred after Uzziah, against the consent of his priests, offered incense in the temple and for which he was stricken with leprosy. [5] This presumptuous act of Uzziah and his consequent affliction with leprosy is also mentioned by the Chronicler (2 Chron. 26 : 18-21). If however the earthquake in question occurred at this juncture of Uzziah's life it must presumably have been towards the end of his reign and probably around 740. [6]

---

[1] In 2 Kgs. 10 : 36; 13 : 1; 13 : 10 and 14 : 23 we respectively read that Jehu reigned 28 years, Jehoahaz 17, Jehoash 16 and Jeroboam II 41, a total of 102.

[2] As presented in *The Westminster Historical Atlas to the Bible*, 1946, p. 15.

[3] *Op. cit.*, p. 39.

[4] See Wiseman, *op. cit.*, p. 56, and Noth, *op. cit.*, p. 257 n. 3. cf. also Thiele, *op. cit.*, pp. 78 ff., and p. 98.

[5] *Antiquities* 9 : 10, 4.

[6] We read that after being stricken with disease Uzziah was confined in a separate house and that his son, Jotham, assumed the burden of government (2 Kgs. 15 : 5), but as he was only 25 years old when he began his reign (2 Kgs. 15 : 23) his regency can scarcely have been more than a few years.

The call of Amos two years before this event would accordingly be in the year 742 B.C. [1]

If this, then, is the most probable date for Amos it is likely that it was the threatening menace of Assyria which primarily moved him to prophesy. In the year 745 Tiglath-Pileser III usurped the Assyrian throne and immediately undertook a series of eastern campaigns. [2] By 743 his armies appeared in the Syrian state of Arpad and he received tribute from Rezin of Damascus and other western rulers. The indolent leaders of Israel (6 : 1 ff.) were indifferent to the consequences of these movements by Assyria, but the far-seeing Amos discerned that in a few years Israel must be invaded. [3] We may therefore assume that it was this critical development in the political history of Syria-Palestine which was the signal for Amos' call to prophesy a year or two later. Discussing the reasons which urged the prophet to his task H. W. Hogg wrote: 'The most natural explanation is that one of the burning questions of the hour was: 'What is Assyria going to do? Will it or will it not come on southwards ... Amos' answer is clear and decided: Yes, the Assyrian will: For triple, nay quadruple iniquity, says Yahweh, I will not turn him back" ...'. [4] It will be observed that this last sentence is Hogg's translation of the refrain which appears so often in the first two chapters of the Book, and which in Hebrew runs thus:

כה אמר יהוה על שלשה פשעי ...
ועל ארבעה לא אשיבנו

---

[1] See here also R. S. Cripps, *op. cit.*, pp. 34-41.

[2] See A. T. Olmstead, *History of Assyria*, 1923, pp. 177 f.

[3] Cripps makes the interesting suggestion that 'Amos selling the wool of his sheep at Damascus would hear the stories about Tiglath-Pileser, convincing him that a new age in Assyrian history had begun', *op. cit.*, p. 37.

[4] 'The Starting-Point of the Religious Message of Amos' in *Transactions of the Third International Congress of the History of Religions*, 1908, 1, pp. 325-327.

The usual translation is, 'Thus says the Lord: For three transgressions . . . and for four I will not revoke the punishment' (*R.S.V.*), but a rendering which emphasises the fact and incidence of sin seems more acceptable in view of the context. It would accordingly seem that it was the Assyrian peril rather than any eschatological expectation which impelled Amos to prophesy, and which indeed remained a dominant theme throughout his preaching.

But in addition to the Assyrian menace Amos also represents the divine visitation in terms of plagues and similar afflictions. Thus in 4 : 10 we find a reference to a 'pestilence after the manner of Egypt', while in 5 : 16-17 there will be much wailing in the streets and public places. According to 6 : 9-10 death mysteriously claims its victims and in 8 : 3 we read, 'the dead bodies shall be many; in every place they shall be cast out in silence'. The prophet's portrait of coming doom further includes the blighting effect of mildew on vineyards and the devouring of the fig and olive by locusts (4 : 9). But such disasters are for the most part normal and frequent occurrences in nature and have here no eschatological significance.

Some writers, however, claim to recognise an allusion to earthquakes in certain passages, and interpret them as evidence for the view that Amos was thinking in terms of a universal catastrophe. Thus, the verse in which Yahweh says 'I will press you down in your place' (2 : 13) is thought by Sellin to refer to an earthquake of world-wide dimensions.[1] But it is obvious from the context that the words apply to the devastation which will be caused by impending war. There appears, of course, to be a reference to a disaster in the natural realm in 8 : 8:

---

[1] *Das Zwölfprophetenbuch*, 1922, *ad loc*. So H. E. W. Fosbroke regards this verse as pertaining to 'the final catastrophe', *loc. cit.*, p. 790.

'Shall not the land tremble on this account,
and every one mourn who dwells in it,
and all of it rise like the Nile,
and be tossed about and sink again
like the Nile of Egypt?'

But it is doubtful if this verse follows easily on 8 : 7 which
seems rather to find its natural sequence in 8 : 10. The fact,
moreover, that the material of 8b also appears in 9 : 5-6
casts doubt on its authenticity. The late character of 9 : 5-6
is in itself obvious, and in any case it is questionable if it
were consonant with the theology and purpose of Amos to
say:

'The Lord, the God of hosts,
he who touches the earth and it melts . . .
and all of it rises like the Nile,
and sinks again like the Nile of Egypt;
who builds his upper chambers in the heavens,
and founds his vault upon the earth;
who calls for the waters of the sea,
and pours them out upon the surface of the earth . . .'

The picture of the earth melting before Yahweh is found
in the late composition of Psalm 46 (vs. 6), while the notion
of Yahweh building his chambers in the heavens and foun-
ding his vault upon the earth is reminiscent of the thought
of Deutero-Isaiah (e.g. 40 : 21-22). Writers like Gressmann,
then, who see such passages as evidence for claiming that
there was an eschatological element in the teaching of
Amos do so on precarious grounds. [1] The passage 'I will
make the sun go down at noon and darken the earth in
broad daylight' (8 : 9) is likewise regarded as an allusion
to a solar eclipse, and therefore as supporting the theory
that Amos conceived of Yahweh's intervention in the na-

---

[1] H. Gressmann, *Die älteste Geschichtschreibung und Prophetie von Israel*,
1910, pp. 327, 356. Cf. also S. B. Frost, *op. cit.*, pp. 49, 56.

tural order in terms of eschatology.[1] This passage is, however, not only suspect in its present context but, because it begins with the characteristically late expression 'On that Day'.

Nor can we base any eschatological claims for Amos on the Epilogue to the present Book (9 : 11-15)[2] which outlines the blissful state of Judah's existence at a future date. Beginning with the words 'In that day I will raise up the booth of David that is fallen and . . . raise up its ruins' it proceeds to mention the restoration of the fortunes of Israel, the rebuilding of her cities and the reclamation of her gardens and vineyards. The late authorship of the passage is, however, commonly recognised by critical students of the Old Testament.[3] The reference to the restoration of the house of David could scarcely be a relevant theme in the mouth of a prophet who was ministering in the northern kingdom, while mention of the breaches and ruins in a context pertaining to Judah presupposes the Babylonian destruction of the land in 586. The post-exilic date of the passage is further emphasised in the final verse which represents Yahweh as saying, 'I will plant them upon their land, and they shall never again be plucked up out of the land which I have given them'.

When we consider Hosea we, likewise, find little evidence of an eschatological trait in his teaching. We hear of Israel's

---

[1] Gressmann, *ibid.* So of 8 : 8-9 C. R. North comments 'What Amos seems to envisage is convulsions of nature on something like a cosmic scale. It is genuine eschatology; Yahweh is "Lord of the End of Things"', *op. cit.*, pp. 126 f. Fosbroke also thinks that we have here 'the idea of an earthquake of far-reaching effect as one of the woes accompanying the great day of final judgment', *loc. cit.*, p. 842.

[2] Sellin (*Das Zwölfprophetenbuch*, p. 225) and E. König (*Geschichte der Alttestamentlichen Religion*, 1924, pp. 343 f.) are amongst those who defended the authenticity of the passage.

[3] See, e.g., W. R. Harper, *Amos, I.C.C.*, 1905, pp. 195 ff.; R. H. Pfeiffer, *Introd. to the Old Test.*, p. 580.

'desolation in the day of punishment' (5 : 9), but this is a punishment which will be inflicted by a marauding army as is denoted by 11 : 5-6:

> Assyria shall be their king . . .
> The sword shall rage against their cities,
> consume the bars of their gates;
> and devour them in their fortresses'.

That this humiliation is due to Israel's sin and disobedience is equally clear from such passages as 10 : 13-14 where we read:

> 'You have ploughed iniquity, you have reaped injustice . . .
> therefore the tumult of war shall rise against your people,
> and all your fortresses shall be destroyed'.

There is, however, no eschatological implication in the destruction and doom envisaged here. Even 1 : 5 which speaks of the 'day' in which Yahweh will break the bow of Israel in the valley of Jezreel, refers, as the context indicates, to the political end of the northern kingdom. We find, indeed, references to 'that day' throughout 2 : 16-21 but whatever meaning we attach to the phrase we can scarcely claim that this material derives from Hosea.

Isaiah is especially regarded as a prophet with an eschatological message. And a passage which is often cited as affording particular evidence for this view is 2 : 12-21: [1]

> 'For the Lord of hosts has a day
> against all that is proud and lofty . . .
> against all the cedars of Lebanon, lofty and lifted up . . .
> against all the high mountains,
> and against all the lofty hills . . .
> against all the ships of Tarshish
> and against all the beautiful craft.

---

[1] Cf. C. R. North, *op. cit.*, p. 217, and S. B. Frost, *op. cit.*, p. 51. So R. B. Y. Scott regards 2 : 12-17 as 'one of Isaiah's earliest messages', *Interpreter's Bible*, 5, p. 185.

And the haughtiness of man shall be humbled . . .
and Yahweh alone will be exalted in that day . . .
In that day men will cast forth their idols of silver
and their idols of gold, which they made for themselves
to worship, to the moles and to the bats,
to enter the caverns of the rocks and clefts of the cliffs,
from before the terror of Yahweh, and from the glory of
his majesty, when he rises to terrify the earth'.

Mowinckel, indeed, remarks that because of its indefinite appellation the 'day' mentioned here has not yet a definite eschatological meaning.[1] But this judgment is valid only if we regard the passage as Isaianic. The references to the cedars of Lebanon recall late passages such as 14 : 8 and 66 : 13, while the high mountains and the lofty hills are reminiscent of the 'lofty mountain and high hill' of the post-exilic verse 30 : 28. The 'ships of Tarshish' of verse 16 seem, likewise, to have a thematic connection with the late oracle against Tyre in chapter 23. The fact, moreover, that chapter 2 begins with an ideal picture of Zion 'in the latter days' suggests that the chapter as a whole is composed of late material. References to 'that day' further appear throughout the Book (e.g., 3 : 18; 4 : 2; 10 : 20; 11 : 10 ff.) but these again are in contexts which are in the nature of post-exilic glosses and interpolations.[2]

The Book of Micah opens with the words:

'Hear, you peoples, all of you,
hearken, O earth, and all that is in it;
and let the Lord God be a witness against you,
the Lord from his holy temple,
For behold, the Lord is coming forth out of his place,
and will come down and tread upon the high places
of the earth. And the mountains will melt under him

---

[1] *Op. cit.*, p. 133, n. 1.
[2] See, e.g., R. H. Pfeiffer, *Religion in the Old Testament*, 1961, p. 122.

and the valleys will be cleft like wax before the fire,
like waters poured down a steep place'.

There is, however, a universality in these words which hardly justify attributing them to Micah. The picture of Yahweh treading upon the high places of the earth is suggestive of Deut. 32 : 13 and Isaiah 58 : 14, while the notion of the mountains melting before him recall such late compositions as Psalm 97 and Nahum 1 : 5. We find in chapter 2 a declaration of woe against those who devise wickedness and are guilty of social evils, and Yahweh himself says:

'Behold, against this family I am devising evil,
from which you cannot remove your necks;
and you shall not walk haughtily,
for it will be an evil time (v. 3).'

That there is a reference here to coming evils is clear, but there is nothing to suggest that the verse should be interpreted eschatologically. Verse 4, indeed, declares

'In that day they shall take up a taunt song
against you and wail with bitter lamentation'

but this material has no logical connexion with what precedes. Similar references to 'that day' appear in 4 : 6 and 8 : 10, but these, again, are clearly of post-exilic origin.

According to the Book of Zephaniah the day of Yahweh is one of punishment for indifference to ethical standards (1 : 7 ff.), and the inhabitants of Jerusalem are the special objects of the divine wrath. We thus read:

'The great day of the Lord is near,
near and hastening fast . . .
a day of wrath is that day, a day of distress and anguish,
a day of ruin and devastation, a day of darkness and gloom,
a day of clouds and thick darkness, a day of trumpet blast
and battle cry against the fortified cities
and against the lofty battlements (1 : 14-16).'

This passage may derive from Zephaniah himself and hence
may be a contemporary reference to an invasion of Judah;
but whatever its origin its conception of the day of Yahweh
is in all essentials the same as Amos' representation of it
as a day of darkness and gloom. Verse 17 which speaks of
distress coming on men 'because they have sinned against
the Lord' may be a continuation of this theme, but verse
18 is obviously later, for the reference to 'all the earth' and
its inhabitants presupposes a universality unknown in
Israel before the teaching of Deutero-Isaiah. It is, moreover,
of the same provenance as 3 : 8 which is itself clearly
post-exilic:

> Therefore wait for me, says the Lord,
> for the day when I arise as a witness.
> For my decision is to gather nations, to assemble kingdoms,
> to pour out upon them my indignation, all the heat of my
>   anger;
> for in the fire of my jealous wrath
> all the earth shall be consumed.'

Such considerations, then, lead us to the conclusion that
there is nothing of an eschatological nature in the genuine
utterances of the great prophets. These men neither reflect an
indebtness to Babylonian sentiments of hope and fear, nor
yet accepted the popular conception of the Day of Yahweh.
Nor indeed can we see how eschatology could be essential
to the purpose of their message. For their concern was
mainly with the course of contemporary events. As Mowinckel says, 'their starting point was always the given,
concrete, historical situation, and nearly always the political
situation'. [1] If they had an interest in the future it was in the
immediate future as it arose out of the present. But it was
chiefly to interpret the events of the present that Yahweh

---

[1] *Op. cit.*, p. 131.

called them. Hence, the call of every great prophet is without exception connected with an historical crisis. The people were asked to turn their attention to the events of the moment and to discern in them the course of future developments. They thus proclaim Yahweh as acting and speaking to the immediate situation; and although sinful Israel deserves defeat and destruction, yet if she even now observes Yahweh's word she may 'live'. As Amos pleaded, 'Seek Yahweh and live, lest he break out like fire in the house of Joseph and devour it' (5 : 6). But it is the continuance of the normal earthly life hitherto lived in the land of Palestine, albeit a life more in accordance with the divine will. In Hosea we similarly find that though Israel's sinfulness involves the divine punishment it is not the end of her existence on earth. The Israelites will continue to live but under reduced circumstances. Yahweh 'would redeem them but they speak lies against' him (7 : 13). For this reason 'the sword shall rage against their cities . . . and devour them in their fortresses' (11 : 5-6). So it is with Isaiah. The people are condemned for their social and religious standards (1 : 11 ff.; 5 : 8, 11 f.) and there will be a consequent 'day of punishment in the storm which will come from afar' (10 : 3). Assyria will effect this punishment, but life will go on for the inhabitants of Judah, though they will be a chastened and more subdued people (10 : 5 f.). It is, thus, not Isaiah himself but a man of a later age who wrote 'the Lord of hosts will make a full end . . . in the midst of all the earth' (10 : 23).

Jeremiah is, again, primarily concerned with speaking a word in season to the Judeans of his day. He foresees doom and destruction, but this is not such as will bring the world to an end. Yahweh 'will utter . . . judgments' (1 : 16) against his people but this is to take the form of discomfiture at the hands of the invading Chaldeans. The majority of the nation will be carried to Babylon but this, again, will not mean the end of life for them. On the contrary, in his letter to the exiles Jeremiah counsels that they should adapt themselves to life in Babylon and make their homes there. It is thus noteworthy that a prophet who was convinced of the imminent end of the nation (7 : 12 ff.; 32 : 27 ff.) should envisage the Judeans living and prospering in another land. Even after the national upheaval Jeremiah assumes that life will continue in Palestine, for he speaks of ultimately possessing family property (32 : 8 ff.) and said 'houses and fields and vineyards shall again be bought in this land' (32 : 15). He regarded the destruction of the nation essential to the advancement of the spiritual life of Israel, but nowhere does he contemplate the cessation of the material order of existence. In other words he does not think in terms of eschatology. [1] And it is equally significant that his conception of man's ideal relationship with God, as transmitted to us in the words of the New Covenant (31 : 31-34), is likewise expressed in terms of life experienced on the earthly plane. He envisages no vague celestial union with God. It is rather life on this earth, where each man will live in full accord with the divine law.

This, then, was the nature of the message of the pre-exilic prophets. In it there is no indication that they visualised in any form the sudden, catastrophic ending of the temporal order. Nor is it likely that such an expectation was entertained even by the popular mind of the day. For eschatology implies a sense of frustration with the present order of existence and a consequent yearning for its end and

---

[1] The passage describing the earth returning to chaos and desolation before Yahweh's anger (4 : 23-26) is, of course, not Jeremiah's, although Frost (*op. cit.*, p. 53) accepts it as genuine and as being 'eschatological in the absolute sense'.

the immediate inauguration of another. But, while we have no evidence that this was the prevalent mood in pre-exilic times, we hear much of the disillusionment and disappointment of the Jews who returned from Babylon. Not only were the city walls and the temple in ruins (Hag. 1 : 9; Neh. 1 : 3) but famine and poverty were widespread (Hag. 1 : 6; Neh. 5 : 1-5). Realising, however, that their circumstances would not readily change on this earth, the Jews now visualised a day in the future when Yahweh would directly act on their behalf. Typical of this hope is a passage in Zephaniah which reads:

> 'On that day it shall be said to Jerusalem:
> Do not fear, O Zion, let not your hands grow weak.
> The Lord, your God, is in your midst,
> a warrior who gives victory . . .
> he will exult over you with loud singing
> as on a day of festival . . .
> At that time I will bring you home,
> at the time when I gather you together;
> yea, I will make you renowned and praised
> among all the peoples of the earth,
> when I restore your fortunes before your eyes
> says the Lord (3 : 16-20)'. [1]

The day when Yahweh manifests himself is now also referred to in terms of the destruction of the earth and its inhabitants (Zeph. 1 : 18; Is. 10 : 23), while we further read of a day when Yahweh will exercise his rule over all the earth (Zech. 14 : 9). Another distinctive feature of the day of the divine activity at this period is the judgment of mankind and the subsequent punishment of the wicked. According to Isaiah 66 : 15-66 'Yahweh will come in fire' and 'execute judgment upon all flesh', while in the Book of

---

[1] So in Micah 7 : 11 we hear of 'a day for the building of your walls'. See also Zeph. 12 : 1 ff.

Malachi we read: 'For behold, the day comes, burning like an oven, when all the arrogant and all evildoers will be stubble; the day that comes shall burn them up, says the Lord of hosts, so that it will leave them neither root nor branch. But for you who fear my name the sun of righteousness shall rise with healing in its wings. You shall go forth leaping like calves from the stall. And you shall tread down the wicked, for they will be ashes under the soles of your feet, on the day when I act, says the Lord of hosts' (4 : 1-3).

It is probable that Persian influence underlies this view of the ultimate destiny of the good and evil. [1] At any rate we read in the Gathas of Zoroaster that through Mazda's 'Ordeal of blazing fire and molten metal to be held up as a sign in the two existences of this world and the next, Destruction' will come 'upon the Followers of the Druj, Blessings upon the Followers of Asha'. [2] But, however this may be, we find in certain writings of the post-exilic age, and particularly in Apocalyptic literature, such notions as the destruction of the earth before the presence of Yahweh, the inauguration of a kingdom in which his will is universally acknowledged, and a day in which judgment is passed on all mankind. And in such concepts it may perhaps be claimed that we reach a stage in Judaic thought which might be termed 'eschatological'. [3]

---

[1] On the question of Persian influence on Jewish Apocalypse and Eschatology see Oesterley and Robinson, *Hebrew Religion*, pp. 388 ff.

[2] Yasna 51 : 9 as translated by D. F. M. Bode and P. Nanavutty in *Songs of Zarathustra*, 1952, p. 100.

[3] However, after examining passages as late as Daniel chapter 12 R. H. Kennett concluded: 'It is my firm conviction that eschatology is not found in the *canonical* Scriptures of the Old Testament, and that it has its origin in later books written in imitation of these Scriptures which ... were not canonised by the Jewish Church', *op. cit.*, p. 186.

INDEX

Subjects

Achan, 130
Adad-Nirari III, 102n
Ahaz, 40, 107
Ahura-Mazda, 151n, 220
Akhenaton, 193
Amarna Age, 93
Amaziah, 103, 176
Ammon, 115, 119
Amos, 33, 47, 52ff, 60f, 75f, 103ff;
  date of, 207ff
Arameans, 105
Asshur, 101, 102, 200
Assyria, 102, 108, 109, 111

Baal, 45, 46; cult of, 54, 78
Baal-zebub, god of Ekron, 101
Babylon, 1, 111, 115; gods of, 121ff
Balaam, 2
Beersheba, 74
Bel, 122
Bel-Marduk, 196
Bethel, 74, 103, 176

Caphtor, 104, 105n
Carchemish, 41, 110
Chaldeans, 110, 111, 112f
Chemosh, god, 45, 100, 101, 119
Chesed, 79, 160n, 172
Covenant, 25ff; new, 165f, 218
Creation, Deutero-Isaiah and, 119ff
Cult, the prophets and, 63ff
Cyrus, 119, 121, 123, 187, 188, 191,
  196

Dagon, god, 2
David, 101, 132, 135
Day of Yahweh, 49f, 202ff
Deborah, Song of, 29, 101
Decalogue, Ritual, 76
Deuteronomy, 33, 89f
Divine justice, 129ff; Jeremiah and,
  137ff; Ezekiel and, 143ff; Deutero-

Isaiah and, 148ff
Dry bones, valley of, 169f
Dualism, 151

Ecstasy, 6ff
Edom, 116
Egypt, 33, 108, 110, 117, 187
El (Baal) Berith, 27, 46
Elijah, 3, 60, 101, 133
Elisha, 3, 132
Enuma Elish, Babylonian epic of
  creation, 97n, 125n, 128n
Eschatology, pre-exilic prophets and,
  199ff; definition of, 202
Ethiopia, 104, 105
Exiles, 41ff, 129, 131, 143f, 148f
Ezekiel, 34, 35, 42f, 115f; date of, 115

Forgiveness, divine, 164, 169, 174
Future hope, Jewish, 202

Gilgal, 74, 78
Gomer, 160n
Grace, divine, 161, 165ff, 170f
Greeks, 125

Hebrews, Epistle to the, 92
Hezekiah, 109
History, God and, 102ff
Hosea, 34, 46, 56ff, 61, 105f; date
  of, 103

Idols, the prophets and, 114, 121ff
Individualism, 132ff, 146f
Individual responsibility, 137, 144ff
Isaiah, 40, 61, 79f, 106ff; date of
  call, 106n; Isaiah ch. 6, 71f, 176n

Jehoiakim, 111
Jeremiah, 20ff, 34, 40ff, 48, 62, 77f,
  110ff; date of, 110
Jeroboam II, 103, 207

Jezebel, 133
Jezreel, 106, 213
Josiah, 110

Karkar, 102
Kir, 104

Lachish Letters, 5n, 113n
Lex talionis, 134, 136
Lydians, 119, 125

Malachi, Book of, 220
Marduk, 122, 128
Medes, 110, 119
Megiddo, 110
Melkart, 119
Mercy, divine, 143, 159f, 166f, 172f
Micah, Book of, 80f, 214
Milcom, god, 45, 119
Miriam, 135
Moabite Stone, 100n
Monotheism, 95ff; Deutero-Isaiah and, 125ff
Morality, the prophets and, 52ff
Moses, 31f, 93f, 98, 100

Nabi, meaning of, 4f
Nahum, Book of, 215
Name, Babylonian doctrine of, 97n, 127; Yahweh's, 169
Nature, the prophets' view of, 46ff
Nebiim, 4, 10ff
Nebo, god, 122
Nebuchadrezzar, 40, 110, 111, 113, 116, 122
Necho, 110
Nephesh, 16
New Year Festival, 197, 204f

Patriarchs, 93
Pekah, 107
Persians, 125
Pharaoh, 118
Philistia, 116
Philistines, 104, 105
Phineas, 135
Priests, 41, 69, 72
Prophecy, in ancient Near East, 2; in ancient Israel, 3; true and false, 18ff

Prophets, originality of canonical, 24 ff, 39ff; false, 69f
Psammetichus II, 115

Rabshakeh, 39, 40, 109
Repentance, the prophets and, 155ff
Revelation, the prophets and, 23
Rezin, 106, 209
Right, Righteousness, 52f; Deutero-Isaiah's conception of, 58 ff
Rimmon, god, 45
Ruach, 16

Sacrifice, the prophets and, 132ff
Salvation, 171, 173
Samaria, 104
Saul, 76, 133
Scythians, 110
Seba, 187
Servant of Yahweh, 182ff
Servant Songs, 178ff
Shalmaneser III, 207
Shamash, god, 102n
Sin, the prophets' view of, 152ff
Sinai, 28, 32, 99
Suffering, problem of, 191f; vicarious, 192ff
Syrians, 105
Syro-Ephraimite war, 106f, 109

Temple, Jeremiah and, 41, 83, 85
Theodicy, problem of, 148ff
Tiglath-Pileser III, 102, 103n, 105n, 107, 208
Tradition, the prophets and, 25ff, 36
Tyre, 116, 117

Uzziah, 208

Vine, wild, Ezekiel and, 167f
Visions, prophetic, 13, 23

Word, of Yahweh, 38f
worship, non-cultic, 84

Yahweh, meaning of term, 95ff; and morality, 49ff; relationship with Israel, 34f

Zechariah, Book of, 87

Zedekiah, 112

Zephaniah, Book of, 215f, 219

Zoroaster, 126, 220

Authors

Albright, W. F., 2n, 4, 26, 94, 96, 107n, 207n

Anderson, G. W., 50n

Arnold, W. R., 5, 97

Balla, E., 189n

Begrich, J., 190, 208

Bertholet, A., 189

Bienemann, G. A., 154n

Blank, S. H., 20n, 186, 188n

Bode, D. F. M., 220n

Bollier, J. A., 53n

Bowman, J., 96

Bright, J., 32n, 94, 95n

Brown, P. E., 26

Burney, C. F., 101n

Černý, J., 199n

Charles, R. H., 199

Cheyne, T. K., 136n

Condamin, A., 188n

Contenau, G., 97n

Cook, S. A., 24, 52, 55n, 61n, 129n

Corhill, C. H., 94

Cripps, R. S., 9, 16n, 36n, 67n, 202n, 209n

Davidson, A. B., 155n, 199

Dodds, E. R., 2n

Driver, G. R., 95

Driver, S. R., 28n, 191n

Duhm, B., 165n, 178, 184n, 188, 189

Dürr, L, 197

Eerdmans, B. D., 66n, 207n

Eichrodt, W., 28, 144n

Eissfeldt, O., 185

Elmslie, W. A. L., 85n

Engnell, I., 70, 205n

Farley, A., 188n

Farr, G., 160n

Finkelstein, L., 131n

Fischer, J., 183n

Fohrer, G., 15n

Fosbroke, H. E. W., 205n, 210n, 212n

Frankfort, H., 200n, 201n, 205n

Frost, S., 199n, 202, 211n, 218n

von Gall, A., 200

Galling, K., 30

Gordis, R., 47n

Gordon, C. H., 93

Gottwald, N. K., 150n

Graham, W. C., 24, 100n

Gray, G. B., 82

Gray, J., 205n

Gressmann, H., 2n, 199, 203, 211

Guillaume, A., 4, 8

Gunkel, H., 67

Halder, A., 2n, 8, 18, 70, 71, 73

Haller, M., 189n

Harper, W. R., 105n, 212n

Hempel, J., 96, 196n

Hertzberg, H. W., 53n

Heschel, A., 9

Hogg, H. W., 209

Hölscher, G., 2n, 4n, 6, 12, 18n, 64, 89n, 203

Hooke, S. H., 84

van Hoonacker, A., 188n

Horst, F., 47n

Hyatt, J. P., 22n, 65, 77n, 136n

Irwin, W. A., 23n, 25, 27, 44n, 137n, 147n

James, F., 95

Jepsen, A., 2n, 6n, 9, 10

Jeremias, A., 200

Johnson, A. R., 68n

Josephus, 208

Junker, H., 67

Kaplan, M. M., 71n

Kaufmann, Y., 95

Kautzsch, E., 63, 79n, 83n, 95

Kennett, R. H., 64, 79n, 184n, 189n, 203, 220n

Keunen, A., 4
Kittel, R., 154n
Klein, W. C., 7, 16n, 22
Knight, H., 7, 12n, 16n, 18n, 19n
Knobel, A., 6
Koehler, L., 28, 133
König, E., 212n

Lattey,C., 75, 77n, 79
Lods, A., 5 7, 98n, 99n

Malamat, A., 110n
Marti, K., 153n
Matthews, I. G., 9, 65, 89n
Mattuck, I. I., 44n
May, H. G., 54n
McFadyen, J. E., 64
Meek, T. J., 4, 72, 96, 99n, 100
Mendenhall, G. E., 25, 29
Meyer, E., 27
Micklem, R. C., 154n
Montefiore, C. G., 85
Montgomery, J. A., 135n, 136n, 148n
Moore, G. F., 101n
Morgenstern, J., 105n, 123n
Mowinckel, S., 22n, 49, 67, 189, 190, 200, 203f, 214, 216
Muilenburg, J., 28, 59n, 184n, 186

Nanavutty, P., 220n
Nehrer, A., 2n
Neubauer, A., 191n
North, C. R., 183n, 184n, 185n, 188n, 196n, 205n, 207n, 212n
Noth, M., 2n, 28, 32n, 146n, 207n

Obbink, H. T., 13n
Obermann, J., 96
Oesterley, W. O. E., 66, 74n, 75, 99n, 220n
Olmstead, A. T., 209n
Orlinsky, H. M., 26n, 35n, 93

Paterson, J., 66
Patterson, C. H., 147n
Payne, E. A., 160n
Peake, A. S., 146n, 147, 148n
Pedersen, J., 16, 68, 72, 169n
Pfeiffer, R. H., 2n, 5, 27, 31n, 47n, 76, 88, 89, 97n, 127n, 134n

Phythian-Adams, W. J., 25
Porteous, N. W., 25, 71n, 86

Quell, G., 20n

von Rad, G., 33n, 202n, 203n
Ringgren, H., 197n
Robinson, H. W., 6n, 8, 11n, 15, 16n, 30, 38n, 66, 81n, 137n, 160n, 169n, 184n, 185, 187, 191, 203n
Robinson, T. H., 6, 7, 76n, 86, 99n, 199n, 220n
Rowley, H. H., 6n, 66, 74n, 75, 79, 85, 87, 88, 94n, 132, 160n

Schian, M., 184n
Schmidt, H., 189n
Schraeder, E., 197n
Schultz, H., 93
Scott, R. B. Y., 9, 15, 22n, 205n, 213n
Seierstad, I. P., 9
Sellin, E., 199, 201, 210, 212n
Simpson, C. A., 27, 156n
Skinner, J., 6, 19n, 20, 64, 76n, 77, 141n, 188
Smend, R., 154n
Smith, G. A., 194n
Smith, J. M. P., 8, 65, 81n, 83n, 199n, 203n
Smith, Sidney, 190
Smith, W. R., 5, 18n, 55n, 65
Snaith, N. H. 106n, 160n
Speiser, E. A., 15n
Stade, B., 4n
Staerk, W., 200n
Sutcliffe, E. F., 133f

Thiele, E. R., 207n, 208n
Thomas, D. W., 5n, 108n, 113n

Volz, P., 93, 189n

Wardle, W. L., 94n
Welch, A. C., 25, 65
Wellhausen, J., 27, 31n, 96, 100n
Widengren, G., 14n
Wilson, J. A., 2n, 3n, 63
Wiseman, D. J., 108n, 111n, 207n
Wright, G. E., 26, 33n, 66n, 95n, 132n, 199n
Zimmern, H., 197, 200